The Writer's Mind

The Writer's Mind

Writing as a Mode of Thinking

Edited by

Janice N. Hays
University of Colorado, Colorado Springs

Phyllis A. Roth
Skidmore College

Jon R. Ramsey
Skidmore College

Robert D. Foulke
Skidmore College

National Council of Teachers of English
1111 Kenyon Road, Urbana, Illinois 61801

Our gratitude is extended to those among the administration and faculty at Skidmore College and to the officers of the New York College English Association whose assistance and cooperation were responsible for the success of "The Writer's Mind" conference at Skidmore. Without the encouragement of the conference participants and the generous support of Skidmore College, this collection would have been impossible. "Understanding Composing" by Sondra Perl first appeared in *College Composition and Communication* 31 (December 1980): 363–369. "Current Brain Research and the Composing Process" by Monica R. Weis SSJ first appeared as "Current Brain Research and the Composing Process: A Call for Interaction" in *The CEA Critic* 44 (January 1982): 22–28.

Book Design: Tom Kovacs for TDK Design

NCTE Stock Number 58668

Library of Congress Cataloging in Publication Data

Main entry under title:

The Writer's mind.

    Bibliography: p.
    1. English language—Rhetoric—Study and teaching— Addresses, essays, lectures. 2. Thought and thinking —Study and teaching—Addresses, essays, lectures. 3. Exposition (Rhetoric)—Addresses, essays, lectures. 4. Creative writing—Study and teaching—Addresses, essays, lectures. 5. Creative thinking (Education)— Addresses, essays, lectures. I. Hays, Janice N.
PE1404.W68 1983   808'.042'01   83-13223
ISBN 0-8141-5866-8

Contents

Introduction   ix

I Language and Mind

1. Rhetoric and Romanticism   3
    Jon R. Ramsey

2. Cognitive Immaturity and Remedial College Writers   15
    Annette N. Bradford

3. Current Brain Research and the Composing Process   25
    Monica R. Weis SSJ

4. Recovering and Discovering Treasures of the Mind   35
    Marilyn Goldberg

5. Understanding Composing   43
    Sondra Perl

6. Written Products and the Writing Process   53
    Lee Odell

7. Modes of Thinking, Modes of Argument   67
    Marie Secor

II The Composing Process

8. On the Relation of Invention to Arrangement   75
    John C. Schafer

9. A Writer's Tool: Computing as a Mode of Inventing   87
    Hugh Burns

10. Invention and the Writing Sequence   95
    Leone Scanlon

11. The Basic Reading and Writing Phenomenon:
    Writing as Evidence of Thinking   103
    Karen M. Hjelmervik
    Susan B. Merriman

12. Revising: The Writer's Need to Invent
    and Express Relationships   113
    Sandra Schor

13. The Development of Discursive Maturity
    in College Writers   127
    Janice N. Hays

14. Building Thought on Paper with Adult Basic Writers   145
    Elaine O. Lees

15. Integrating Instruction in Reading, Writing,
    and Reasoning   153
    Marilyn S. Sternglass

16. Writing and Reading as Collaborative or Social Acts   159
    Kenneth A. Bruffee

17. Reuniting Rhetoric: Theoretical and Pedagogical
    Considerations   171
    Richard A. Katula
    Celest A. Martin

18. Writing and Thinking in a Postliterate Society   181
    William V. Costanzo

III The Writer as Interpreter

19. The Intelligent Eye and the Thinking Hand   191
    Ann E. Berthoff

20. Interpreting and Composing: The Many Resources
    of Kind   197
    James F. Slevin

21. Re-Viewing Reading and Writing Assignments   211
    Phyllis A. Roth

22. Metaphor, Thinking, and the Composing Process   221
    Donald McQuade

23. The Other Speaking: Allegory and Lacan   231
      Robert Viscusi

24. The Writer's Mind: Recent Research
    and Unanswered Questions   239
      Richard L. Larson

Contributors   253

Introduction

Over the last decade, we have heard much about the "literacy crisis" in the United States, a phenomenon that has become evident at every level of the educational process. Although the "crisis" may be exaggerated in the media, the findings of the National Assessment of Educational Progress, the steady drop in SAT scores, and simply the anecdotal reports of high school and college instructors all attest to the reality of poor student writing—and, we think, to a related phenomenon: students' very limited abilities to read with perception and discrimination. One substantial response has been a series of demands that we return, in our teaching of writing, to "the basics"—although it is not always clear to which "basics" such petitioners allude. For the most part, they probably mean usage, punctuation, and spelling. Yet elementary and secondary schools have been teaching, and continue to teach, these fundamentals, and still students do not seem to write clearly and intelligently.

Equally troubling, but hardly surprising, high school and college students do not seem to be thinking very well—in other words, to be addressing substantial issues with analytic sophistication and with coherence. Recently, Charles Cooper and his associates studied the writing of regularly admitted freshmen at the State University of New York, Buffalo—a selective university whose students are chosen from among better qualified college applicants. The study revealed that these freshmen wrote in ways that were almost entirely correct in usage and grammar but revealed a banality, superficiality, and triviality suggestive of fundamental inabilities to think analytically about complex phenomena. These students failed to reflect upon current social problems in ways that acknowledged their scope and intricacy.[1] To the extent that freshmen at SUNY-Buffalo may be typical of their peers throughout the country, this analysis offers a far from comforting prospect for the future, for we live in a world that increasingly requires the types of thinking which writing makes possible. A study like the one at SUNY-Buffalo points up the need for educators to foster the development of sophisticated cognitive abilities.

ix

The papers in *The Writer's Mind: Writing as a Mode of Thinking* assume that an intimate relationship exists between good writing and good thinking. If college students write in ways that are, in Susan Miller's words, "juvenile and extraordinarily innocent of complication,"[2] and if in their writing many college students perform, in Piaget's terms, at a concrete-operational level of cognitive functioning, they may well do so precisely because they have not done enough writing to develop complex thought. For, uniquely, *written* language makes logical and analytic thought possible. According to Jerome Bruner,[3] formal thought assumes the very structure and order that written language imposes: "writing, by objectifying words, and by making their meanings available for much more prolonged and intensive scrutiny than is possible orally, encourages private thought."[4]

We have known for a long time that language is an instrument of thought, but only recently has writing's importance for the development of specific types of intellection become clear. Bruner makes a useful distinction between "communicative competence" and "analytic competence." Communicative competence, which he sees as analogous to Piaget's concrete operations, involves the speaking and understanding of concrete messages about immediate reality. It is the kind of language we use dozens of times each day in order to speak to other people and to transact ordinary business with them. But such language—a language, incidentally, in which our students are often highly fluent—does not lead to the development of a particular analytic competence, for it depends heavily upon the immediate context of conversation. Analytic competence, on the other hand, is sometimes described as the "context-free elaboration" of language because it does not depend for its meaning upon the speaker's intentions or the listener's reactions in a specified physical, social, or other conventional setting. Of course, no written discourse is totally free of a context—in the sense of an implied rhetorical relationship between writer and reader which encompasses the purpose, tone, and effect of the discourse—but in a written text that context is secondary and remote rather than primary and immediate. In developing analytic competence, writers learn to disentangle meaning from the situations in which it is used so that it can begin to operate upon itself. Analytic competence, then, "involves the prolonged operation of thought processes exclusively on linguistic representations, on propositional structures accompanied by strategies of thought and problem solving appropriate not to direct experience with objects and events but with ensembles of propositions. [Analytic thinking] is heavily meta-linguistic in nature . . . involving operations on the linguistic code, to assure its fit to sets of observations and . . . more often than not, it generates new notational systems like mathematics, or more powerfully elaborated forms of the natural language like poetry."[5] Thus, in Bruner's words, "reality becomes secondary to possibility."[6]

The ability to separate one's thoughts from immediate reality and to operate upon the products of language itself can take place only through writing—in part because short-term memory restricts what can be held in immediate consciousness, but also in part because it is the structure and linearity of written language that impose form and order. (In the classroom, much academic discourse is the speaking out loud of "written language.") Thus, as Janet Emig also argues,[7] it is the act of shaping thought *in writing* that makes possible the elaboration of ideas, the establishing of relationships among those ideas, and the consequent manipulations of those relationships that we associate with complex thought. This fact has always been one premise of a liberal arts education, and it has been an important reason why liberal arts institutions have resisted short-answer, objective tests as an index of learning: we do not genuinely "know" a subject until we have written about it, nor can we begin to think it through thoroughly until we have qualified, subordinated, correlated, and synthesized aspects of that subject in the structures of written language.

The Writer's Mind, then, addresses itself to the connections and interdependencies between writing and cognition. Only through more fully grasping these relationships will we be able to make the case for extensive writing as an instrument of learning—a case that badly needs to be made in a period of increasing emphasis on vocational and technological education. Only by making such a case will we be able to resist the pressures, particularly acute upon secondary school teachers, to adopt "quick-fix" solutions to the literacy crisis, solutions that, by ignoring the more fundamental question of the development of critical thinking through writing, exacerbate the very situations they are intended to cure. For instance, when the "return to basics" focuses exclusively or even primarily on developing students' consciousness of "rules" ("do not begin a sentence with *and* or *but*"), students memorize seemingly inflexible and often inappropriate dicta without ever understanding the principles that inform them and that enable skilled writers to use them—or ignore them—to advantage. Novice writers then often conclude that writing provides only an opportunity to fail, not the means to learn. Only in understanding how writing is a mode of thinking will we be able to teach writing in ways best calculated to promote cognitive development—and to argue for the small class sizes that make feasible such teaching, absolutely linked as it must be to extensive amounts of student writing.

Origin and Themes of *The Writer's Mind*

The Writer's Mind grows out of the New York College English Association conference on the same topic held in October, 1980, at Skidmore College. That conference drew together educators, researchers, and theoreticians primarily from the Northeast but also from as far away as Colorado and Texas. For two days and nights, participants listened to papers addressing the subject of writing and thinking, discussed the issues raised, and exchanged ideas in an atmosphere that was both highly stimulating and at the same time sufficiently relaxed to encourage prolonged and thoughtful discussion. Participants included not only those whose primary interest was the theory and teaching of writing but also literary specialists concerned with finding bridges between discourse theory and literary theory.

The essays in *The Writer's Mind* are among the conference's best, reworked after the occasion itself to incorporate and respond to ideas generated there. The resulting collection reflects the conference's focus. That is, *The Writer's Mind* is neither exclusively a presentation of a single theoretical position nor primarily a collection of essays detailing practical measures for the classroom. Rather, the selection and arrangement of essays in the volume provide both a theoretical context in which instructors can better understand and modify their teaching of writing and an analysis of effective teaching techniques that have developed out of theory.

The Writer's Mind offers perspectives on nearly every aspect of the mental activities that inform expository writing. Often, discussions of one aspect will overlap with, indeed appear in the context of, discussions of other considerations, suggesting just how complex are the workings of the writer's mind and the degree to which its operations interact with one another. The several sections of the book reflect the explicit distinctions among three main topic areas. The first section, "Language and Mind," includes discussions of brain physiology, language acquisition and development, and the fundamental cognitive processes which influence student writing. The second section, "The Composing Process," focuses more directly on the experiences of writers as they plan topics, invent ideas, develop coherent presentations, and reshape their efforts, and on the teaching strategies which might aid this complex, recursive process. And finally, the essays grouped under the heading "The Writer as Interpreter" examine some of the philosophic, literary, and psychological connections among thinking, reading, interpreting, and writing, exploring the principles of thought and organization associated primarily with works of art. We can no longer relegate these creative activities of mind exclusively to the domain of art because the articulate imagination embraces all the social, economic, and political realities of daily life. *The Writer's Mind* concludes with Richard L. Larson's overview of current composition research. Most of the developments in writing research that Larson discusses and many of the questions raised by these developments are addressed in *The Writer's Mind.*

Beyond these major structural divisions, essays in the volume implicitly engage in dialogue with one another about invention, revision, cognitive development as it affects writing development, the roles of formal structure and intuitive thought in composing, the interaction between reading and writing, and strategies for adapting theory and research findings to classroom use. Often the dialogue is complementary, one essay extending or adding dimensions to issues treated in another; occasionally it is contradictory, as one writer challenges assumptions that another takes for granted. We will not attempt to reconcile these various and sometimes conflicting viewpoints, for they are inherent in the present dynamic state of writing theory, research, and application. Rather than formulate premature answers to fundamental questions, *The Writer's Mind* contributes to this questioning and rethinking of writers' processes.

The Mind and the Composing Process

One of these fundamental questions concerns the "workings of mind" itself as they affect composing processes. Jon Ramsey provides some background for understanding contemporary discussions as he examines Wordsworth and Coleridge's theories of the imagination, theories about the mind's workings in relation to writing and to creativity. Ramsey reminds us that the study of cognition and creativity is neither new nor exclusively the province of empirical research. Annette Bradford's theoretical paper, "Cognitive Immaturity and Remedial College Writers," explores several developmental models of language acquisition and concept formation and particularly tests the implications of Piaget's stages for the composing processes of developmental writers. Implicitly, and sometimes explicitly, as in Monica Weis's review of current research on the brain's hemispheric functions, many of our contributors assume a model of mental functioning that

includes more than the rational, whether those writers conceptualize
this functioning as "intuition" as Marilyn Goldberg does in "Recovering and Discovering Treasures of the Mind," or as the "felt sense"
Sondra Perl describes in "Understanding Composing." Drawing upon
her protocol studies of writers in the act of writing, Perl suggests that
the composing process itself is one of creative discovery, of bringing
into consciousness and making explicit the ideas that are only half
formed and implicit until the act of composing shapes them. In "The
Intelligent Eye and the Thinking Hand," Ann Berthoff challenges the
"positivist" dichotomy between reasoning and feeling, an artificial
division which consigns imagination to the "affective domain." She
argues for a more sophisticated philosophy that would "reclaim imagination as the forming power of mind." Since the imagination is, in
Berthoff's view, the mind's primary agency for perceiving and giving
shape to experience, it is also the informing power of all thinking and
writing activities.

Ann Berthoff's attention to literary and philosophic perspectives
on the writing process also provides the focus for other essays in this
collection. In "Metaphor, Thinking, and the Composing Process,"
Donald McQuade extends the insights of Paul Ricoeur toward a
theory of metaphor and its importance to expository as well as creative
writing. Robert Viscusi's essay, "The Other Speaking: Allegory and
Lacan," provides a speculative journey into Jacques Lacan's psychoanalytic linguistics and Dante's understanding of allegory. Viscusi
suggests that all activities of thinking and writing involve the construction of allegory, and that the allegorizing process, when properly
understood, liberates rather than constrains the writer's efforts to
produce "meaning."

Models for the Composing Process

Another fundamental issue that *The Writer's Mind* raises is the scope
and complexity of an adequate model of the composing process and
the essential interrelatedness of that model's components. In a much
cited discussion of the shift in "paradigm," Richard Young has noted
the replacement of "product" with "process" in our understanding of
writing.[8] Yet recent work—especially in literary theory and in discourse and reading studies—has demonstrated that a complete model
of writing must include both product and process, and that the
workings of each are even more complex than research to date has
established. A more traditional "product" orientation has focused
intensively upon organization and style, whereas the newer "process"

model tends to stress invention and revision. Yet questions about the mind's functioning in writing relate directly to problems both of invention and revision and of organization and style. For example, in "Written Products and the Writing Process," Lee Odell examines the strategies that professional and student writers use in thinking about their topics, strategies reflected in their syntactic and semantic choices. In "Modes of Thinking, Modes of Argument," Marie Secor discusses the thinking activities which shape different forms of written arguments, arguing persuasively that the way in which we go about writing different types of arguments reflects the ways in which we apprehend the world and organize our experience of it.

As our understanding of the writer's mind widens, we will probably find that the answers we seek will not be matters of either/or but of both/and. It is, for example, already clear that in teaching invention we need both intuitive and rational heuristics, although we may not yet know what the exact characteristics of each are, what the precise mix between them ought to be, or how we can help students integrate and shape them.

John Schafer's article, "On the Relation of Invention and Arrangement," gives an excellent overview of these problems, reviewing classical distinctions between the inventing and arranging of ideas, showing how these distinctions have been used (and sometimes misused) in modern rhetorical theory, and describing the different expository situations in which writer-based inventing can be treated apart from or in relation to the more reader-based activities of structuring the paper as a whole. Schafer also suggests some practical considerations in applying heuristic procedures. Hugh Burns describes a technique to stimulate invention in which students carry on a printed and personalized dialogue with the computer. The computer serves as their examiner and so externalizes one of the internal processes by which the exploration of a problem takes place.

In "Invention and the Writing Sequence," Leone Scanlon employs James Britton's view that expressive writing provides the matrix for other types of writing to design a sequence of exercises involving students personally with the inventing and arranging process. Also emphasizing the personal dimension, Karen Hjelmervik and Susan Merriman, in "The Basic Reading and Writing Phenomenon: Writing as Evidence of Thinking," argue that we need to build students' confidence through a program that integrates their reading, thinking, and writing experiences. Other writers in the volume offer additional insights and techniques for helping students generate material in and for writing.

Extending the concern for an adequate and organic model of writing, a number of essays address questions about teaching writing through the teaching of structure. Several writers suggest that a too narrow emphasis upon structure, an emphasis that divorces it from or elevates it above the subject matter it embodies, leads to stultified writing and reductionism (the most notorious extremes of which are probably the five-paragraph theme and the "models" approach to teaching writing). Sandra Schor, in "Revising: The Writer's Need to Invent and Express Relationships," discusses students' revision practices in a research project emphasizing whole structures; Schor finds that despite the project's focus upon large elements of the work, students generally revised either for neatness and correctness or by the rigid and often inappropriate application of prescriptive rules.

Other writers suggest the use of structures or genres as ways of understanding reality and as strategies for shaping and commenting upon it, holding that such structures can both stimulate thinking and enable students to develop a repertoire of forms for generating and arranging discourse. James Slevin, in "Interpreting and Composing: The Many Resources of Kind," calls for a "poetics of discourse" founded on historical and epistemological study of traditional literary and expository genres.

Phyllis Roth also applies a literary perspective, specifically that of reader response theories, to an understanding of the composing process. Roth describes courses in writing about reading that encourage students to revise, that is to re-see, their highly individual reading and writing in terms of an academic community and a public audience. Other contributors also discuss revision, and implicit in all these discussions is the recognition that revision is also generation and arrangement: that it is, in part at least, a successive and ever more complex "reseeing" of the reality being written and of the structures which writers use to embody it. Such assumptions are implicit also in many of the writing sequences that essays in *The Writer's Mind* propose, sequences that move students toward higher levels of complexity and abstraction as they think about their subjects.

Cognitive and Writing Development

Also fundamental to such sequences is the notion of cognitive and writing development. Several writers address this question directly and suggest ways of promoting cognitive development in the writing classroom. In "The Development of Discursive Maturity in College Writers," Janice Hays examines, in relation to the developmental stages outlined by William G. Perry, the necessity of advancing student thinking and writing beyond their concrete and descriptive stages toward the formation of concepts and ideas. Hays argues that such cognitive growth constitutes the center of a college education and is promoted largely through practice in expository writing. Elaine Lees's "Building Thought on Paper with Adult Basic Writers" makes a similar case for a cognitive and linguistic partnership and outlines some classroom procedures which foster this mutual development. In "Reading, Writing, and Reasoning," Marilyn Sternglass draws upon current research in psycholinguistic models of reading, Piaget's model of cognitive development, and a process-centered approach to writing in order to structure a reading and writing course geared to concept formation, taking students through a step-by-step process whereby they generate, analyze, and synthesize materials from reading for writing.

These analyses can provide only a tentative model of writing. We do not yet have answers to numbers of fundamental questions about writing development in college students: To what extent is such development innate and to what extent is it determined by environment and education? Is it the product of writing itself? Exactly what are the stages of *writing* development once we have moved beyond "concrete" narrative and descriptive writing? To what extent can we teach different levels of writing, and do they depend upon maturation? Another major area that needs addressing is symbolic development. In what ways and in what sequence does the child's ability to make up a lively story develop into the mature writer's ability to create and explain complex symbols? How do we teach or encourage such development?

Writing development also bears upon invention, another example of the model's recursiveness. That is, if there is a sequence in the development of writing ability, are certain heuristic strategies more appropriate to certain stages of that development? Is there a sequence in which the ability to utilize particular heuristic strategies emerges? Numbers of writers in this volume and elsewhere have commented upon the distinctions between Linda Flower's concept of "reader-based" and "writer-based" prose[9] and their correlation to cognitive development, and both James Moffett and James Britton have suggested relationships between writing development and the kinds and forms of discourse. We need, however, to know more about the characteristics of such stages of discursive development. For example, if students and professional writers view and structure reality differently as they write about it, then as Lee Odell suggests in this volume, these differing perceptions may be linked to age and maturity.

These questions and others suggest the interrelatedness of various parts of the writing process and the thinking processes linked to writing. The composing process is also related to allied mental activities. Drawing upon the insights of L. S. Vygotsky and Thomas Kuhn, Kenneth Bruffee argues that learning to write need not be a lonely, silent, isolated endeavor but should be, instead, "a social or collaborative act," for the writing process relies heavily on "internalized speech," which presupposes an audience both of the self (a dialogue made manifest as "thought") and of "a community of knowledgeable peers." Bruffee's analysis has an interesting application in Richard Katula and Celest Martin's essay on "Reuniting Rhetoric." The authors describe their efforts to combine the "rhetorical" requirements of both public speaking and expository writing in a single communications course. In "Writing and Thinking in a Postliterate Society," William Costanzo discusses the relationship of both oral and visual communication to writing. Costanzo distinguishes among oral, literate, and visual modes of thinking and communicating, but he urges as well that the presuppositions of visual and oral culture must inform our writing instruction to enable us to build a bridge from the experiences of our students to our writing-centered larger culture.

Some Uses of *The Writer's Mind*

It may be a long time before we have an adequate model of the mind's operations as they pertain to writing. The construction of that model will probably draw upon such various disciplines as neurophysiology, psychology, psychoanalysis, linguistics, literary criticism, studies in reading, and the philosophy of language, in addition to the results of current research in the composing process. Yet in the teaching of writing, we cannot always afford to wait for these answers. We do know that too narrow an emphasis upon linear/sequential/hierarchical processes leads, as many of this volume's writers have noted, to formulaic, banal, dead writing; too exclusive a focus upon "intuitive," associational processes leads to interesting writing that is amorphous, incoherent, and often private. Clearly, both kinds of functioning are essential to the writer's work, but the perplexing question for composition teachers is *how*, on the one hand, to encourage and help students think and write creatively and intelligently and, on the other, also to help them structure and shape that writing so that it is coherent and logical. Until we have a more adequate model of "mind," we may not be able to evolve techniques that will prove entirely satisfactory in the classroom—nor will we be able to find answers to the questions Richard Larson raises about how and why writers decide to write in the first place, answers that we need in order to help our students write. Many of the researchers Larson discusses and many of our contributors do, however, offer some partial or provisional solutions to these problems and some suggestions for directions in which solutions might be found.

Moreover, the essays and structure of *The Writer's Mind* reveal that, whatever their differences in model and methodology, theorists and researchers are today agreed that writing and thinking are part of the same continuous and recursive mental process, that writing is indeed a mode of thinking. Within the context of the issues raised in the papers, secondary school and college teachers can both understand and appreciate the implications of divergent philosophies and explore the uses of specific techniques in teaching writing.

Finally, *The Writer's Mind* offers composition instructors and literary critics alike a bridge between discourse theory and contemporary critical thinking, a bridge suggesting ways by which the study of the creation and ascription of meaning to a text in the act of reading are intimately bound up with the writing process. This is an exciting and rewarding area of investigation, for contemporary literary theory in many of its manifestations seems, to some, alien from the classroom and even from the reading and interpreting act. Thus, from the standpoint of both theory and application, these papers together offer a view of writing and thinking that includes the humanistic and the empirical, the "transactional," or "referential," and the imaginative perspectives, a view that firmly establishes the role of writing in all our educational endeavors.

Notes

1. Charles Cooper, Roger Cherry, Rita Gerber, Stefan Fleischer, and Barbara Copley, "Writing Abilities of Regularly-Admitted Freshmen at SUNY/Buffalo" (Unpublished study, State University of New York at Buffalo, 1980), 82–83 *passim*.

2. Susan Miller, "Rhetorical Maturity: Definition and Development," in *Reinventing the Rhetorical Tradition,* ed. Aviva Freedman and Ian Pringle (Conway, Ark.: L&S Books, 1980), 121.

3. J. S. Bruner, "Language as an Instrument of Thought," in *Problems of Language and Learning,* ed. Alan Davies (London: Heinemann, 1975), 79–80.

4. J. Goody and I. Watt, as cited in *The Development of Writing Abilities (11–18),* ed. James Britton, Tony Burgess, Nancy Martin, Alex McLeod, and Harold Rosen (1975; rpt. London: Macmillan Education, 1977), 201.

5. Bruner, 72–73.

6. Bruner, 70–79 *passim.*

7. Janet Emig, "Writing as a Mode of Learning," *College Composition and Communication* 28 (May 1977): 122–28. The resemblance of this book's title to Emig's is a deliberate acknowledgment of indebtedness.

8. Richard E. Young, "Paradigms and Problems: Needed Research in Rhetorical Invention," in *Research on Composing, Points of Departure,* ed. Charles R. Cooper and Lee Odell (Urbana, Ill.: NCTE, 1978), 29–48.

9. Linda Flower, "Writer-Based Prose: A Cognitive Basis for Problems in Writing," *College English* 41 (September 1979): 1–12.

I Language and Mind

1 Rhetoric and Romanticism

Jon R. Ramsey
Skidmore College

Current research on the writing process is in essential respects redis-covering what great writers, particularly literary artists, have always known: that unspoken, spoken, and written language provides the symbol system through which much of our knowing about things occurs, and that words carry an enormous power to promote or obscure understanding. The perspectives we now use to discuss "the writer's mind" and "writing as a mode of thinking" are especially indebted to Romantic literary theory. The Romantics felt compelled, as we do, to discover "in what manner language and the human mind act and re-act on each other."[1] Their attention shifted away from earlier product and audience-centered views of writing toward the writer's (specifically the poet's) state of mind and soul.[2] The ways in which intuition, inspiration, perception, reflection, and memory impinge upon the writing process became for the Romantics an explicit, major literary topic. They regarded the reformation of lan-guage, moreover, as central to the social and psychological revolution they hoped to foster.

Although our methods of inquiry, degree of idealism, and conclu-sions about the composing process may separate us from the Roman-tics, we are linked with them in believing that the activity of writing influences, even radically reshapes, what we know of ourselves and the world. In fact, we first encounter in Romantic inquiries an epis-temological and psycholinguistic interest very much like our own. As a means of pointing out some shared territory, I want to sketch a few Wordsworthian and Coleridgean perspectives on the writer's mind and the composing process.

4 *Language and Mind*

Wordsworth and Coleridge on Language

When Coleridge and Wordsworth collaborated on their great literary
manifesto *Lyrical Ballads* and the "Preface" which accompanied the
second edition, they were trying to revolutionize the sensibility of
their age. The revolution, they believed, would occur not through the
political and social upheavals of a French Revolution or through
legal and social reforms, though all these modes of change might be
the harbingers of a more profound psychic revolution. Instead, the
poets were intent upon defamiliarizing the formulas of perception,
thought, and expression which preserved the status quo of ignorance
and injustice. This mental reorientation would take place largely
through a reordering of the language system, the means by which we
configure things external to ourselves, reflect upon their significance
and relationship to us, and examine our own thinking processes.

Recognizing that Coleridge and Wordsworth did not share equally
in this faith or in the assumptions about language that underlie
Lyrical Ballads, we can see nevertheless that the volume they nurtured
together raises many points about language and consciousness which
contemporary composition research has pursued as well. Through an
amateur understanding of anthropology, through psychological inquiry and sheer polemic, the "Preface" to *Lyrical Ballads* sets out the
intimate relationships among "the beautiful and permanent forms of
nature" (Zall, p. 18), uncorrupted perception of the forms, the consequent mental and moral condition of people living in touch with
nature, and the language of the beautiful and permanent. For the
audience addressed in *Lyrical Ballads,* entrenched, unnatural "habits
of association" (Zall, p. 17) stand as the chief obstacle to the full
apprehension of beauty and truth: an oppressive weight of habit in
our use of language and acts of perceiving and thinking has obscured
nature's beauty and permanence, which should find their analogue in
the natural order of our internal life. It is the poet's task, then, to find
words "which are the emanations of reality and truth" (Zall, p. 50).

The difficulties of finding such perfect symbols and at the same
time "creating the taste" by which such a language could be comprehended by a corrupted audience did not escape Wordsworth's and
Coleridge's attention. Nor did they settle easily on a source from
which the true voices of things "emanated." Wordsworth tended to
regard nature as the inspiring source of our best passions, and words
as the embodiment of those passions; he also treated words not merely
as conventional signs but "as *things,* active and efficient, which are of
themselves part of the passion" (Zall, pp. 13–14). At times he also, as

in the "Essay upon Epitaphs" (written ca. 1810), takes a less object-oriented, more symbolist view of language formation as primarily a mental phenomenon:

> Words are too awful an instrument for good and evil to be trifled with; they hold above all other external powers a dominion over thoughts. If words be not . . . an incarnation of the thought, but only a clothing for it, then surely they will prove an ill gift. . . . Language, if it do not uphold, feed, and leave in quiet, like the power of gravitation or the air we breathe, is a counter-spirit, unremittingly and noiselessly at work, to subvert, to lay waste, to vitiate, and to dissolve. (Zall, pp. 125–126)

The word as "incarnation of the thought" is a goal which poetry and prose can only approach. Wordsworth knew that language often proved a "counter-spirit" to unity of being, even when the poet's moral aesthetic regarded the articulate imagination as a means of grace.

This is not the place to review Coleridge's complex epistemology of language or his critique of the linguistic assumptions he had helped Wordsworth bring into focus for the 1800 "Preface." It is sufficient to remark that Coleridge anticipates the concerns of modern language theory more clearly than Wordsworth. Coleridge felt more freedom to speculate on the linguistic interplay of signifiers themselves, on meanings generated less by the signs' connections to signified objects and events than by a system of verbal relationships which *is* consciousness. Thus when Coleridge wrote in *The Stateman's Manual* (1816) that the word as symbol "always partakes of the reality it renders intelligible," he was more likely than Wordworth to be thinking of "reality" as the mind's most powerful internal workings. In *Biographia Literaria* (composed 1815) Coleridge wrote, in the context of distinguishing his epistemology of language from Wordsworth's: "The best part of human language . . . is derived from reflection on the acts of mind itself. It is formed by a voluntary appropriation of fixed symbols to internal acts, to processes and results of imagination."[3]

Despite their many philosophic differences, Wordsworth and Coleridge shared a sense of urgency about reforming language and mind; to both authors the internalized, spoken, and written dialect of the tribe seemed the crucial target. Language becomes the implicit and often the explicit topic throughout the poems in *Lyrical Ballads*. Nearly every phenomenon of a subjective or objective kind explored in *Lyrical Ballads* speaks a language of its own. The poet's most difficult task in the ballads is to show how the separate tongues can

6   *Language and Mind*

communicate with one another, how all experiences can join in harmonic discourse yet still preserve the sacredness of their several dialects and accents. The belief that language, particularly the language of metaphor, is a vital participant in every aspect of human experience becomes the main article of faith in this revolutionary volume. The poet's function is to return consciousness to an organic wholeness "more consonant to nature" (Zall, p. 72). Language in *Lyrical Ballads* is the vehicle of reunification. Just as insincere, formulaic, and distorted language accompanies and to some extent occasions the fall from unified perception, so too redemption depends on our discovering the genuine voices of things. Sometimes the several tongues seem alien and strange, as they did to many of the first readers of *Lyrical Ballads;* nevertheless, the ballads give expression, Wordsworth argues, to feelings, situations, people, and even objects "such as men *may* sympathise with, and such as there is reason to believe they would be better and more moral beings if they did sympathise with" (Zall, p. 75).

Romantic Themes in *The Writer's Mind*

Of all the essays in *The Writer's Mind*, Robert Viscusi's meditation on Dante, Lacan, and the cognitive leaps made possible through allegory (see chapter 23) comes closest to the highest aspirations of Romantic language theory. It appears that allegory's claims upon the Logos are not different in spirit, for example, from Wordsworth's most confident celebration of the word's ontological significance:

> . . . Visionary Power
> Attends upon the motions of the winds
> Embodied in the mystery of words.
> There darkness makes abode, and all the host
> Of shadowy things do work their changes there,
> As in a mansion like their proper home.[4]

Donald McQuade, in "Metaphor, Thinking, and the Composing Process" (see chapter 22), explores the importance of metaphoric thinking to expository (as well as creative) writing. He acknowledges his debt to Ricoeur and to poets and novelists. The Romantics in particular, we remember, extolled not only the sensuous delight of metaphor but its heuristic necessity as well: metaphor was for them a primary agent for discovering and expressing things inaccessible to discursive language, for creating constellations of meaning in a decentered world.

Each section of *The Writer's Mind,* as the introduction points out, addresses "the connections and interdependencies between writing and cognition." Ann Berthoff's essay (chapter 19) provides our most direct link to a Coleridgean perspective. Central to her argument for a more philosophic, less mechanistic understanding of the composing process is a revitalization of "imagination" as Coleridge defined it in *Biographia Literaria:* "the living power and prime agent of all human perception."[5] She argues that "empirical" psychologists have misunderstood the *shaping* agency of mind and imagination, and that this "positivist" influence dominates contemporary research in composition. The essays in *The Writer's Mind,* however, avoid mechanistic descriptions of language and mind and dull formulas for teaching writing; rather they offer a far more detailed, useful, and still exciting understanding of the mind's interinvolvement with words. Composition research is in very basic ways confirming, and making available to our teaching, the insights which literary artists carry around as their common property.

The conclusions presented and questions posed in the best of our current research are not usually of a philosophic nature; but the very close observation of the actual thinking, writing, and revising practices of experienced and inexperienced writers is not alien to the efforts of Coleridge and Wordsworth, who subjected their own sensory experiences, reflections, and writing efforts to the most exhaustive scrutiny (as in *The Prelude, Biographia Literaria,* and Coleridge's *Notebooks*). Coleridge and Wordsworth were if anything too fascinated with the concrete and specific; "research" which could reveal the minute workings and precise patterns of thinking and writing would certainly have interested them. Moreover, a celebration of the shaping power of language is implicit even in the more academically subdued essays in *The Writer's Mind.* The names that are invoked repeatedly in this volume—Bruner, Perry, Piaget, Luria, Vygotsky, Lennenberg—lend an almost messianic purpose to the book's close studies of brain functions, teaching techniques, developmental patterns, and writing strategies. Perry is cited, for example, for his insightful descriptions of the stages of cognitive development, which lead away from a bondage to the concrete and operational toward the relativistic and contextual, and toward the necessity of making intellectual and moral choices in a world offering few compelling structures of belief. Composition researchers embrace Bruner precisely because he describes written language as a shaping force upon our thinking patterns and stresses the need (for which Coleridge often argued) to "separate one's thought

from immediate reality and to operate upon the products of language
itself." Luria and Vygotsky promote the view, as Annette Bradford
notes in chapter 2, that language is "'the most decisive element in
systematizing perception.'" Even the physiological research represented in this volume, such as Monica Weis's review of brain functions
(see chapter 3), is undertaken to help "students gain insights into how
language shapes and gives meaning to their experience."

Romantic Theory Illuminates Composition Research

Composition research is, evidently, consistent with many of the
philosophic and linguistic insights which germinate from the experience of literary artists. Researchers and writers alike will agree with
Marilyn Goldberg's reiteration of Jerome Bruner's view (see chapter
4): When written language is working at its best, "there is an elegant
isomorphism between the structures of our minds and the structures
of our writing." If we have moved closer than did the Romantics to a
functional description of that isomorphism, there remain other key
issues in current research with which the Romantics might help us:
Romantic literature holds implications especially for prewriting and
invention, rewriting and recursiveness, and the stubbornly nonverbal
components of our experience.

Prewriting and Invention

Keats's letters, Shelley's prose and poetry, and many of Wordsworth's
and Coleridge's writings are filled with agonized probings and ecstatic
descriptions of the early stages of the creative process. The poets
wonder, for example, whether prewriting, as we might call this stage
of creativity, springs from unconscious sources or from something
available to conscious control. Does it begin in an idea, an image, or a
felt sense? Is creativity promoted by a particular environment? Does
one keep writing *until* inspiration comes or begin to write *when*
inspiration finally pays a visit? Can the writer's creative energy be
sustained over a long period of time, or is the brief lyric (perhaps for
us the short essay) the natural home for creative outbursts? The
Romantics explored these and related questions with insights worthy
of any composition teacher's attention. In fact, many of the great
Romantic poems are essentially detailed accounts of inventing or
creating. Even a quick rereading of "Tintern Abbey," the "Intima-
tions Ode," "Ode to a Nightingale," or "Dejection: An Ode" reminds

us that these poems are efforts to find out what to say, think, or feel
about something: how to recollect the past and rekindle its fading
intensity; how to define and emerge from one's own melancholy,
describe an inexplicable sense of loss or ennui; how to reflect upon
the direction of one's own thoughts, or distinguish genuine inspiration from a mere rush of nervous energy; and so on. We note too that
these poems often speculate without concluding or resolving. They
sometimes even wait until the work's endpoint to ask the most fundamental questions: "Was it a vision or a waking dream? / Fled is
that music:—Do I wake or sleep?"

Wordsworth's *Prelude,* from beginning to end a poem which gets
invented before our eyes, is a great storehouse of reflections on every
stage of the thinking-writing process. The poem eventually traces
"the growth of a poet's mind," but the work's first three hundred
lines actually record the search for a topic worthy of so many lines.
The difficulty of beginning right stems in part from the nonlinear,
nonsequential nature of psychological causes and effects, which seem
to violate chronology and change their significance to us each time
we examine them:

> Hard task, vain hope, to analyse the mind,
> If each most obvious and particular thought
> . . . .
> Hath no beginning.   (*Prelude* [1850], 2. 228–232)

The Prelude, like so many other Romantic poems, affords us mag-
nificent examples of "writer-based" composition ("the record and the
working of [the writer's] own verbal thought," according to John
Schafer's definition). We are taken through all the emergent patterns
of memories, anticipations, images, ideas, and specific word cues
which gradually unfold the poem's elaborate structuring principles.
Anyone who wants precise lessons in every facet of invention will
study *The Prelude.*

Rewriting and Recursiveness

Closely linked with our interest in beginnings is the need to understand how writers proceed to refine their ideas, bring a thesis into
focus, develop an overall design to the essay, and search for *le mot
juste* and the finely crafted phrase. We no longer think of such
revising as solely a concluding activity but rather, thanks to Janet
Emig, Linda Flower, Sondra Perl, and Nancy Sommers, as an ongoing "recursive" process. Here too the Romantics have preceded us

by retaining the evidence of recursiveness in their finished poems and essays. We know from Romantic manuscripts, of course, how heavily revised were the "spontaneous" compositions of these poets; indeed, they expunged many false starts and unfruitful lines of thought from the poems they actually published, and they often continued to revise after publication. But since theirs was the art of imitating organic growth, they carefully structured their works to reveal the means by which they had gathered evidence, altered their first impressions, and reformulated major ideas. Rather than striving for a product which preserved only their final decisions and conclusions and the experiences which supported those ends, the Romantics valued (more than we might in the final draft of an essay) the surprises, modifications, and contradictions which characterize the process of inquiry itself. They developed art forms that embody the poet's tortuous efforts to invest the chaos of experience with order and meaning, or at least to move toward some "momentary stay against confusion."

In most of their poems, and in their essays as well, we see this continuous process of reassessment and refocusing, both through a refinement of word choices and a subtle recasting of ideas. When, for example, "Tintern Abbey" opens with "Five years have passed; five summers, with the length / Of five long winters," we confront first a simple fact of chronology, which quickly refocuses on the particular season (summer) to which memory and emotion cling, and finally the complete transformation of the external measurement of time into a metaphorical assessment of the poet's internal, emotional life. As it turns out, this movement from outer to inner, from observed objects and events to psychological responses, and from past to present sets the tone and establishes an ordering principle for the entire poem.

This very detailed record of the recursive writing process is characteristic of Romantic literature, whose ontology centers on the "field effect" of phenomena as they mutually define and reshape one another. Sondra Perl's succinct formulation of recursiveness suggests a good way of reading the Romantics: "recursiveness in writing implies that there is a forward-moving action that exists by virtue of a backward-moving action." Coleridge's description of the way in which "a *legitimate* poem" achieves organic form and affects its reader coincides remarkably with this principle. The poem repeatedly pauses, reiterates images and ideas, reflects upon itself, looks for evidence of an emergent form, then moves forward again, now anticipating with more confidence its structural destiny. And the reader's pleasure depends on this recursive design:

> The reader should be carried forward, not merely or chiefly by the mechanical impulse of curiosity, or by a restless desire to arrive at the final solution: but by the pleasureable activity of mind excited by the attractions of the journey itself. Like the motion of a serpent, which the Egyptians made the emblem of intellectual power; or like the path of sound through the air; at every step he pauses and half recedes, and from the retrogressive movement collects the force which again carries him onward.[6]

The same patient, serpentine gathering of energy gives shape to Coleridge's "conversation" poems. For both Coleridge and Wordsworth the recursive becomes a principle of artistic form, a pattern of consiousness, and a mode of apprehending reality. It is a means of access to Wordsworth's "ennobling interchange" between mind and external world and lies at the heart of his "sense sublime / Of something far more deeply interfused." On the other hand, the recursive can also become, the Romantics attest, a monster of the composing process, "a redundant energy, / Vexing its own creation" (*Prelude* [1850], 1. 37–38), a surfeit of energy and self-scrutiny which "makes a toy of Thought" (Coleridge, "Frost at Midnight," line 23). So on the dark side of the "sublime" benefits of the recursive principle we meet with *Frankenstein*, the central Romatic parable of creative energy doubling back narcissistically, destructively upon itself. *Frankenstein* evokes so many fascinations and anxieties inherent in the creative process; certainly one of the monstrosities suggested is the retrograde motion of creativity, the point at which the backward tug begins to overpower the energy to move forward again. While few writers ever confront an inertia of such demonic proportions, all writers need to learn how and when to look back at their own work and when to press on without reviewing, revising, and perhaps fixating on the lines already written. To help our students toward this balance between unfettered, unself-conscious writing and the need to reperceive their work while it develops, we discourage premature editing for surface correctness and shift their attention to the larger structure which the essay gradually brings into being. Sandra Schor makes the crucial point that "a good revision has all the creative implications of a new piece of work." Even the finished, elaborately structured products of Romantic literature reveal the writer's struggle to "revise" in this larger sense.

Nonverbal Components of Experience

One aspect of the writer's struggle to invent, develop, and revise is, of course, "the sad incompetence of human speech" (*Prelude*, 6.593)—

the writer's apprehension of things inherently nonverbal or frustrat-
ingly preverbal. Romantic poetry, in its sinuous movement toward
closures which are never entirely attainable (nor probably desirable),
seems always in pursuit of phenomena which word symbols cannot
quite embrace. We are in familiar territory, then, when Sondra Perl,
Eugene Gendlin, and others speak of a "felt sense," "intuitions," and
"Eureka moments," the largely sensory and nonconscious antecedents
to the composing process (see chapter 5). This "felt sense," says Perl,
"is always there, within us. It is unifying, and yet, when we bring
words to it, it can break apart, shift, unravel, and become something
else." Neither Romantic nor modern rhetoric, however, stands silently
in awe of the ineffable. Romantic efforts to express the inexpressible,
to coerce all experiences into language, remind us of our own determination to heal the old dualism between *res et verba*.

The poets' strategies for making the "felt sense" accessible to
language differ from ours; like us, however, they sought ways of
extending the epistemological limits of the composing process. Wordsworth developed an entire cast of mediating characters, even a "silent
poet," to establish points of contact between his verbal art and the
experiences which remain "far hidden from the reach of words" (*Prelude* [1850], 3.187). Coleridge's most intriguing response to the challenge of the non-verbal is "Kubla Khan," a compelling "vision" of
the supreme creative moment. No architects work long hours to plan
Kubla's gardens and "pleasure dome," nor do we see workmen haul-
ing materials, constructing, modifying the original design; instead,
Kubla has the power to "decree," and upon that instant create, a
world in which opposite and discordant qualities are perfectly recon-
ciled. As we would expect from the Romantic dialectic, Xanadu is
only a temporary construct, "a miracle of rare device" whose organic
coherence is short-lived. We have caught a glimpse, nevertheless, of
the imagination unmediated by rhetorical stratagems.

Current rhetorical theory is less speculative, revolutionary, and
apocalyptic than its Romantic antecedents. It is more experimentally
sound, precise, cautious in its logic, and it is teachable. Ours remains,
however, a very hopeful rhetoric. Nearly all the composition research
confirms our belief in the importance of writing as an agent of
knowledge. There is an excitement generated by our enhanced understanding of the mind's involvement with words, and by the mounting
evidence that better writing and thinking *can* be taught in an osten-
sibly postliterate age. We share with the Romantics this excitement
about language. Their art not only foreshadows our research but offers
extraordinary reflections upon the writer's mind at work.

Notes

1. William Wordsworth, "Preface to *Lyrical Ballads*," in *Literary Criticism of William Wordsworth*, ed. Paul M. Zall (Lincoln: University of Nebraska, 1966), 39. Hereafter cited in the text as Zall.

2. For discussions of the shifts from classical to romantic to modern rhetorical theory, see especially Richard Young's "Arts, Crafts, Gifts and Knacks: Some Disharmonies in the New Rhetoric," and Aviva Freedman and Ian Pringle's "Epilogue: Reinventing the Rhetorical Tradition": both essays in *Reinventing the Rhetorical Tradition*, ed. Aviva Freedman and Ian Pringle (Conway, Ark.: L & S Books, 1980), 53-60, 173-185. Also see Frank D'Angelo, *A Conceptual Theory of Rhetoric* (Cambridge, Mass.: Winthrop, 1975), for a discussion of certain "romantic" dimensions of contemporary rhetorical theory.

3. *Biographia Literaria*, ed. George Watson (New York: Dutton, 1965), 197.

4. *The Prelude*, ed. Ernest de Selincourt and rev. Helen Darbishire, 2nd ed. (Oxford: University Press, 1959), 170. Hereafter cited in the text.

5. *Biographia*, 167.

6. *Biographia*, 173.

2 Cognitive Immaturity and Remedial College Writers

Annette N. Bradford
Rensselaer Polytechnic Institute

One of the most common complaints made by teachers of freshman writers is this: My students just don't think. The students most guilty of this indictment are common in two classrooms: the first is the regular freshman English class, where their usually good command of grammar and mechanics leaves the teacher complaining, "He said *nothing*, but he said it so correctly"; the second is the remedial English class where students have neither mechanical excellence nor carefully conceived, mature discussion to recommend their writing.

Neither of the traditional approaches to teaching freshman writing—the content/reader approach or the form/how-to approach—has been really effective in dealing with such students. The basis of their problem seems to be cognitive immaturity and lack of training in studies which might lead to concept formation. Yet many times when I have talked with students who were having writing problems, I have found them quite able to explain verbally what they intended to express in the written assignment. But when these students were forced to take this synthesis one step farther, to the level of written communication, they failed.[1] The problem is not simply a matter of concept formation: it is complicated by the college requirement that students present ideas in written form.

As an introduction to the problem, I will discuss the role of language in concept formation. I will then examine two of Piaget's now-classic developmental stages—Concrete Operations and Formal Operations—in light of the developmental theories of Eric Lenneberg, A. R. Luria, and Lev Vygotsky, and propose a model for integrating Piaget's levels of cognitive development with abstraction theory and stages of physiological development. Finally, I will suggest some ways in which traditional college English programs can adapt to the particular needs of cognitively immature students.

Theories of Concept Formation

In his advice to teachers, educational theorist Robert Gagné outlined eight progressively complex types of learning, ranging from "signal learning" to "problem solving."[2] The more advanced of these types of learning, Gagné contends, "can take place only when a person has mastered a large variety of verbal associations."[3] Levels six, seven, and eight—concept learning, principle learning, and problem solving— emphasize the developmental maturity necessary for the adolescent to draw from the various sectors of his or her experience to synthesize a new concept, a process "of constructing a complex representation of the world (including oneself) and using these representations for the purpose of directing behavior."[4] Eli Saltz defines the process of concept formation as "learning that a great many disparate objects or events belong together in a single category," which helps the learner "deal with novel stimuli in terms of past experience."[5]

Luria and Vygotsky identify the fundamental role of language in concept formation as "the most decisive element in systematizing perception."[6] Language as a symbol system is a person's first and most basic tool of generalization. Even in the use of the individual word, the two year old has accomplished a primitive abstraction when he or she is able to divorce the auditory/linguistic sign "doggie" from its physical referent, the dog. Vygotsky explains:

> A word does not refer to a simple object but to a group or to a class of objects. Each word is therefore already a generalization. Generalization is a verbal act of thought and reflects reality in quite another way than sensation and perception reflect it.[7]

The combination of words to form sentences, even the primitive two- and three-word utterances of three year olds, introduces mediation— that is, the "particular organization of concepts in which each concept is capable of reminding the subject of every other concept in the set."[8] The simplest and most frequently occurring illustration of this inter-concept system, Saltz writes, is the sentence.[9]

Piaget's Stages and Other Developmental Theories

In our culture, as in Piaget's, each of Piaget's developmental periods is initiated by some corresponding stage in language acquisition and cognitive development (see figure 1). At age two, when the child begins the Concrete Operations period, he or she begins to learn

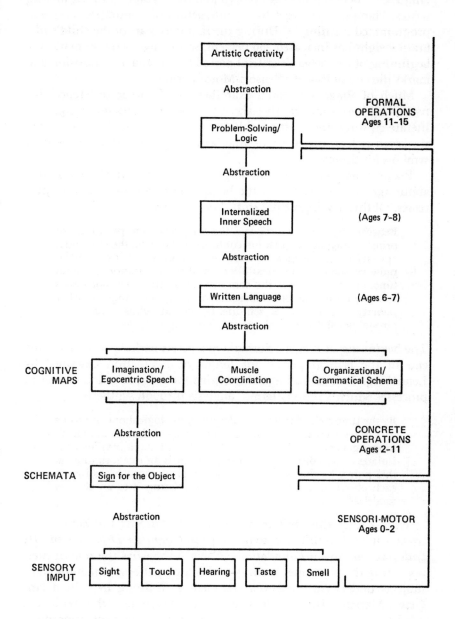

Figure 1. A model of abstraction and concept formation as related to Piaget's Developmental Stages.

language. "Between the ages of two and three years," Eric Lenneberg writes, "language emerges by an interaction of maturation and self-programmed learning."[10] During the first two years of the child's life, brain weight has increased 350 percent, so that age two also marks the beginning of Lenneberg's critical period for language acquisition and marks the end of Piaget's Sensori-Motor period.

Much of Piaget's research examines the dramatic differences between children from ages five–six and those from ages seven–eight. In literate cultures, the most notable rite of passage associated with ages six–seven is learning to write—the beginnings of abstracting written symbols for things.

Piaget's last developmental stage, Formal Operations, is initiated about age eleven and marks the beginning of abstract thought processes. Of this developmental shift, Lenneberg writes:

> Between the ages of three and the early teens the possibility of primary language acquisition continues to be good; the individual appears to be the most sensitive to stimuli at this time and to preserve some innate flexibility for the organization of brain functions to carry out the complex integration of subprocesses necesary for the smooth elaboration of speech and language. After puberty, the ability for self-orientation and adjustment to the physiological demands of verbal behavior quickly declines.[11]

The beginning of Piaget's Formal Operations period, then, marks the end of the critical period for language acquisition described by Lenneberg. This critical age also begins the reorganization of logical processes which Vygotsky terms "analysis through synthesis":

> By the time a child reaches adolescence, the logical operations he uses to reflect reality have undergone a marked change. . . . He no longer generalizes on the basis of his immediate impressions but isolates certain distinct attributes as the basis for categorization; at this point, he draws inferences about phenomena by assigning each object to a specific category (by relating it to an abstract model).[12]

What causes this shift from concrete/situational thinking to abstract/categorical thinking to develop? In *Cognitive Development: Its Cultural and Social Foundations*, Luria emphasizes the role of literacy, citing the phenomenal shifts in thinking patterns which his adult subjects underwent after even rudimentary training in written language. Margaret Donaldson is yet another researcher who credits the manipulation of written language with the power to create concepts.[13]

Concrete and Formal Operations

Why is it that a large number of college freshmen have not acquired an ability which most theorists link with ages eleven through thirteen? What is the basis for the cognitive immaturity that makes these students unable to deal with higher levels of abstraction? Part of the problem, I believe, lies in our too rigid notions of Piaget's stages and their corresponding ages of appearance, which are now classic theory. Even though age two is the point where most theorists mark the onset of language, variations of up to six months on either side of this age are not uncommon—which is to say four plus one or only a 67 percent probability that language acquisition will begin precisely at age two. When children enter school around age six, individual developmental variations are easily observed. This margin for variance becomes even greater when one tries to establish an absolute age for each child to enter puberty.

The problem with Piaget's stages is that they hold true only for the "average" student. The average college freshman can deal with abstractions well enough to perform at the required level in a regular freshmen English class. But my concern is with those students who cannot handle adequately the required abstractions of freshman writing. I contend that while age eleven may mark the beginning of Formal Operations, this period may extend into early adulthood, ages nineteen to twenty, before the ability to abstract concepts is fully developed. Remedial writers may even, in fact, retain some characteristics of the Concrete Operations stage. An understanding of these characteristics as they manifest themselves in remedial writers requires a brief review of the Piagetian stages of Concrete Operations and Formal Operations.

Flavell outlines the accomplishments and limitations of a child at the Concrete Operations stage. Unlike the "before-the-eye reality" required by the Pre-Operational child the Concrete Operational child "is beginning to extend his thought, as Piaget phrases it, from the *actual* toward the *potential*."[14] The limitations of a child at this stage of thinking are important ones. First, by definition, concrete operations are concrete: the child's "structuring and organizing activity is oriented toward concrete things and events in the immediate present."[15] The Concrete Operations child may delineate all possibilities as he or she approaches a problem and then may try to discover which of these possibilities really does occur. Second, the Concrete

Operations child is bound to "the phenomenal here and now"; "he
has to vanquish the various physical properties of objects and events
one by one because his cognitive instruments are insufficiently detached and disassociated from the subject matter they bear upon,
to permit a context-free, once-for-all structuring."[16] The final characteristic, in Flavell's analysis, is the unconnected nature of the Concrete
Operations child's logical groupings: the "concrete-operational systems. . . . do not interlock to form a simple, integrated system by
which the child can readily pass from one substructure to another in
the course of a single problem."[17]

On the other hand, the very significance of the word "formal" in
the expression Formal Operations "refers to the fact that the thinker
can follow the form of an argument but disregard its specific content."[18] Through an integrated group lattice structure which Piaget
terms *structure d'ensemble,* the Formal Operations thinker approaches
a problem by envisioning, through the combination of experimenta-
tion and logical analysis, all the possibilities before arriving at reality.[19]
The new cognitive orientation has several characteristics. First, the
average adolescent's cognitive strategy is fundamentally hypothetic-
deductive in character.[20] Secondly, the formal thinking of this state is
"above all *propositional* thinking, in which the adolescent manipu-
lates abstractions and statements, not raw data."[21] Finally, "this
property of formal thought is closely affiliated with the newly developed orientation towards the possible and the hypothetical."[22] This
shift in mental processes is expressed concisely by Luria in his review
of Vygotsky's theories:

> In his analysis of the fundamental developmental changes in
> mental processes . . . Vygotsky observed that although the young
> child thinks by remembering, the adolescent remembers by think-
> ing. Thus the formation of complex forms of the reflection of
> reality and activity goes hand in hand with radical changes in the
> mental processes that affect these forms of reflection and underlie
> activity.[23]

Finally, it is valuable to examine two of these behavioral stages
drawn by Piaget for adolescent behavior. First, "while the child deals
largely with the present, with the here and now, the adolescent extends
his conceptual range to the hypothetical, the future and the spatially
remote."[24] And secondly, adolescence represents a third "high water
mark" of egocentrism, taking the form of "naive idealism, bent on
intemperate proposals for reforming and reshaping reality. . . . cou-
pled with cavalier disregard for practical obstacles."[25] Piaget describes
this late egocentrism thus:

> The adolescent goes through a phase in which he attributes unlimited power to his own thoughts so that the dream of a glorious future or of transforming the world through ideals . . . seems to be not only fantasy but also an effective action which in itself modifies the empirical world. This is obviously a form of the cognitive egocentrism.[26]

Immature remedial writers still exhibit qualities of Piaget's Concrete Operations stage in their writing. For example, when dealing with imaginative literature, these students's essays will be very concrete; instead of tracing a theme or character, the remedial student will resort to plot summary. Hypothetical, theoretical questions based on reading yield confused and concrete responses, usually based not on the reading, but on the readers' own lives or experiences. This reaction to creative literature suggests another of Piaget's characteristics of the Concrete Operations child: the inability to express in writing any but a context-bound reaction to the work. A topic, for example, which compares themes or ideas in two poems will elicit independent and unrelated summaries of each work. A final characistic of the early adolescent still very much in evidence in remedial writers is an embarrassing egocentrism. Assignments meant to be logical explorations of a topic based on an experience with an essay or a piece of literature often elicit confessional writing from remedial writers. They produce embarrassingly personal pieces impossible to grade without students' construing an attack on their approach to the topic as an attack on their personal feelings. Thus, although these students have entered Formal Operations, it is wrong to assume that, like clockwork, every adolescent emerges from Formal Operations at age fifteen, ready to deal with high-level abstractions and logical thought processes.

Implications for Teaching Remedial Writers

If we can conclude from the previous discussion that cognitive immaturity and the inability to handle abstract thought processes, especially in writing, are major difficulties facing remedial writers, what implications does this fact have for the teaching of freshman writing? Luria was able to help his adult subjects make the transition from concrete-situational thinking to abstract-categorical thinking through training in writing. Could the teacher of freshman writing do the same for his or her students?

At least the rudiments of abstract thought might be taught through practice and through exposure to assignments and subject matter which demand that the student form new concepts from existing structures. Vygotsky emphasized that the active process of concept formation "emerges and takes shape in the course of a complex operation aimed at the solution to a problem," that the mere mechanical linking of a word and object are not sufficient.[27] This theory might offer possibilities for several alterations of the traditional freshman English curriculum, enabling it to deal with *all* of its students. In the same manner that various "Honors" programs adjust to college freshmen who are exceptionally cognitively mature, a remedial writing program built around the teaching of abstraction would respond to students who were cognitively immature.

One possibility might be a test of abstract writing and thinking developed to screen cognitively immature students and place them in remedial classes. The same purpose would be served by a freshman English curriculum flexible enough to allow remedial students to shift out of regular freshman writing classes into smaller classes geared to deal with the problems of the remedial student; such an arrangement would be easier to incorporate into an existing program. The college cannot, after all, wait for the cognitively immature to "grow up," for these students need as quickly as possible to develop the thinking and writing skills required for success in their other college courses.

The goal of such courses would be to help students emerge from Formal Operations with confidence in their ability to handle high-level abstractions in oral and written communications. As Andrea Lunsford suggests, such classes should be student-centered (not teacher-centered) workshops in which learners arrive at concepts by drawing inferences from relevant particulars rather than having those concepts simply handed to them by their teachers. Lunsford suggests the following structures for the basic writing classroom, structures derived from an abstract thought theory:

1. Basic writing classes should never be teacher-centered. [Avoiding set lectures, the teacher should conduct the class in] small workshop groups in which all members are active participants.
2. Class time should be spent writing, reading what has been written aloud to the group audience and talking about that writing.
3. Such sessions require an atmosphere of trust, and they demand careful diagnosis and preparation by the teacher.[28]

I agree with Lunsford: experience tells me that small groups of remedial students learn from each other and actively benefit from the social atmosphere of the classroom. Luria emphasizes the role of such an environment when he laments that psychology "has avoided the idea that many mental processes are social or historical in origin."[29] Citing Piaget, Phillips too agrees that a classroom in which a student is working to establish formal operations cannot be teacher-centered: "Every time you teach a child something, you keep him from reinventing it."[30] The role of the teacher, then, in the basic writing classroom is that of guiding students and providing them with materials and exercises which lead them to synthesize new relationships from existing information.

Notes

1. Andrea Lunsford contends that, "while these writers may have little difficulty in dealing with familiar everyday problems requiring abstract thought based on concepts, they are *not aware of the processes they are using.* Thus they often lack the ability to infer principles from their own experience." ("Cognitive Development and the Basic Writer," *College English* 41 [September 1979]: 39.)

2. Gagné's eight progressively complex types of learning:

"1-*signal learning*—involuntary response
2-*stimulus-response learning*—voluntary action reinforced through operant conditioning
3-*chaining*—S/R bonds in specific sequence
4-*verbal association*—learning of complex S/R bonds
5-*multiple discrimination*—learning to respond differently to similar verbal associations as they grow in number and become more complex
6-*concept learning*—responding to things or events as a class
7-*principle learning*—learning to combine or relate chains of concepts
8-*problem solving*—learning to combine principles in a way which permits application to a wide variety of new situations."

As quoted in Robert F. Biehler's *Psychology Applied to Teaching* (Boston: Houghton Mifflin Company, 1971), 207-208.

3. Gagné in Biehler, 207.

4. Margaret Donaldson, "The Development of Conceptualization" in *The Development of Cognitive Processes,* ed. Vernon Hamilton and Magdelene D. Vernon (London, San Francisco, and New York: Academic Press, 1976), 278.

5. Eli Saltz, *The Cognitive Bases of Human Learning* (Homewood, Ill.: The Dorses Press, 1971), 29.

6. A. R. Luria, *Cognitive Development: Its Cultural and Social Foundations,* trans. Martin Lopez-Morillas and Lynn Solotaroff, ed. Michael Cole (Cambridge, Mass. and London: Harvard University Press, 1976), 50.

7. L. S. Vygotsky, *Thought and Language,* ed. and trans. Eugenia Hanfmann and Gertrude Vakav (New York, London, and Cambridge, Mass.: MIT Press and John Wiley and Sons, Inc., 1962), 5.

8. Saltz, 310.

9. Ibid., 310.

10. Eric Lenneberg, *Biological Foundations of Language* (New York, London, and Sydney: John Wiley and Sons, Inc., 1967), 162.

11. Ibid., 142.

12. Luria, 52.

13. According to Donaldson, "it seems likely that the change from concrete to categorical thinking is closely linked to the process of becoming literate. . . . Oral language is always language embedded in some kind of context (though its referent may or may not be in the here and now). Written language endures unchanging across space and time, and by virtue of this there is pressure for it to become explicit, self-sufficient, context free" (p. 295).

14. John H. Flavell, *The Developmental Psychology of Jean Piaget* (New York: Dvan Nostra, Ltd., Company, 1963), 203.

15. Ibid., 205.

16. Ibid., 204.

17. Ibid., 205.

18. John L. Phillips, *The Origins of Intellect: Piaget's Theory* (San Francisco: W. H. Fresman and Co., 1976), 103

19. Flavell, 204.

20. Ibid., 205.

21. Ibid., 206.

22. Ibid., 206.

23. Luria, 11.

24. Flavell, 223.

25. Ibid., 224.

26. Piaget as quoted in Flavell, 224–225.

27. Vygotsky, 54.

28. Lunsford, 41.

29. Luria, 3.

30. Piaget in Phillips, 120.

3 Current Brain Research and the Composing Process

Monica R. Weis SSJ
Nazareth College

> I wish to God that some neurologist would sit down and figure out how the improviser's brain works, how he selects, out of hundreds of thousands of possibilities, the notes he does and at the speed he does—how, in God's name, his mind works so damned fast! and why, when the notes come out right, they are right. . . . Composing is a slow, arduous, obvious, inch-by-inch process, whereas improvisation is a lightning mystery. In fact, it's the creative mystery of our age.[1]

Alec Wilder's wish, quoted in a 1973 *The New Yorker*, articulates for the field of jazz the basic question facing serious teachers of composition. What really happens in the composing process? Why does a flash of intuition often make the crucial difference between a merely artificial piece of writing and a sincere, authentic voice? Not only *why* does it make a difference, but precisely *how* does it make a difference? In focusing on this question, I would like to summarize current areas of brain research that provide information about hemispheric asymmetry—information that *should* influence the direction of teaching composition.

Research in Hemispheric Asymmetry

It has long been suspected that the two cortical hemispheres of the brain are concerned with different operations or modes of knowing: that is, the left hemisphere, which controls the production of speech, perceives the world logically, critically, and sequentially, whereas the right hemisphere is involved in intuitive, holistic patterning, visual, spatial, musical apprehension. Because thinking is such a complex operation of largely unmeasurable interacting elements, no precise and conclusive data really isolates and explains what happens. However, by examining patients who for medical reasons have only one operative hemisphere, neurosurgeons and scientists are discovering some surprising information about brain activity. A. R. Luria, the Russian psychologist, worked with a musician who, after his stroke, composed better music than before his illness. Although he could no longer speak or write down the notes, he could play them and remember them. It would seem that some dimension of his musical ability was developed or released after his speech faculties were impaired. In effect, he was communicating in a new way through music.[2] Similarly, it is not unusual for a speech or physical therapist to succeed in getting some aphasic stroke victims to write, indicating that perhaps cerebral integration can overcome or bypass the injured site.[3] Recently, at New York University, Andrea Glass taught an eighty-four-year-old woman in rehabilitation who could neither speak nor understand speech to communicate via shaped and colored plastic symbols.[4]

Experiments with split-brain individuals (epileptics who have undergone commissurotomy, which severs the corpus callosum between the cortical hemispheres to reduce the occurrence of seizures) support this data and provide the additional advantage of presenting problem-solving tasks to two separate and functioning brains. If the subject uses special contact lenses, information presented to the left visual field (LVF) is processed only in the right hemisphere (RH), and information presented to the right visual field (RVF) is processed only in the left hemisphere (LH). Milner and Taylor (1972) found that the right hemisphere demonstrated superior visuo-spatial performance. When a design was presented to the right hemisphere, the left hand drew more accurate pictures than when the design was presented to the left hemisphere for right hand response.[5] This is not just a case of better muscle coordination, as has been demonstrated in another experiment by Gazzaniga. His split-brain patient was asked to duplicate an arrangement of blocks and then to duplicate a three-dimensional drawing of a cube. The right hand (responding to information processed by the left hemisphere) was unable to perform either task; that is, the left hemisphere could not process the visual and spatial information being presented to it.[6]

In addition to visuo-spatial perception, the right hemisphere seems capable of generating emotional reactions. Sperry and Gazzaniga flashed a picture of a nude to the LVF-RH of a split-brain woman who, while she *said* that she had seen nothing (and indeed, that hemisphere had seen nothing), blushed and then broke into a slow grin. When asked why she was laughing, the woman made a lame excuse: "Oh, that funny machine!" The dominant (or left) hemisphere has also been documented as interfering with the nondominant hemisphere. There are instances in problem-solving tasks in which the right hand will interrupt the left hand drawing a picture, or in which the right hand will tear down a block arrangement being built by the left hand. It is as if the left or dominant hemisphere did not want the right or nondominant hemisphere to succeed in an activity—as if the dominant hemisphere resented the competition.[7]

In another experiment, Gazzaniga flashed the word "heart" to the patient—the "he" portion to the LVF-RH and the "art" portion to the RVF-LH (he - art). Thus each hemisphere was simultaneously receiving different information. When speaking, the patient would say he had seen "art"; when pointing to a card with the left hand, the patient invariably pointed to "he." As Gazzaniga reports, "both hemispheres had simultaneously observed the portions of the word available to them and in this particular case the right hemisphere, when it had the opportunity to express itself, had prevailed over the left."[8] Gazzaniga's work with split-brain patients has led him to conclude that each of the two hemispheres is capable of mental functions of a high order. Why then is the right hemisphere, the nondominant one, so subjugated?

Or to rephrase this question to echo Alec Wilder's remarks, cited at the paper's opening: in the composition classroom, why does a moment of intuition come so rarely? Why are students unable to get their brilliant ideas onto paper? One hypothesis is that after age two or three, when left hemisphere dominance is firmly established, whatever "language" is learned by the right hemisphere in early childhood becomes functionally suppressed, perhaps lost or erased, and the corpus callosum assumes the role of a traffic cop transmitting language information primarily in one direction—that is, to the critical, analytic left hemisphere which leans toward ordered, structured outlines and passes judgment on the intuitive flashes of the right hemisphere. Some studies are being done with amobarbitol to paralyze the left hemisphere temporarily, which relieves "competition" so that the primitive linguistic abilities of the right hemisphere can be activated.

A similar phenomenon has been recorded in dream research: the left hemisphere (that is, the critical faculty) acts as an objective "watcher" or monitor during the dream sequence. At other times, however, the left hemisphere is either inaccessible to consciousness or engaged in data dumping. Then the right brain, what Erich Fromm calls the "forgotten language," acts freely. What is important in dream research for this consideration of intuition and composition is the information it provides about right hemispheric activity: all creative acts accomplished in the dream state are "quintessentially pattern-recognition . . . not analytic."[9] You may recall the famous example of Friedrich Kekulé, who in 1865 struggled over a linear concept of the benzene molecule until he dreamed of a rotating ring of atoms—fantasized as a snake biting its tail—and realized that the molecule was an hexagonal ring of carbon atoms. Contemporary writer and journalist, Donald Murray, insists he still has difficulty convincing his wife and daughter that when he is faced with an editorial problem and deals with it by taking a nap on the couch in his office, he is really "working"—what Arthur Koestler would call "thinking aside."[10]

Notice that this brief list is composed of experiments based on observation of behavior. More recently, some landmark research into the biological underpinnings of brain plasticity indicate that Lenneberg's critical period hypothesis may not be entirely accurate. Now, instead of believing that the development of the cortex is fixed at puberty, Lynch and Wells report that the constituents of the adult brain, that is, the neurones and glia, possess "considerable capacity for growth." Bennett (1976) reports a change in the shape of dendrites of mature rats exposed to an enriched environment. These results, say Lynch and Wells, suggest a new hypothesis: "an ever-changing brain capable of growing new circuitry rather than a static structure which simply modifies the strength of its embryologically defined wiring pattern."[11] Evoked responses monitored by electroencephalogram (EEG) recordings seem to support this new speculation (Wood 1971). "Subjects were asked to discriminate between the stop consonants *ba* and *da* (a linguistic discrimination) and between fundamental frequency of *ba* at 140 Hz and *da* at 104 Hz (a non-linguistic discrimination). The EEG responses for the two tasks differed significantly in the left hemisphere, showing that there were different neural consequences depending on whether the type of processing required was linguistic or non-linguistic, even though the acoustic signals were identical."[12]

Admittedly, there are many more experiments that could be discussed here. My purpose, however, has been merely to present a brief sampling of research in hemispheric asymmetry. We can conclude broadly that the right hemisphere seems to be qualitatively different from the left; environment and conditioning seem to affect the neocortex; growth and rearrangement of neural circuitry seem possible. These generalizations suggest a right hemisphere capable of both interrelated and independent intuitive activity—a right hemisphere which is often the overlooked component in the process of composing.

Encouraging the Creative Component in Writing

As composition specialists, we recognize the need to encourage the creative component in writing. We are beginning to understand more accurately that making sense of the world around us involves not only the logical, analytic ordering predominant in left hemispheric activity but also the intuitive patterning process predominant in right hemispheric activity—processes that can be taught as well as learned. John Dixon, the English educator, has said: "The intuitive act is not absolutely beyond the writer's control; it can be nourished and encouraged."[13]

Let me illustrate this nourishment by using as an example one of my students at the University of Virginia last fall. Students in ENWR 101 were asked to write an essay about something that was bothering them—something they wanted to know more about—and to phrase that topic as a question. One young man was experiencing anxiety about being on the swim team. Faced with this dissonance—the "disequilibrium" Piaget claims is essential for learning—my student phrased his situation this way: Why am I still on the swim team? The filtering process of language which produced this expression suggests the student already has an untested hypothesis about his anxiety. Then he toyed with possible answers to his question—in this exploration stage, the student engages in what John Dixon calls valuable "gossip," essential for "recalling experience, getting it clear, giving it shape and making connections, speculating and building theories."[14] Such dallying with experience leads the student to the work of selecting, arranging, organizing his data. My swim team student at first saw his reasons for remaining on the team organized into physical, psychological, social, and financial advantages. But with some teacher guidance and classroom experiences in appropriate heuristics to strengthen right hemispheric activity, a student could begin to see other possible groupings of the raw data: individual, family, school, and community reasons for remaining on the team; on-campus and off-campus advantages; the value for personal development, for job hunting, for raising children in future years.

In this stage of experimenting with categories—of seeing the range, the aspects, and the other classes of the phenomenon—the students may reach a Eureka moment when they discover what they really want to write about; that is, students gain insights into how language shapes and gives meaning to their experience. They discover a plan that fits their purposes in writing. In other words—critical judgment (hemispheric activity more toward the left end of the thinking continuum) affirms the choice of pattern. But as often happens in the midst of the composing process, when the writer already has begun a rough draft, the writer comes upon the unexpected. The surprising discovery may be an additional right hemispheric insight about language use, a new intuition about the arrangement of the data that more closely fits a perception of reality, or a problem in describing an experience to an audience (that is, problems with conventions of spelling or with the dialect/register grid). Then the writer has to alter the strategy. As Thomas Kuhn explains so well in *The Structure of Scientific Revolutions,* new data or insights necessitate restructuring the web of knowledge.[15] The whole process of composing, and more specifically the stages of rhetorical invention, demonstrates the recursive quality of thinking that is actualized by the interplay of right and left hemispheric activity.

In past decades, we have emphasized the logical thought and analytical judgment of the argumentation essay or the perfect Harvard outline to the detriment of holistic perception. And yet in the history of great ideas, the flash of insight has triumphed and made people famous. How many students know, for instance, that Einstein dreamed up his generalization about the time-space continuum while sick in bed? As can be demonstrated by some of the experiments mentioned above, when free from the logical, neat categorizing of left brain activity, new discoveries of possible—or even impossible—combinations can be entertained.

So what about my student who was experiencing anxiety over being on the swim team, and what about specific heuristic techniques to aid the creative process? Paul, despite a background of ten years of swim team competition, discovered through this composing experience that he really wanted something else from his college career; he subsequently quit the team. And by the way, the essay was his best of the semester.

As for heuristic procedures to encourage the flash of insight, my primary concern is that the technique be consistent with what we know about hemispheric activity. For example, Rohman's prewriting, writing, editing schema provides a system for generating ideas, but his notion of the three stages is based on a sequential concept of the composing process. Although experimental testing of his particular program indicates that students achieve better results with the heuristic than without it, brain research indicates that the writing process is not linear but recursive. Kenneth Pike's tagmemics help a student investigate a topic by contrast, range of variation, and distribution in class, context, and matrix. The value of this method, according to Pike, is the set of questions it provides to help the student begin writing. My own experience with using a modified version of this strategy with students is that, although answering the questions does start the students writing, I'm not convinced it leaves ample room for true right brain activity and the moment of insight. Students, and particularly poor students, are apt to entangle themselves in the technique, not sensing when to let it go to celebrate a new intuition. Brainstorming, free writing, problem solving—whatever the heuristic—must be more than a memory retrieval aid and must allow sufficient time and respect for the recursive stages of invention.

Questions for Further Research

My comments leave us with some crucial and as yet unanswered questions: If Piaget is correct that the young school child is an intuitive thinker, how important is an experience-based curriculum for older students? Are Peter Elbow's and Ken Macrorie's approaches to freeing students to write sufficient, or should there be a more guided program of writing experiences? If the left hemisphere acts as the primary audience to intuitive thinking, is there any way to stimulate right hemispheric activity while tempering the critical judgment of the left hemisphere? Is there something we can learn from an interaction of the linear nature of spoken and written discourse and Susanne Langer's description of the simultaneous impact of a contextualized art form?

While we have no facile answers to these questions and, indeed, in some instances no real hypotheses, I sense that a major contribution to understanding the composing process can come from current trends in brain research. As Carl Sagan points out in *The Dragons of Eden:*

> There is no way to tell whether the patterns extracted by the right hemisphere are real or imagined without subjecting them to left hemisphere scrutiny. On the other hand, mere critical thinking, without creative and intuitive insights, without the search for new patterns, is sterile and doomed. To solve complex problems in changing circumstances requires the activity of both cerebral hemispheres: the path to the future lies through the corpus callosum.[16]

If the right hemisphere is qualitatively different, as research seems to indicate, perhaps in working with older students we need hard data on the effects of visual stimuli in the classroom, development and testing of spatial-concept warm-up exercises before a composing session, and new hypotheses about the holistic effect of music as a direct stimulus to creative thinking. But above all—and this can be accomplished almost immediately—we need to make students comfortable with the presence of mystery in the composing process and particularly in the stages of rhetorical invention. Here, more than in any other stage of the composing process, students freeze because they have not been reassured about the recursive nature of the stages of invention, nor have they been taught anything about the alternation of interaction of right and left hemispheric activity. Students often regard their inability to formulate an adequate outline—whatever that is—as a failure of their writing skills, or worse, as a failure of themselves as persons. And while there is at present little coordinated and substantiated data from research on functions of right and left hemispheres, students desperately need to be reassured that their groping for ideas is a wonderful, albeit painful, phenomenon of languaging that allows them to shape their own world according to their own intuitive patterning.

As composition specialists we cannot afford to overlook current theories of possible brain growth and development. We need to build on the research efforts of colleagues like Dixie Goswami and Janet Emig, who are now charting the composing habits of aphasics. We need to design heuristic strategies built on sound scientific theories. The cooperation of disciplines is not only valuable for science, but contributes to one of the most important aspects of developing man, for as James E. Miller, Jr. says in *Word, Self, Reality:*

> In the process of sorting through his thoughts, or of disentangling and examining his tangled experiences, he is in effect defining himself, outlining himself, asserting and proclaiming himself. There can be no more vital activity for the individual. . . .[17]

Notes

1. Alec Wilder in "Profile" by Whitney Balliet, *The New Yorker,* 9 July 1973, 45; also quoted by Janet Emig in *The Writing Processes of Students,* ed. Walter T. Petty and Patrick J. Finn, Conf. Report No. 1 (Buffalo: SUNY, 1975), 13-14.
2. Maya Pines, *The Brain Changers: Scientists and The New Mind Control* (New York: NAL, 1973), 136.
3. E. Weigl, "Written Language: Acquisition and Disturbances," in *Foundations of Language Development: A Multidisciplinary Approach,* vol. 2, ed. Eric and Elizabeth Lenneberg (New York: Academic Press, 1975), 386.

4. Pines, 142.

5. Gillian Cohen, *The Psychology of Cognition* (New York: Academic Press, 1977), 193.

6. Michael S. Gazzaniga, "The Split-Brain in Man," in *Language*, ed. Clark, Eschholz, and Rosa (New York: St. Martin's Press, 1977), 131.

7. Pines, 137.

8. Gazzaniga, 128.

9. Carl Sagan, *The Dragons of Eden* (New York: Ballantine Books, 1977), 179.

10. Arthur Koestler, *The Act of Creation* (London: Macmillan, 1964), 145–177.

11. G. Lynch and J. Wells, "Neuroanatomical Plasticity & Behavioral Adaptability," in *Brain and Learning*, ed. Timothy Teyler (Stamford, Conn.: Greylock Pub., 1978), 106.

12. Cohen, 207.

13. John Dixon, *Growth Through English* (Oxford: NATE, 1978), 1–2.

14. Dixon, 7.

15. Thomas S. Kuhn, *The Structure of Scientific Revolutions*, (Chicago: University of Chicago Press, 1970), 2 ff.

16. Sagan, 190–191.

17. James E. Miller Jr., "Discovering the Self" from *Word, Self, Reality*, in *The Conscious Reader*, ed. C. Shrodes, et al. (New York: Macmillan, 1974), 27.

4 Recovering and Discovering Treasures of the Mind

Marilyn Goldberg
The Pennsylvania State University

One justification for any kind of education is that the human brain, unlike other internal organs of the body, is capable of functioning the way human beings consciously choose for it to function. That is, intelligent intervention can improve the otherwise automatic and spontaneous operations of the brain. Consciously, educators can mold and shape and strive to perfect the activities of their students' minds.*

Throughout the years of schooling, much of that intervention fulfills either of two quite different objectives. The first is quantitative: through education we increase the amount of information stored in the mind. The second objective is pragmatic: through education we improve the skill with which people store, retrieve, and organize information. In the best of all possible worlds, the two objectives work together: as we increase the amount of information stored in the mind, we also improve the efficiency of the mind's operations—generally as a result of frequent repetitions of those operations.

In this essay, we will examine some ways that composition teachers intervene to improve the activities of their students' minds. One basic premise is that we work far more vigorously to fulfill the second objective—improving cognitive skills—than we do the first. However, we do teach some information, and in order to teach it effectively, we need to understand something about the way learners store it—in concepts. Further, insights into concept learning can help us recognize some isomorphic features in thinking and writing and also some particular ways in which writing necessitates significant memory searches. Thus we can understand how our intervention enables our students to improve thinking skills—often discovering in the process some treasures lurking unseen in their own minds.

---

* I use the word "brain" here to refer to the physiological organ. Throughout the paper, however, I use the word "mind" to denote the psychological construct that seems to originate in the brain.

Conceptual Learning

Some students enter my classes with clear concepts of the technical vocabulary of sentence structures: they know exactly what I mean when I talk about clauses, phrases, sentences, and paragraphs. But most of them do not, even though they can repeat definitions like "a sentence is a complete thought with a subject and a verb." These students possess information but they have no conception of its significance. They have learned meaningless information by rote. What rote learning does is render the information available to the conceptualizing processes, but if these further cognitive activities fail to take place, the grammatical and rhetorical information will be useless.

Conceptual learning differs from rote learning, not in degree but in kind, and we must be aware of the difference when we try to teach information in a composition course. Furthermore, as Vygotsky notes in *Thought and Language*, confusing rote learning with concept learning is a natural error. Success with tests that seek memorized information or that require completed exercises does not necessarily indicate successful learning, even though in theory such success indicates mastery. The feedback on both rote learning and real learning, especially in the pursuit of high-level concepts, can be the same. How, then, can we know when our students have mastered the concept of, for example, verbs or sentences? We must constantly check their ability to utilize these concepts: they need to find verbs in the clauses they read and write, and they need to write all kinds of sentences and clauses—and non-sentences as well. In other words, we can move from the plane of the concept itself to the exemplar, and if our students can use the concept frequently in various ways over a period of time, then we will know that they know it.

The difficulty of teaching concepts that must be attained, as distinct from information that can be memorized, is compounded by another problem that is particularly pernicious for teachers of composition. We ask our students to focus upon the most ordinary of their skills, the skills of using language and of thinking. What we want them to understand are their own most intimate thoughts and their most intuitively regular mental operations, qualities that they know so well that the conscious effort to recognize them is extremely demanding. As Chomsky indicates, "One difficulty in the psychological sciences lies in the familiarity of the phenomena with which they deal. A certain intellectual effort is required to see how such phenomena can pose serious problems or call for intricate explanatory theories."[1] He quotes others who recognize the same quality of consciousness—

Wittgenstein, for example: "The aspects of things that are most important for us are hidden because of their simplicity and familiarity."[2] Vygotsky alludes to the problem and suggests a solution citing a "law of awareness" by which "an impediment or disturbance in an automatic activity makes the actor aware of that activity."[3] That is, we are rarely aware of our usual activities until they are disturbed or until, as Murphy's Law states, something goes wrong. What qualities of human life could be more usual, more simple and familiar, more intuitively regular to our students than their own language and their own thoughts? We could easily paraphrase Chomsky's comment: "One difficulty in the teaching of composition lies in the familiarity of the phenomena—thought as well as language—with which we deal."

Organization of Ideas

Overly familiar concepts and rote learning provide substantial hazards in the teaching of composition. If our efforts to teach concepts of language structure are successful, however, some unanticipated learning can develop. That is, if our students do truly learn what we can teach, they can learn more than the skill of writing: they can gain insight into their own minds. Consider some of the terminology we use. When we teach arrangement or organization of ideas in a paper, for example, we teach concepts such as *thesis sentence, topic sentence, subordination, coordination,* and so on. These terms apply also to the organization (or potential organization) of ideas often loosely confederated in the mind. Again, we may introduce the concept of outlining with its parallel structures and its superordinate and subordinate ideas. Furthermore, some composition teachers follow a syllabus that demands from students a number of papers written in different modes, organized according to different logical formats: inductive or deductive organizations, classifications, comparison, analyses, and so on. Finally, some of us talk about levels of abstractions: for example, using the metaphor of a camera—its lenses of varying lengths zooming in and zooming out while trained on a subject—we can describe some ways of changing the perspective in students' descriptions and narratives and comparisons. All of these explanations of organizing writing, of using different modes, and of varying perspectives are also explanations of some aspects of the organization and functions of our thought processes.

Jerome Bruner, the director of the Center for Cognitive Studies at Harvard University until 1972, has developed a model describing the mind's hierarchical arrangements of concepts. The mind, Bruner demonstrates, receives information and stores it according to its ability to place the information into established categories. And these categories are embedded within each other to form classes subsuming classes, ever increasing the dimensions of abstraction. The process of categorizing, Bruner wrote in 1965, gives us a way "to render discriminably different things equivalent, to group the objects and events and people around us into classes, and to respond to them in terms of their class membership rather than their uniqueness."[4] Brief examples of Bruner's classification system include animals, cats, my cat Charlotte; or Third World People, Kenyans, and Jomo Kenyatta; or topic sentences and restrictives; or superordinate, coordinate, and subordinate elements. In other words, there is an elegant isomorphism between the structures of our minds and the structures of our writing, and understanding this relationship can become an exciting learning experience for our students.

Obviously, our methods of teaching thinking are not those of the philosopher or the logician. We do not try to create awareness of bonding and deductive procedures by lecturing about those procedures; nor do we insist that our students master skills of syllogistic reasoning. Rather, we instruct them in the nature of logic by our attention to their organization of ideas in every stage of the composing process, from outline to completed paper. We must insist that students avoid using chronological relationships exclusively, those that slip most spontaneously into consciousness. By insisting that they classify ideas or exemplify them, we are forcing them to rearrange or consciously manipulate the information stored in their memories. Thus, we are establishing a framework for attacking the problem of overfamiliarity; students can become aware of some structures of their own thinking.

Outlining and the Superordination of Concepts

One major source of understanding their own thinking processes is the outlining procedure, for that outline, properly contrived, recapitulates the categorizing or embedding process that Bruner describes. One of the most difficult concepts to teach thoroughly is the superordinate relationship between the thesis sentence and the major ideas subordinate to it, and then the further subordinate relationship of the details to those major ideas. Students are often capable of performing the activities of organizing without understanding the logic or the mental operations of outlining. And they often fail to recognize why they should understand what they can do intuitively, an argument used even more effectively against the demand that they learn their intuitively derived grammar. But with patient efforts to exemplify, to extricate from other writing, to diagram with circles and ladders, most students experience a mild "eureka," and they do understand. Once they gain that important insight, once that high-level abstraction is clear, it is likely that they can understand not only their conscious and controlled writing efforts, but also their spontaneous thinking efforts. They can recognize the way that their minds jump, for example, from the experience with a teacher to hasty generalizations about that teacher, from their single experience with a minority person to their likely generalizations about all members of that minority, from their scanty encounters with news from television newscasts to their major, often compelling opinions about their country and their world. They can experience the emptiness of their generalizations and the poverty of their supporting knowledge. They can discover the need to challenge generalizations, to support their views rigorously, and to modify or even reverse their original opinions.

Thus, we show our students the relationship between the formal, conscious logic of their writing and the pervasive, spontaneously developed logic of their thinking. And while they are recognizing the processes of thinking, they are also encountering their own thoughts, increasing their familiarity with what they know. In teaching writing, we teach our students to clarify their ideas in their sentences and to organize them in their papers, forcing them to confront what they think as they develop the contents of their own memory structures.

Memory Scanning

How do they search through memory and choose specific ideas for elaboration in their papers? In his book, *Cognitive Psychology*,[5] Ulric Neisser suggests that people use the same procedures when searching through memory that they use when their senses are searching through the world beyond themselves. Describing in full the activities of sensory perception, notably visual perception, Neisser postulates that the process takes two steps: when the eyes are open or any of the senses is alert, a vast field of possibilites impinges upon them; then instantaneously, reflexively, the eye, directed by the brain, chooses some small portion of that field to perceive. In other words, human beings constantly scan the passing world and then immediately focus on selected portions of it. These portions are not selected at random. The choice is made by what Neisser calls an "executive," a decision-making mechanism named for its counterpart in computers. Likewise with memory: all of memory is potentially available, but at any given moment, only certain portions are selected for retrieval, again, by a kind of "executive." The processes of both perception and memory retrieval continuously proceed automatically, involuntarily. However, they can be trained. Intervention can create procedural habits so that the "executive" selects information that will fulfill some preconceived plan voluntarily and deliberately. That human intervention takes the form of education.

Teachers can assist students in the mechanical experience of scanning and make them conscious of some executive decisions of focusing: the development of these thinking skills is possible in a class in composition. We help to train our students' thinking processes by providing writing assignments that demand scanning and focusing on memories. Then students can deliberately select those they want to use and carefully organize them. As noted above, this exercise of an "executive" is necessitated by composition assignments that diminish reliance on chronology as an organizing principle, assignments that force students to develop other kinds of mental operations.

I explain this shift from chronological to logical organization in my classes. Recently, one of the students was writing about different kinds of hands, and to describe the hands of old people, she reflected on those of her grandmother. During one class, I directed her to recall a number of occasions when she observed those hands, and then I asked her to put these different experiences together to derive a generalization about her grandmother's hands, and then, in a larger abstraction, about the hands of old people. Thus we were able to clarify the inductive thinking process (along with the perils of that process); in addition, we could share the student's experience of scanning her memory and then focusing on selected portions of it. We could establish that the segments of memory were often long separated in time and that, reordered in a nonsequential way and treated collaterally, they became logical. Through this simple, exemplary thinking experience, the students could recognize that an "executive" was continuously confronting decisions.

Although Neisser does not link his observations on memory searches with Piaget's observations on reflective thinking, the concepts are similar. Piaget, also, links perception and reflective abstraction as two sources of information that can feed the ever-constant process of creating an individual structure of intellect (or mind). And his concept of intelligence is not unlike Neisser's concept of the executive. Intelligence, a highly elaborated word in Piaget's special terminology, is the activity or operation of coordination, and that coordination mediates not only the structure of intellect with the impinging environment, but also the structure of intellect with itself—in reflective abstraction. That is, the structure of intellect can feed upon itself, constantly refining and recoordinating itself as a result of its adjustment to its own new products. And it works this way by re-placing or re-storing previously stored information. Presumably that restorage process will result in what Piaget calls "equilibration," the constantly elusive goal toward which mental activities tend, the relaxation of tension between the world as it is perceived and the world as it may truly exist. For Piaget as for Neisser, this activity of the mind upon information already stored in the mind is a major source of practice in the development of intellectual skills.

Recovering Treasures

The act of reaching consciously into the clumped-up structures of memory, of re-searching through the sometimes dusty and rarely activated elements of its construction, can reveal some treasures, some original and profound nuggets of special value, nuggets worth displaying in writing. We can distinguish between recovering and discovering such treasures: recovering results from the uncomplicated act of seeking a treasure where we know it is stored and then finding it; discovering it—a far more pleasurable experience—results from a creative act, largely one of synthesis, that produces a thought never before suspected. We cannot always account for the origin of the creative thought, but sometimes seeking to recover a memory, a reflective thinker discovers his or her new treasure—a new formula, a new interpretation of a Joycean enigma, a new synthesis of old thoughts previously existing in unconnected compartments of memory. We are describing a new consciousness of some pre-existing possibilities, an awareness of some familiar and often unexamined material in memory, often material to which we have become so habituated that it rarely if ever comes to conscious thought.

Creating the necessity for a new analysis, composition classes offer the opportunity for a new synthesis. The act of writing demands that concepts, generally global or even imagistic in storage, be forced into the linear patterns of writing, patterns organized by the analytical determination of thesis, sub-theses and details. The act of analysis, then, implements thinking skills: students select parts of their concepts and arrange them logically—side by side or embedded within each other. Students write them clearly in sentences and then gather those together in paragraphs. At the same time, the act of analysis creates a new familiarity with the concepts stored in memory: with all of this conscious manipulation of their own thoughts, students are likely to come to some conscious understanding of those thoughts. They might even discover some hidden generalizations that motivate much of their behavior; they might even fulfill a major goal of education by controlling their thinking processes—and those generalizations—by making conscious executive decisions.

Clearly this kind of consciousness and control will not characterize the thinking of all graduates of our classes, but the possibility does exist, and, if we understand it, we can exploit it. If we ascertain that our students do indeed learn what we teach, and if we demand that students not lapse into the easy efforts of their old accept-it-as-it-is-stored thinking, then we can improve the odds that our students will come to know their old thoughts, discover new ones and, at the same time, develop conscious skill in thinking.

Notes

1. Noam Chomsky, *Language and Mind* (New York: Harcourt Brace Jovanovich, 1972), 24.

2. Ibid., 25.

3. L. S. Vygotsky, *Thought and Language,* ed. and trans. Eugenia Hanfmann and Gertrude Vakar (Cambridge, Mass.: The M.I.T. Press, 1962), 16.

4. Jerome Bruner, Jacqueline J. Goodnow, and George A. Austin, *A Study of Thinking* (New York: Science Editions, 1965), 1.

5. Ulric Neisser, *Cognitive Psychology* (Englewood Cliffs, N.J.: Prentice-Hall, 1967), 279.

5 Understanding Composing

Sondra Perl
Herbert H. Lehman College, CUNY

Any psychological process, whether the development of thought or voluntary behavior, is a process undergoing changes right before one's eyes. . . . Under certain conditions it becomes possible to trace this development.[1]

L. S. Vygotsky

It's hard to begin this case study of myself as a writer because even as I'm searching for a beginning, a pattern of organization, I'm watching myself, trying to understand my behavior. As I sit here in silence, I can see lots of things happening that never made it onto my tapes. My mind leaps from the task at hand to what I need at the vegetable stand for tonight's soup to the threatening rain outside to ideas voiced in my writing group this morning, but in between "distractions" I hear myself trying out words I might use. It's as if the extraneous thoughts are a counterpoint to the more steady attention I'm giving to composing. This is all to point out that the process is more complex than I'm aware of, but I think my tapes reveal certain basic patterns that I tend to follow.

Anne
New York City Teacher

Anne is a teacher of writing. In 1979, she was among a group of twenty teachers who were taking a course in research and basic writing at New York University.[2] One of the assignments in the course was for the teachers to tape their thoughts while composing aloud on the topic, "My Most Anxious Moment as a Writer." Everyone in the group was given the topic in the morning during class and told to compose later on that day in a place where they would be comfortable and relatively free from distraction. The result was a tape of composing aloud and a written product that formed the basis for class discussion over the next few days.

43

One of the purposes of this assignment was to provide teachers with an opportunity to see their own composing process at work. From the start of the course, we recognized that we were controlling the situation by assigning a topic and that we might be altering the process by asking writers to compose aloud. Nonetheless, we viewed the task as a way of capturing some of the flow of composing and, as Anne later observed in her analysis of her tape, she was able to detect certain basic patterns. This observation, made not only by Anne, leads me to ask, "What basic patterns seem to occur during composing?" and "What does this type of research have to tell us about the nature of the composing process?"

Recursiveness in Writing

Perhaps the most challenging part of the answer is the recognition of recursiveness in writing. In recent years, many researchers including myself have questioned the traditional notion that writing is a linear process with a strict plan-write-revise sequence.[3] In its stead, we have advocated the idea that writing is a recursive process, that throughout the process of writing, writers return to substrands of the overall process, or subroutines (short successions of steps); writers use these to keep the process moving forward. In other words, recursiveness in writing implies that there is a forward-moving action that exists by virtue of a backward-moving action. The questions that then need to be answered are, "To what do writers move back?" "What exactly is being repeated?" "What recurs?"

To answer these questions, it is important to look at what writers do while writing and what an analysis of their processes reveals. The descriptions that follow are based on my own observations of the composing processes of many types of writers including college students, graduate students, and English teachers like Anne.

Writing does appear to be recursive, yet the parts that recur seem to vary from writer to writer and from topic to topic. Furthermore, some recursive elements are easy to spot while others are not. The most visible recurring feature or backward movement involves rereading little bits of discourse. Few writers I have seen write for long periods of time without returning briefly to what is already down on the page. For some, like Anne, rereading occurs after every few phrases; for others, it occurs after every sentence; more frequently, it occurs after a "chunk" of information has been written. Thus, the unit that is reread is not necessarily a syntactic one, but rather a semantic one as defined by the writer.

The second recurring feature is some key word or item called up by the topic. Writers consistently return to their notion of the topic throughout the process of writing. Particularly when they are stuck, writers seem to use the topic or a key word in it as a way to get going again. Thus many times it is possible to see writers "going back," rereading the topic they were given, changing it to suit what they have been writing or changing what they have written to suit their notion of the topic.

There is also a third backward movement in writing, one that is not so easy to document. It is not easy because the move, itself, cannot immediately be identified with words. In fact, the move is not to any words on the page nor to the topic but to feelings or non-verbalized perceptions that surround the words, or to what the words already present evoke in the writer. The move draws on sense experience, and it can be observed if one pays close attention to what happens when writers pause and seem to listen or otherwise react to what is inside of them. The move occurs inside the writer, to what is physically felt. The term used to describe this focus of writers' attention is "felt sense."

The term "felt sense" has been coined and described by Eugene Gendlin, a philosopher at the University of Chicago. In his words, felt sense is

> the soft underbelly of thought . . . a kind of bodily awareness that . . . can be used as a tool . . . a bodily awareness that . . . encompasses everything you feel and know about a given subject at a given time. . . . It is felt in the body, yet it has meanings. It is body and mind before they are split apart.[4]

This felt sense is always there, within us. It is unifying, and yet, when we bring words to it, it can break apart, shift, unravel, and become something else. Gendlin has spent many years showing people how to work with their felt sense. Here I am making connections between what he has done and what I have seen happen as people write.

When writers are given a topic, the topic itself evokes a felt sense in them. This topic calls forth images, words, ideas, and vague, fuzzy feelings that are anchored in the writer's body. What is elicited, then, is not solely the product of a mind but of a mind alive in a living, sensing body. When writers pause, when they go back and repeat key words, what they seem to be doing is waiting, paying attention to what is still vague and unclear. They are looking to their felt experience, and waiting for an image, a word, or a phrase to emerge that captures the sense they embody. Usually, when they make the decision to write, it is after they have a dawning awareness that something has clicked, that they have enough of a sense that if they begin with a few words heading in a certain direction, words will continue to come which will allow them to flesh out the sense they have.

The process of using what is sensed directly about a topic is a natural one. Many writers do it without any conscious awareness that that is what they are doing. For example, Anne repeats the words "anxious moments," using these key words as a way of allowing her sense of the topic to deepen. She asks herself, "Why are exams so anxiety provoking?" and waits until she has enough of a sense within her that she can go in a certain direction. She does not yet have the words, only the sense that she is able to begin. Once she writes, she stops to see what is there. She maintains a highly recursive composing style throughout, and she seems unable to go forward without first going back to see and to listen to what she has already created. In her own words, she says:

> My disjointed style of composing is very striking to me. I almost never move from the writing of one sentence directly to the next. After each sentence I pause to read what I've written, assess, some-times edit and think about what will come next. I often have to read the several preceding sentences a few times as if to gain momentum to carry me to the next sentence. I seem to depend a lot on the sound of my words and . . . while I'm hanging in the middle of this uncompleted thought, I may also start editing a previous sentence or get an inspiration for something which I want to include later in the paper.

What tells Anne that she is ready to write? What is the feeling of "momentum" like for her? What is she hearing as she listens to the "sound" of her words? When she experiences "inspiration," how does she recognize it?

In the approach I am presenting, the ability to recognize what one needs to do or where one needs to go is informed by calling on felt sense. This is the internal criterion writers seem to use to guide them when they are planning, drafting, and revising.

Drawing on the Felt Sense

The recursive move, then, that is hardest to document but is probably the most important to be aware of is the move to felt sense, to what is not yet in words but out of which images, words, and concepts emerge. The continuing presence of this felt sense, waiting for us to discover it and see where it leads, raises a number of questions.

Is "felt sense" another term for what professional writers call their "inner voice" or their feeling of "inspiration"?

Do skilled writers call on their capacity to sense more readily than unskilled writers?

Rather than merely reducing the complex act of writing to a neat formulation, can the term "felt sense" point us to an area of our experience from which we can evolve even richer and more accurate descriptions of composing?

Can learning how to work with felt sense teach us about creativity and release us from stultifyingly repetitive patterns?

My observations lead me to answer "yes" to all four questions. There seems to be a basic step in the process of composing that skilled writers rely on even when they are unaware of it and that less skilled writers can be taught. This process seems to rely on very careful attention to one's inner reflections and is often accompanied with bodily sensations. When it's working, this process allows us to say or write what we've never said before, to create something new and fresh, and occasionally it provides us with the experience of "newness" or "freshness," even when "old words" or images are used.

The basic process begins with paying attention. If we are given a topic, it begins with taking the topic in and attending to what it evokes in us. There is less "figuring out" an answer and more "waiting" to see what forms. Even without a predetermined topic, the process remains the same. We can ask ourselves, "What's on my mind?" or "Of all the things I know about, what would I most like to write about now?" and wait to see what comes. What we pay attention to is the part of our bodies where we experience ourselves directly. For many people, it's the area of their stomachs; for others, there is a more generalized response and they maintain a hovering attention to what they experience throughout their bodies.

Once a felt sense forms, we match words to it. As we begin to describe it, we get to see what is there for us. We get to see what we think, what we know. If we are writing about something that truly interests us, the felt sense deepens. We know that we are writing out of a "centered" place.

If the process is working, we begin to move along, sometimes quickly. Other times, we need to return to the beginning, to reread, to see if we captured what we meant to say. Sometimes after rereading we move on again, picking up speed. Other times by rereading we realize we've gone off the track, that what we've written doesn't quite "say it," and we need to reassess. Sometimes the words are wrong and we need to change them. Other times we need to go back to the topic, to call up the sense it initially evoked to see where and how our words led us astray. Sometimes in rereading we discover that the topic is "wrong," that the direction we discovered in writing is where we really want to go. It is important here to clarify that the terms "right" and "wrong" are not necessarily meant to refer to grammatical structures or to correctness.

What is "right" or "wrong" corresponds to our sense of our intention. We intend to write something, words come, and now we assess if those words adequately capture our intended meaning. Thus, the first question we ask ourselves is "Are these words right for me?" "Do they capture what I'm trying to say?" "If not, what's missing?" Once we ask "what's missing?" we need once again to wait, to let a felt sense of what is missing form, and then to write out of that sense.

Retrospective Structuring

I have labeled this process of attending, of calling up a felt sense, and of writing out of that place, the process of retrospective structuring. It is retrospective in that it begins with what is already there, inchoately, and brings whatever is there forward by using language in structured form.

It seems as though a felt sense has within it many possible structures or forms. As we shape what we intend to say, we are further structuring our sense while correspondingly shaping our piece of writing.

It is also important to note that what is there implicitly, without words, is not equivalent to what finally emerges. In the process of writing, we begin with what is inchoate and end with something that is tangible. In order to do so, we both discover and construct what we mean. Yet the term "discovery" ought not lead us to think that meaning exists fully formed inside of us and that all we need do is dig deep enough to release it. In writing, meaning cannot be discovered the way we discover an object on an archeological dig. In writing, meaning is crafted and constructed. It involves us in a process of coming-into-being. Once we have worked at shaping, through language, what is there inchoately, we can look at what we have written to see if it adequately captures what we intended. Often at this moment discovery occurs. We see something new in our writing that comes upon us as a surprise. We see in our words a further structuring of the sense we began with, and we recognize that in those words we have discovered something new about ourselves and our topic. Thus when we are successful at this process, we end up with a product that teaches us something, that clarifies what we know (or what we knew at one point only implicitly), and that lifts out or explicates or enlarges our experience. In this way, writing leads to discovery.

All the writers I have observed, skilled and unskilled alike, use the process of retrospective structuring while writing. Yet the degree to which they do so varies and seems, in fact, to depend upon the model of the writing process that they have internalized. Those who realize that writing can be a recursive process have an easier time with waiting, looking, and discovering. Those who subscribe to the linear model find themselves easily frustrated when what they write does not immediately correspond to what they planned or when what they produce leaves them with little sense of accomplishment. Since they have relied on a formulaic approach, they often produce writing that is formulaic as well, thereby cutting themselves off from the possibility of discovering something new.

Projective Structuring

Such a result seems linked to another feature of the composing process, to what I call projective structuring, or the ability to craft what one intends to say so that it is intelligible to others. A number of concerns arise in regard to projective structuring; I will mention only a few that have been raised for me as I have watched different writers at work.

1. Although projective structuring is only one important part of the composing process, many writers act as if it is the whole process. These writers focus on what they think others want them to write rather than looking to see what it is they want to write. As a result, they often ignore their felt sense and they do not establish a living connection between themselves and their topic.

2. Many writers reduce projective structuring to a series of rules or criteria for evaluating finished discourse. These writers ask, "Is what I'm writing correct?" and "Does it conform to the rules I've been taught?" While these concerns are important, they often overshadow all others and lock the writer in the position of writing solely or primarily for the approval of readers.

Projective structuring, as I see it, involves much more than imagining a strict audience and maintaining a strict focus on correctness. It is true that to handle this part of the process well, writers need to know certain grammatical rules and evaluative criteria, but they also need to know how to call up a sense of their reader's needs and expectations.

For projective structuring to function fully, writers need to draw on their capacity to move away from their own words, to decenter from the page, and to project themselves into the role of the reader. In other words, projective structuring asks writers to attempt to become readers and to imagine what someone other than themselves will need before the writer's particular piece of writing can become intelligible and compelling. To do so, writers must have the experience of being readers. They cannot call up a felt sense of a reader unless they themselves have experienced what it means to be lost in a piece of writing or to be excited by it. When writers do not have such experiences, it is easy for them to accept that readers merely require correctness.

In closing, I would like to suggest that retrospective and projective structuring are two parts of the same basic process. Together they form the alternating mental postures writers assume as they move through the act of composing. The former relies on the ability to go inside, to attend to what is there, from that attending to place words upon a page, and then to assess if those words adequately capture one's meaning. The latter relies on the ability to assess how the words on that page will affect someone other than the writer: the reader. We rarely do one without the other entering in; in fact, again in these postures we can see the shuttling back-and-forth movements of the composing process, the move from sense to words and from words to sense, from inner experience to outer judgment and from judgment back to experience. As we move through this cycle, we are continually composing and recomposing our meanings and what we mean. And in doing so, we display some of the basic recursive patterns that writers who observe themselves closely seem to see in their own work. After observing the process for a long time we may, like Anne, conclude that at any given moment the process is more complex than anything we are aware of; yet such insights, I believe, are important. They show us the fallacy of reducing the composing process to a simple linear scheme, and they leave us with the potential for creating even more powerful ways of understanding composing.

Notes

1. L. S. Vygotsky, *Mind in Society*, trans. M. Cole, V. John-Steiner, S. Scribner, and E. Souberman (Cambridge, Mass.: Harvard University Press, 1978), 61.

2. This course was team-taught by myself and Gordon Pradl, associate professor of English Education at New York University.

3. See Janet Emig, *The Composing Processes of Twelfth Graders*, NCTE Research Report No. 13 (Urbana, Ill.: NCTE, 1971); Linda Flower and J. R. Hayes, "The Cognition of Discovery," *College Composition and Communication* 31 (February 1980): 21–32; Nancy Sommers, "The Need for Theory in Composition Research," *College Composition and Communication* 30 (February 1979): 46–49.

4. Eugene Gendlin, *Focusing* (New York: Everest House, 1978), 35, 165.

6 Written Products and the Writing Process

Lee Odell
Rensselaer Polytechnic Institute

The distinction between written products and the writing process is not so great as we sometimes assume. By examining written products, we can identify analytic skills that writers might use both in exploring facts, ideas, and feelings and in formulating their thoughts on a given subject. Of course, there are certain kinds of information which cannot be obtained by analyzing a completed piece of writing. For one thing, we cannot learn about the sequence of activities a writer went through in the process of producing a draft. If, for instance, we want to learn about the interrelated activities that Linda Flower and John R. Hayes label *generating, organizing,* and *goal-setting,*[1] we will have to observe writers while they are engaged in the act of composing. Moreover, we cannot assume that a written product reflects all of the writer's conscious analytic activity. For example, analogies or distinctions that occurred to a writer early in the composing process may later be discarded because they seem irrelevant or invalid.

These limitations notwithstanding, we can reasonably talk about the thinking reflected in a piece of writing. Although problematic,[2] this inquiry rests upon three assumptions. The first is that, as Frank D'Angelo argues,[3] the attempt to understand a subject requires that one look for relationships in the phenomena one is writing about. The second assumption, which I share with both D'Angelo and Ross Winterowd,[4] is that some of these relationships are made explicit in the linguistic structure of a written text. And the final asssumption, advanced by cognitive psychologists and reading theorists, is that thinking is not governed solely by intuition but is guided by "plans" or "schemata," strategies for "gathering, sorting, or transforming information."[5] On the basis of these assumptions, I argue that writers' choices of language, syntax, and content have epistemological significance. These choices reflect ways of knowing; they involve strategies or plans or schemata for thinking about a given topic.

Professional and Student Writing Samples Contrasted

Since the significance of these strategies seems clearest when one examines contrasting pieces of writing, I shall compare student writing with professional writing on each of two topics. One set of student papers is in response to this assignment:

> Write about a childhood experience to which you had a strong emotional reaction; perhaps the experience was sad or funny or frightening. The time span of the experience should be brief, no more than two or three hours *at most*.

The other set of papers was written in response to this assignment:

> Assume that you are looking at a car (not your own) with one or more bumper stickers on it. What reasonable guesses can you make about the personality, attitudes and/or experience of the person who owns the car you are looking at?

For purposes of contrast, I shall discuss passages from published essays on similar topics: Truman Capote's "A Christmas Memory" and Jim Hougan's article on graffiti, "Kilroy's New Message." After completing my analysis of this writing, I shall comment on the appropriateness and the limitations of my comparisons. The basis for my analysis in this article will be a set of categories derived from tagmemic theory: *focus, contrast, classification, change, reference to sequence, reference to physical context.*[6]

Focus

Near the beginning of "A Christmas Memory," Truman Capote gives readers a first glimpse of a close boyhood friend, an elderly cousin who will figure prominently in his narrative:

> A *woman* with shorn white hair is standing at the kitchen window. . . . *She* is small and sprightly, like a bantam hen; but, due to a long youthful illness, *her shoulders* are pitifully hunched. *Her face* is remarkable—not unlike Lincoln's, craggy like that, and tinted by sun and wind; but it is delicate too, finely boned, and *her eyes* are sherry-colored and timid. [italics mine]

The succession of grammatical subjects in this passage suggests a series of visual images, much as though a camera were focusing first on *a woman*, then zooming in to focus on *her shoulders*, on *her face*, and last on *her eyes*. With each new *grammatical focus* (a term I will use interchangeably with grammatical subject of a clause), Capote is led to make a new observation about his friend. At the risk of straining the syntax/camera metaphor, I suggest that each change in grammatical and visual focus brings the narrator closer to his subject and hence brings into view details that would not be readily apparent from a greater distance.

Jim Hougan begins his article on graffiti with this paragraph:

> Slowly and almost unnoticed, the *Men's Room* has become politicized. On its walls—in London, Amsterdam, Paris, New York—*an ideological storm* rages multilingually. Imperialism is roundly denounced. *World leaders* are deflated in witty pentameters that cannot be reprinted in the public press. *Liberation* is demanded for Angola, Mozambique, Surinam, . . . *Revenge* is summoned on behalf of Kent, Attica, and the Eniwetok Atoll. [italics mine]

Grammatical subjects in this passage do not suggest the sort of specific visual examination found in the passage by Capote. Yet by shifting from *Men's Room* to *ideological storm* to *world leaders* to *liberation* and *revenge,* Hougan has introduced several important facets of his subject: the setting in which graffiti are found, the people who are objects of graffitists' wrath, the messages conveyed in the "new" graffiti, and the fervor (the "storm") with which those messages are expressed.

This shifting of focus appears throughout the passages by Hougan and Capote. Only a relatively small percentage of Hougan's clauses have as their subject a word that is also used as the subject of one or more other clauses. And the most frequently repeated grammatical subject (the names of a scholar Hougan refers to often) appears in less than ten percent of the clauses I examined. Capote, too, is relatively unlikely to dwell upon a single grammatical subject. The most frequently repeated subject (the pronoun *we*) appears in only twenty-seven percent of the clauses in his writing.

Student writing, on the other hand, does not show nearly as much variation in focus. In both their exposition and narration, over half their clauses are likely to have the same word as grammatical subject. For example, in a very typical bumper sticker essay, a student focused extensively on the owner of a car that bore the bumper sticker "Thank God I'm an American":

> Obviously, *the person* who owns this car is proud that *he* or *she* lives in America. *The person* might also be fed up with other people who have stickers that say Thank God I'm Irish or some other country. *The person* might have realized that after all of the trouble in the world, the best place to be is in America. [italics mine]

The limitations of this passage become particularly clear if we contrast it with another student essay, one of the very few essays in our sample in which the student writer shifted focus effectively:

> The *bumper sticker* read, "Honk if you're horny," and was stuck on the man's bright orange sports car. Looking very straight and conservative, *he* seemed somewhat embarrassed. Dressed in a brown suit, white shirt, and brown tie, *he* looked very meek and mild. *He* seemed as if *he* did not want to look around at the other drivers or passengers of the cars stopped at the red light. *His attention* was fixed only on the top of the steering wheel. *I* imagined the *orange car* could not have been his own; maybe *it* was his daughter's or his son's. As *we* both sat at the red light, with cars surrounding us on both sides, a *young kid* in the car behind him beeped his horn. *The man* looked up very quickly, wishing maybe that the light had changed. No, it was still red. Only *the color of the man's face* had changed—to bright red. I could see in his face he was thinking of the sticker. . . . [italics mine]

There may be several ways to account for the differences in the use of focus in these two passages. For purposes of this analysis, the important thing is that the shifting of focus in the second passage reflects a strategy for perceiving and understanding a scene, a strategy that is not found in the first passage.

As did both Hougan and Capote, students often focused on human *Agents;* the subject slot of a clause was likely to be filled with a noun referring to people who act, do something to, have some influence upon the topic at hand. But Hougan also focused on people or objects that are *Affected* by the actions or phenomena he is discussing (*"World leaders* are deflated") and Hougan occasionally focuses on *Actions* ("The *liberalization* of laws relating to obscenity has had its effect . . ."). Students, by contrast, were somewhat less likely to focus on grammatical categories other than *Agent.* Only 6 percent of the clauses in these essays focused on something other than *Agent.* But 37 percent of Hougan's clauses focus on *Affected* or *Actions.*

Both Capote and Hougan also shifted focus to some aspect of the physical context in which one finds the experiences/phenomena they were discussing. For example, after describing a long day of gathering and shelling pecans, Capote wrote:

> The *kitchen* is growing dark. *Dusk* turns the window into a mirror: our *reflections* mingle with the rising moon as we work by the fireside in the firelight. At last, when the *moon* is quite high, we toss the final hull into the fire and, with joined sighs, watch it catch flame. [italics mine]

In one sense, Capote's subject here is the feeling that comes at the end of a day. But he has conveyed that feeling, in part, by commenting on aspects of his physical surroundings—the kitchen, dusk, the moon. In the passage I examined, 21 percent of Capote's clauses have this sort of grammatical focus. Hougan never focused on physical context so frequently in a short passage. Nonetheless, 11 percent of his clauses focus on (and, hence, make some comment about) the physical contexts in which graffiti appear. Student writing showed very little focus on physical context. Only 5 percent of the clauses in narrative essays had an element of physical context as subject of the clause, and only 2 percent of the clauses in student expository writing had this sort of subject.

Throughout this analysis, I have been assuming that grammatical focus is extremely important, that the grammatical subject of a clause influences the direction or at least the emphasis of a clause.[7] A change in grammatical subject suggests a shift in a writer's attention; it obligates a writer to comment on a new aspect of the subject at hand. Although repetition of the same grammatical subject may be appropriate in some circumstances, failure to shift grammatical focus, at least in student essays considered here, can suggest a restricted examination of the subject at hand.

Contrast

Part of understanding anything (an action, feeling, motive, value, idea) requires that we contrast it with other things, determine what it is not, see how it differs from other things. Hougan and Capote have used two kinds of contrasts. First, they appear to have noted differences between two or more facets of experience that actually exist: feelings that are being or have been felt; actions that are taking or have taken place; ideas that have been or are being expressed; objects that have existed or currently exist. Hougan notes: "Unlike their political counterparts, [certain graffitists] have no obvious social program. . . ." Hougan also comments that "Of all repressive efforts [to thwart graffitists] the blackboard is the *most naive,* the sandy paint the *most totalitarian.*" As Capote and his friend are shelling a large bowl of pecans, Capote tells his readers that "now and again my friend sneaks [for the dog] a mite, *though* insisting we deprive ourselves." When they make fruitcakes, they have the problem that "of the ingredients that go into our fruitcakes, whiskey is the *most expensive* as well as the *hardest* to obtain."

In addition to citing differences between two things that actually exist, Hougan and Capote also noticed differences between what actually exists and what could or should exist. In speaking of the "other people" with whom he and his friend live, Capote says, ". . . *though they have power over us and frequently make us cry, we are not,* on the whole, too much aware of them." Here Capote has contrasted an actual state of affairs (lack of awareness) with what one might assume to be the case when the "other people" have so much power. Hougan cites the same sort of contrast when he remarks that "the graffitist has *not* been awarded his proper stature or importance."

In their narration and in their exposition, students used some of the same kinds of contrasts that Hougan did. But students' use of contrast differed from Hougan's and Capote's in several ways. In general, students' writing shows relatively little attention to contrasts between two items that actually exist; students noted this sort of contrast less than half as often as did Hougan and Capote. In their narratives, students were—unlike Capote—especially interested in the disparity between what existed and what might have existed. For instance, one student narrated a childhood experience in which his older brother and sister, left to baby-sit with their younger brother, put their brother to bed early so that they could invite friends over for a party:

> By that time, it must have been all of six o'clock, and I was getting hungry, since they *had not given* me any dinner before I went to bed. I yelled downstairs for something to eat. . . . After much begging and pleading, my brother asked me if I'd like a banana, I was ecstatic. "Yes! Yes! Yes!" I screamed, while jumping up and down on my bed. "Well, we *don't have any,*" replied my brother. [italics mine]

In each of the underlined passages, the writer mentions a conflict between a possible state of affairs (having a certain kind of food for dinner, being fed dinner before being sent to bed) and an actual state of affairs (lacking food, being sent to bed without dinner).

In their expository writing, students were often concerned with a third sort of contrast (one that Capote and Hougan used only rarely), a contrast between two hypothetical items. For example, one student noted that the driver of a car with a certain bumper sticker "might know karate, might *not* know the bumper sticker is there, and lastly might *not* appreciate your honking." *Might not know* and *might not appreciate* suggest a disparity between one hypothetical state (*knowing* and *appreciating*) and a more likely hypothetical state (*not knowing, not appreciating*).

Certainly it can be useful to note contrasts between what is actual and what is possible and between two hypothetical conditions. These types of contrasts seem appropriate in the passages cited above. But they do lead one away from direct examination of existing phenomena. They may serve to complement the first type of contrast, but—judging from Capote's and Hougan's writing—they need not completely overshadow it.

Classification

Almost a corollary of contrast is the attempt to find similarities, points at which a given aspect of a topic has something in common with other things. This process is readily apparent in Hougan's and Capote's use of analogy and in their labeling.

As one might expect, Capote's work contains a number of analogies: his small savings consist of "dollar bills, tightly rolled and green as May buds. . . . nickels and quarters worn as smooth as creek pebbles"; his friend is "small and sprightly as a bantam hen. . . ." Curiously enough, however, "A Christmas Memory" contains an even larger number of instances in which Capote classifies by labeling: "We are cousins"; "She . . . was a child"; "She is still a child." In each of these clauses, the predicate nominative indicates a larger class of things, of which the grammatical subject is a member or instance. Occasionally, the labeling is not literal ("We are cousins") but metaphoric ("She [a woman in her sixties] is still a child").

Since Capote's writing is highly personal and highly expressive, his use of analogy is not surprising. But Hougan's work, which is much more impersonal and explanatory than is Capote's, also relies heavily on metaphor. Sometimes this appears in explicit analogy (articles printed by underground papers, Hougan asserts, "tend to have the same satirical, anti-authoritarian character as graffiti"), but frequently his metaphor is implicit in syntactic structures that indicate labeling. In commenting on the textured paint used by some restaurant owners to deter graffitists, Hougan says, "It [textured paint] is the teargas of the W. C., a weapon whose purpose it is to discourage, confuse, and disperse." The subject/linking verb/predicate nominative structure and the appositive structure indicate labeling. But, of course, reference to paint as teargas, even to paint as a weapon entails an imaginative leap, an unsuspected connection that is at the heart of successful metaphor.

Students used analogies less frequently than did Hougan and Capote. In Capote's work, analogies appear almost twice as often as in students' work. Moreover, even when Hougan classifies by labeling, his labels frequently have the metaphoric quality I mentioned above.

Yet this sort of metaphoric labeling never appears in any of the students' expository essays. Moreover, students' labeling tends to be uninformative. Not infrequently, one finds syntactic structures that indicate labeling, but convey relatively little information. For example, one student wrote: " 'Thank God I'm Italian' and 'D'Amico for Sheriff' are bumperstickers I have seen lately." Obviously these are bumperstickers; in this context, it is unlikely that they would be anything else. The phrase *bumperstickers I have seen lately* provides almost no new information about "Thank God I'm Italian" or "D'Amico for Sheriff."

Change

In "A Christmas Memory," Capote pays considerable attention to the ways things change or are changed. In most instances, Capote talks about overt, perceptible changes. He notes, for example, that his friend's face has been *"tinted* by sun and wind," that she can "tame hummingbirds . . . till they balance on her finger," and that her shoulders have become "hunched" due to an illness. Occasionally Capote reports on nonperceptible changes—variations in mood, feelings, attitudes—but even in these instances he is likely to express changes through some metaphor. He refers, for example, to "the Christmas time of year that exhilarates her imagination and *fuels* the blaze of her heart."

Although Hougan refers to both perceptible and nonperceptible changes, he does so in proportions that are nearly the opposite of those found in Capote's essay; he refers most frequently to changes in feelings, attitudes, ideas. Occasionally, he expresses these changes metaphorically (through the work of graffitists, "World leaders are deflated. . . ." and "images are punctured.") But in just over three-fourths of his references to change, he uses words such as *discourage, confuse, challenge,* and *frustrate* to indicate that some internal, nonperceptible change has taken place.

Students' references to change—in both narrative and expository writing—seem more like Hougan's than Capote's. As did Hougan, students commented chiefly upon internal nonperceptible changes—in feelings, attitudes, or understanding. Unlike the student who wrote about the "Honk if you're horny" bumper sticker, students were most likely to say, for example, that someone became embarrassed rather than noting that "only the color of the man's face had changed—to bright red." Unlike Hougan and Capote, few students expressed changes metaphorically. In the childhood experience essays, students referred to perceptible changes only about half as often as did Capote.

Physical Context

Earlier, I noted that both Hougan and Capote focused on (that is, made grammatical subject of a clause) physical context as part of the effort to explore a topic or convey a mood. There are several other similarities in their references to physical context:

1. For both writers, references to a scene (or objects within a scene) provide a location/setting for people's activities.

2. Both writers indicate where objects in the physical context are located in relation to other objects in the physical context. For example:

   > But one way and another we do each year accumulate Christmas savings, a Fruitcake Fund. These moneys we keep hidden in an ancient bead purse under a loose board under the floor under a chamber pot under my friend's bed.

3. Each writer talks about aspects of the physical context as though they were capable of acting. Capote notes that, on a given day, "the fireplace commenced its seasonal roar"; he refers to his friend's face as being "tinted by sun and wind." Hougan points out that a blackboard (placed in restrooms in the hope of diverting the graffitists) "contravenes the illicit character" of the game graffitists play with the establishment.

4. After referring to a given object, both Hougan and Capote frequently mention a rather restricted feature of that object. Capote refers to the house in which his story will take place, then to the kitchen of that house, then to the kitchen window, and finally to a pane of glass in that window. Similarly, Hougan mentions the men's room, the walls of the men's room, the textured paint on those walls, and the graffiti that appear on those walls.

In their references to physical context, the two writers differ slightly. But differences between the two writers are not nearly so great as are differences between the professional writers and student writers. Student papers simply do not reflect the same analysis of physical context that we find in the professional writers' work. It was very unusual for students to refer to a more limited feature of an object they mentioned elsewhere in their papers. And, it was relatively unusual for students to refer to physical context as active (rather than passive). In their expository writing, students were rather unlikely to refer to the physical context as a location for people's actions. Their most frequent reference to physical context was a reference to the car on which a bumper sticker appeared. But with very few exceptions (such as we find in the "Honk if you're horny" essay) students did not locate the car in a larger setting, nor did they focus in on specific features of the car that might have given more significance to the message on the bumper sticker.

In their narrative writing, students frequently referred to physical context as a location for people's actions. The following excerpt from one narrative illustrates this general trend and also contains two exceptions to the practice of most of the student writers. Having described a fight she once had with her sister, one student wrote:

> . . . I decided to march in the house and tell my mother the situation. Well, my sister insisted on teasing me about being a big baby and followed after me. Trying to avoid her I ran into the house and shut the glass door behind me. To my surprise there she was making funny faces at me through the glass. I became so aggravated with her I wanted to punch her in the face. Not realizing the glass would break and might hurt someone, I forced my fist through the glass. The door went to a million pieces of glass and all in my sister's face.

As did most other students, this writer refers to the house, the general setting in which action took place. However, unlike most other students, this student refers to a more specific aspect of the physical context (the glass door) and refers not only to the ways she acted upon the physical context (shutting the door, striking the glass) but also refers to the physical context as an actor ("The door went into a million pieces of glass and all in my sister's face.")

Sequence

Hougan began his essay by remarking that "slowly and almost unnoticed, the Men's Room has become politicized." "There was a time," he observes, "when these same walls were the home of the filthy limerick, the inviting telephone number, the obscene drawing. . . . however today the Men's Room . . . is a political forum par excellence." After locating his subject in a time sequence, Hougan speculated about several cause-effect sequences:

> Just why the pornographers should have abandoned the world's privies to ideologues and Cartesians is not difficult to surmise. Certainly the liberalization of laws relating to obscenity had had its effect in the WC's transformation from the domain of Eros to the demesne of Marx and Descartes. Its suppression over, pornography is today more a commodity than a cri de coeur. Its relation to the rest room is forever changed.

Capote too made frequent references to time sequence. He began his story by locating his experience in time: "Imagine a morning in late November. A coming of winter morning more than twenty years ago. . . . Just today the fireplace commenced its seasonal roar." He also commented—infrequently—on causal sequence: his friend's shoulders are hunched "due to a youthful illness"; the "others" in the house occasionally cause Capote and his friend to cry; he and his friend have to close their "Fun and Freak Museum" (which consisted of a three-legged chicken and a stereopticon with slides of New York and Washington) *"due to* the demise of the main attraction."

The students differ from the professional writers in their references to temporal and causal sequence. In narration, students referred to cause-effect sequences almost twice as frequently as did Capote, usually to explain why they felt or acted as they did. But in exposition students made relatively few references to causal sequences; Hougan made almost three times as many such references as did students. It would appear that in narration, where reference to time sequence was especially appropriate, students tended to refer to causal sequence more frequently than they might have, and in exposition, where reference to causal sequence seems especially appropriate, students tended to emphasize time sequence. Moreover, students' references to causal sequence often have a quality that is not usually found in Hougan's or Capote's writing. When students mention a causal sequence, they frequently seem to be responding to the question, "Why did you make that last assertion?" Capote and Hougan rarely explain why they felt or thought as they did. Typically, their references to cause-effect sequence explain why others acted or felt as they did or why certain phenomena existed.

Conclusion

These samples of student and professional writing reflect quite different ways of thinking about a subject. Although these distinctions seem very significant to me, I want to be careful not to claim too much. I do not suggest these distinctions would necessarily appear in other pieces of writing done by the professionals and students. Indeed, for both student and professional, writing done in other circumstances or for other purposes might reflect quite different ways of knowing.[8] Further, I do not assume that student writers are incapable of engaging in the same intellectual activities that are reflected in the professionals' writing. And finally, I do not want to make value judgments on the basis of the distinctions I have pointed out. When I am reading a set of papers done in response to the same assignment, an analysis of *contrast*, for example, may help me explain to a student why a particular passage seems especially well- or poorly-thought out. But to be fair to the students whose work I have examined, that sort of judgment is inappropriate here. Comparisons I have made are useful only in *describing* the intellectual processes that may be reflected in student writing.

Bearing in mind these reservations and others I mentioned at the outset of this article, I suggest that the sort of analysis I have illustrated may be particularly useful in the teaching of writing. We have good reason to think we can teach student writers to make conscious use of certain intellectual processes as they try to formulate their ideas. As we assess the "intellectual style" reflected in written products, we may be able to give students much more help with the process of formulating and revising their ideas. For example, reference to physical context had seemed to me a relatively simple matter. In teaching students to use this as a heuristic procedure, I have simply encouraged them to think of settings in which a phenomenon would (and would not) likely exist. But the analysis of Capote's and Hougan's writing makes it clear that there's much more involved. One may refer to physical context simply in order to establish a setting for some object, person, action, or attitude. But one may also, for example, explain how objects in the physical context are located in relation to other objects; observe ways the physical context is acted upon; think of ways in which the physical context acts; examine smaller aspects of some item already mentioned.

Or in place of simply suggesting that students vary grammatical focus, we can suggest specific ways they might shift focus so as to explore a topic more thoroughly. Rather than merely urging students to note contrasts or changes, we can indicate some of the different kinds of contrasts or changes they might look to as they determine what they want to write about. Obviously, this sort of help does not guarantee that students will automatically begin to write like professional writers. But to the extent that effective writing depends on careful, sensitive thinking, we can at least help students increase their chances of finding something interesting to say. And we can begin to make useful connections between written products and the writing process.

Notes

1. Linda Flower and John R. Hayes, "The Dynamics of Composing: Making Plans and Juggling Constraints," in *Cognitive Processes in Writing,* ed. Lee Gregg and Erwin Steinberg (Hillsdale, N.J.: Lawrence Earlbaum, 1980).

2. See Anne Gere's discussion of this point in "Written Composition: Toward Theory of Evaluation," *College English* 42 (September 1980): 48.

3. Frank J. D'Angelo, *A Conceptual Theory of Rhetoric* (Cambridge, Mass.: Winthrop Publishers, Inc., 1975).

4. W. Ross Winterowd, "The Grammar of Coherence," in *Contemporary Rhetoric: A Conceptual Background with Readings* (New York: Harcourt Brace Jovanovich, 1975), 225–233.

5. For a review of this scholarship, see Anthony R. Petrosky's article "From Story to Essay: Reading and Writing," *College Composition and Communication* 33 (February 1982): 19–36.

6. For a discussion of procedures for identifying these relationships in a written text, see my article "Measuring Changes in Intellectual Processes . . . ," in *Evaluating Writing,* eds. Charles Cooper and Lee Odell (Urbana, Ill.: NCTE, 1977, 107–132.

7. For a discussion of the importance of the grammatical subject, see Wallace Chafe, *Meaning and the Structure of Language* (Chicago: The University of Chicago Press, 1970), 210–212.

8. See Carl H. Frederiksen, "Effects of Context-Induced Processing Operations on Semantic Information Acquired from Discourse," *Cognitive Psychology* 7 (1975), 139–166. Although Frederiksen is describing processes by which we comprehend discourse, I believe his argument applies to ways we understand other phenomena.

7 Modes of Thinking, Modes of Argument

Marie Secor
The Pennsylvania State University

In *Language and Mind,* Noam Chomsky begins by asking what contribution the study of language can make to our understanding of human nature.[1] As rhetoricians dealing with the written and spoken products of our language-making faculty, we often ask a similar question: What contribution can our study of written discourse make to our understanding of human nature? And we often extend Chomsky's assumption that language reflects the structure of the mind and assume that written discourse too reveals something about the way we think, about the way we apprehend reality.

I think most of us are willing to accept the reasonableness of that assumption; certainly it underlies both ancient and contemporary discourse theory. But notice what happens to it in the following statement made by Frank D'Angelo in *A Conceptual Theory of Rhetoric:* "Thus from the existence of conceptual patterns in discourse, we infer the existence of similar patterns of thought; from the existence of conceptual patterns of thought, we can infer the existence of corresponding patterns in discourse. One of the tasks of the rhetorician is to relate the structure of thought to the structure of discourse."[2] D'Angelo sees the relationship between the mind and discourse as reversible: not only does the structure of discourse tell us something about patterns of thought, but from these patterns of thought we infer the existence of patterns of discourse. I am willing to believe that written or spoken discourse reveals a good deal about the way we think, but I am less certain we can identify conceptual patterns of thought apart from the discourse they reside in. Where do these patterns exist? Are they modes which reside "in the mind" somehow? If so, where?

I can answer these questions only by distinguishing between talking about patterns of thought or the structure of the mind and talking about understanding human nature. We still know very little about the mind. We know rather more about human nature as it is reflected in our discourse producing activities, and have for centuries. We know the kinds of discourse we produce, the ways writing affects audience, and the types of appeals which operate in discourse. This understanding of human nature has been facilitated by the analytic descriptions philosophers and psychologists have developed and rhetoricians have adopted. The link between rhetoric and psychology has a long and honorable history which reaches all the way back to Aristotle, Quintilian, and Campbell; it is not a recent invention.

Argument Defined

What exactly is argument's place in a theory of modes? James Britton places it on the far end of a scale with the use of language in the spectator role at one end and the use of language in the participant role on the other: "Informing people, instructing people, arguing, explaining, setting forth the pros and cons and coming to a conclusion—these are participant uses of language to get things done."[3] Chaim Perelman defines arguing as "using discourse to influence the intensity of an audience's adherence to certain theses."[4] Both of these definitions usefully see argument as a purpose, an intention which a writer or speaker directs at an audience.

It is also useful to distinguish between argument and persuasion. In his *Theory of Discourse* Kinneavy defines persuasion as "that kind of discourse which is primarily focused on the reader and attempts to elicit from him a specific action or emotion or conviction."[5] But I would like to define persuasion as the more inclusive term, and argument as only one means by which it is accomplished. Argument is not the only means of persuasion: I can be persuaded or moved to action by a strong push, by a knife at my throat, or by a bribe. Nor is argument the only verbal means of persuasion: I can be equally persuaded or moved by written threats or bribes. But to go back to Perelman's definition, argument is the only verbal means of persuasion which attempts to gain my adherence to a position, to convince me, not just to bring about my action. If we accept this distinction, propaganda and advertising fall more often under the category of persuasion than of argument, especially when they are more interested in getting me to act than in convincing me.

As an aim, argument uses other kinds of discourse as means. To borrow Alexander Bain's classification of modes for a moment, argument might use narration to tell a relevant story, description to help an audience visualize something it might otherwise ignore, even exposition to inform an audience unaware of certain conditions. Argument always springs from a sense of the inadequacy of a prevailing view and a sense of the intellectual, emotional, and ethical needs of its audience. Thus refutation of other positions and accommodation to a particular audience are driving forces behind, or elements in, every argument. They shape the discourse and determine its content, but they are not really the substance, the essence, of argument. To translate this theory into practical terms: when we teach argument, we need to pay attention to refutation and accommodation, but we also need to remember that argument is not essentially negative, a tearing down of what others have said, and not cynical manipulation of an audience's weaknesses or susceptibilities.

I would add one more "not" here, one more definition of what we teach when we teach argument. Argument is not formal logic. As we all learn from experience in the classroom, the ability to manipulate statements in and out of Venn diagrams and to construct syllogisms has very little to do with the ability to produce convincing arguments. Philosophers of rhetoric like Chaim Perelman and Stephen Toulmin have carefully distinguished between the logic of argument and formal logic, and Aristotle, too, carefully defines logic as a tool; syllogisms are not kinds or modes of arguments.

Similarly, the terms *induction* and *deduction*, though useful to describe variations in the arrangement of arguments (that is, whether the thesis comes at the beginning or at the end), do not really describe modes of argument or separate contrasting ways the mind operates,[6] and the exact distinction between the two is a matter of some controversy among theorists.[7]

Types of Argument

I would call the classification of arguments I am about to present a theory of types rather than a theory of modes, in order to avoid confusion with the terminology of other discourse theories. These categories describe the typical content of arguments as products of our intentions, and they give us some clues about the typical structures or arrangements of these arguments. This classification begins with the multitude of propositions or theses which can serve as subjects for arguments. We can distinguish here four main types of theses, each of which answers a different question: (1) What is this thing? (2) What caused it or what effects does it have? (3) Is it good or bad? and

(4) What should we do about it? Propositions which answer these questions are, respectively, categorical propositions, causal statements, evaluations, and proposals. The thesis of any argument falls into one of these categories. The first two, which correspond to the classical *topoi* of definition and cause and effect, demand their own kinds of arguments with distinctive structures, while arguments for the third and fourth, evaluations and proposals, combine the other two in a variety of possible arrangements of these structures.

I will describe each type briefly. A categorical proposition is a statement which places its subject in the category of its predicate. If I wish to argue that "All art is illusion" or that "The Emperor Caligula was a spoiled brat" or that "Ballet dancers are really athletes," supporting such a statement is always a matter of showing that the subject belongs in the category of or has the attributes of the predicate. That predicate must be defined and evidence or examples given to link the subject up with it. The arguer for a categorical proposition, then, works under two constraints: the definition of the predicate must be acceptable to the audience, and the evidence or examples about the subject must be convincing and verifiable. The emphasis in the argument can be placed either on the definition or on the evidence, depending on the audience's needs.

The second type of proposition, the assertion of cause and effect, requires quite a different kind of argument because it represents a different way of thinking about reality. It is supported not so much with a definition, either assumed or explicit, but with an appeal to or an argument for agency, a basic belief about what can cause what. Just as people who speak the same language share a set of definitions, so do people in the same culture share many causal assumptions. We have a commonsense understanding, for instance, of such natural agencies as light, heat, and gravity, as well as many accepted human agencies whose operations we accept as readily as we believe in the operation of physical law. Whether or not we articulate agency (that connection between a cause and its effect) in argument depends largely on audience. For example, if we argue that a significant cause of teenage drug abuse is parental drinking and drug abuse, the agency between these two is imitation: children imitate their elders. Since most audiences will accept imitation as a motive here, we would not have to stop and argue for it. But if we claimed that wearing a plastic mouth plate can improve athletic performance, we will have to explain how, explain agency. The substance of causal arguments then will be devoted to either identifying plausible causes or showing how they produce their effects.

A third kind of argument judges; it is an evaluation, a statement like "*Jane Eyre* is a great novel." In form, an evaluation looks exactly like a categorical proposition and is argued for similarly: by identifying criteria, assumptions, or definitions of value, and applying them to the particular subject under discussion. For example, to argue for the greatness of *Jane Eyre*, I must construct a plausible definition or set of criteria for great novels which fits the evidence from the book. But evaluations deserve separate consideration because their criteria or standards can easily include good or bad consequences or effects as well as qualities; thus evaluations often require causal arguments showing that the subject does indeed produce a particular effect. To argue, for example, that it was right to bring the Shah of Iran to the U.S. for medical treatment, I might classify that decision as a humanitarian one, or I might argue that the decision was wrong by exploring its consequences in a causal argument.

The fourth and final type of proposition is the proposal, which answers the question, "What should we do?" A proposal requires a special combination of smaller arguments. We can see how that structure works if we imagine arguing for a proposal such as "Wolves should be reestablished in the forests of northern Pennsylvania." Most audiences will feel no need for action unless they are first convinced that a problem exists which needs this solution. Thus an opening categorical proposition argument might establish the existence of a situation, in this case the absence or rarity of wolves in certain areas. An audience might also need the bad consequences or ethical wrongness of this situation pointed out to it; here causal argument pointing to the overpopulation of deer or a negative evaluation might be useful. Another preliminary step might be a causal argument singling out the dominant reason for the problem. If, for example, wolves have become almost extinct because of unrestricted hunting, then a ban on hunting wolves ought to help. And once the specific proposal is disclosed, it can be supported with another series of arguments pointing out good consequences, ethical rightness, and feasibility.

I have just outlined four categories of arguments, classified according to the kind of question each asks about reality and described according to the structure and arrangement of the content. Obviously, evaluations and proposals are not separate ways of knowing but combinations of definition and causal arguments directed by different intentions. It is possible, therefore, to regroup this classification another way into two main divisions instead of four. To borrow what Richard Weaver calls a "primitive metaphysic," we can think of ourselves as knowing things either as being or becoming, either as essences or as entities altered by time. (Weaver, in fact, takes this distinction a step further and calls definition the "highest order of appeal" and cause and effect a "less exalted source of argument.")[8] I prefer to see them simply as different, complementary ways of knowing, not necessarily arranged in a hierarchy: we apprehend reality either as static or changing, as things with definitions and attributes or as things affecting others. Thus we can and do still understand discourse by describing the patterns we find in it, and we can see these patterns as descriptions of the way the mind interacts with reality, if not of the mechanism by which that interaction is accomplished.

Notes

1. Noam Chomsky, *Language and Mind*, enlarged ed. (New York: Harcourt Brace Jovanovich, 1972), 1.
2. Frank J. D'Angelo, *A Conceptual Theory of Rhetoric* (Cambridge, Mass.: Winthrop Publishers, 1975), 16.
3. James Britton, *Language and Learning* (London: Penguin Books, 1953), 22.
4. Chaim Perelman and L. Olbrechts-Tyteca, *The New Rhetoric* (Notre Dame, Ind.: University of Notre Dame Press, 1969), 66.
5. James Kinneavy, *A Theory of Discourse* (New York: W. W. Norton, 1971), 211.
6. Induction and deduction are sometimes seen as descriptions of separate mental operations as different as up and down, induction reaching a generalization from particulars and deduction affirming a particular from a generalization. The discussion of induction and the classification of four types of arguments were developed jointly with Jeanne Fahnestock. We explore both in more detail in our article, "Teaching Argument: A Theory of Types," *College Composition and Communication* 34 (February 1983): 20–30.
7. Irving M. Copi defines the two not as complementary forms of reasoning, but as reasoning toward a certain conclusion (deduction) and reasoning toward a probable conclusion (induction). *Introduction to Logic*, 5th ed. (New York: Macmillan, 1978), 23–26; also see Karl Popper, *Conjectures and Refutations: The Growth of Scientific Knowledge* (New York: Harper and Row, 1963), 46–47.
8. Richard Weaver, "Language Is Sermonic," in *Rhetoric and Composition*, ed. Richard L. Graves (Rochelle Park, N.J.: Hayden Book Co. 1976), 31–32.

II The Composing Process

II. The Composing Process

8 On the Relation of Invention to Arrangement

John C. Schafer
Humboldt State University

In his article, "Paradigms and Problems: Needed Research in Rhetorical Invention," Richard Young identified an emphasis on product and a lack of attention to the composing process as a distinguishing feature of an approach to composition teaching which he labeled "current traditional rhetoric."[1] Professor Young argued that the product approach—assigning papers, correcting them, and handing them back—wasn't working and that it was high time we abandoned it, or at least supplemented it with some other strategies. It appears that many people have accepted the arguments of Young and others. The "current traditional rhetoric" paradigm is breaking down and the slogan "Teach writing as a process not a product" is rapidly becoming a commonplace in the profession.

Even before this slogan became popular, a rediscovery of classical rhetoric was occurring, prompted by people like Edward P. J. Corbett, whose *Classical Rhetoric for the Modern Student*[2] argued convincingly for the continued relevance of some ancient principles, including those having to do with invention (one of the five canons of classical rhetoric, the others being arrangement, style, memory, and delivery). The emphasis on process and the renewed interest in invention complemented each other: concentrating on invention as a stage of the composing process has been one way for teachers and textbook writers to make their programs more process-oriented.

In 1965, the same year that Corbett's textbook was published, D. Gordon Rohman published an influential article, "Pre-Writing: The Stage of Discovery in the Writing Process,"[3] in which he advocated three prewriting techniques: keeping a journal, practicing religious meditation, and using analogies. Although the prewriting techniques Rohman suggested were obviously different from the invention techniques outlined in the classical rhetorics, he was, like those arguing for a revival of classical invention, pointing out to teachers some things that could be done to shift attention away from product toward the earlier stages of the writing process. Recently several adaptations of classical invention and a host of prewriting techniques have been described in professional articles and rhetoric textbooks. Teachers committed to making their teaching more process-oriented are now faced with the difficult task of deciding which techniques to teach. I don't intend to survey all these techniques but rather to discuss an issue that comes up no matter what technique one presents: namely, the relation between two aspects of composing, specifically the relation between invention and arrangement.

Classical Models of Invention and Arrangement

In the classical tradition that we've inherited from Plato, Aristotle, Cicero, and Quintilian, invention and arrangement were in one sense separate processes. Invention, in the words of Cicero, was "the discovery of valid . . . arguments to render one's cause plausible"; arrangement was "the distribution of arguments thus discovered in their proper order."[4] First one discovered the arguments, then one arranged them. As described by classical rhetoricians, composing is a linear, lock-step process. Although in one sense invention and arrangement were separate in classical rhetoric, in another sense they were not—not nearly as separate as these processes are presented in many modern rhetorics. The ancients considered both invention and arrangement to be audience-based activities. One might invent first and arrange later, but one had to be sensitive to one's purpose and audience during both processes. The would-be orator was not urged to ignore his purpose and audience and invent arguments in a vacuum. Classical invention was not a free association technique; it was instead a focused search through a storehouse of tried and true arguments for ones that would be useful in getting a particular audience to adopt a particular position on an issue.

An orator following classical principles first considered what was at issue—whether the case involved a question of fact, or definition, or value. After the orator was clear as to the issue, he chose from a storehouse of *topoi*, or lines of argument, those that would be most effective in helping him win his case. These *topoi* included many of the devices that we now know as methods of development—arguing from causes, arguing by logically dividing one's subject, arguing from opposition or contrast, for example.

Arrangement in the classical system was even more solidly based in the rhetorical situation. How one constructed any of the six parts of the oration—exordium, narrative, partition, confirmation, refutation, peroration—depended on whom one was addressing and the view one wanted this person to accept. Orators were told to use one kind of exordium, for example, if their audience was hostile to the position they were advocating and another kind if it was receptive to their views.

Contemporary Views of Prewriting

Like the classical rhetoricians, Rohman and his followers, who prefer to speak of prewriting rather than invention, also present writing as a linear process. Usually they break the process down into prewriting, writing, and rewriting, the implication being that the writer proceeds through these stages one at a time. The prewriting strategies they recommend, however, are writer- and subject-centered, not audience-centered as were the techniques of classical invention. Advocates of prewriting believe that students have to develop in certain ways before they are ready to write purposeful, audience-directed discourse. According to Rohman, prewriting devices are necessary to "enlighten [students] concerning the powers of creative discovery within them."[5] He chose his three techniques—journal keeping, religious meditation, and analogies—because he thought they would help students achieve this enlightenment. Other advocates of prewriting recommend different techniques: brainstorming, collage making, metaphor making, free writing, or asking questions based on the five senses. Most theorists and teachers who believe in these and similar techniques (Ken Macrorie, for example) are committed to writing programs emphasizing personal growth, to what Rohman called the "self-actualization" of the writer.

As part of the process of promoting personal growth, advocates of prewriting want to help students overcome mild to severe cases of writer's block. They believe students should achieve fluency first and argue that students won't become fluent if teachers force them from the start to adhere to rigid standards of correctness and rhetorical effectiveness. Many prewriting techniques thus are writer-, not audience-centered because their advocates believe that excessive concern for audience early in the writing process impairs fluency.

One of the early advocates of the fluency first idea was Peter Elbow. In *Writing without Teachers*,[6] Elbow argued that students will write better and in a more authentic voice if they don't try to create and edit simultaneously. He encouraged students to write freely first, and then, after they have generated fairly long stretches of prose, to put on their reader's hat and start editing, or "mopping up," as he called it. Researchers who use protocols—tape recordings of writers instructed to compose outloud—to investigate the writing process are providing empirical support for Elbow's notion that creating and editing should be kept separate. Sondra Perl, for example, says that the inexperienced writers she investigated wrote poorly at least in part because they edited prematurely—before they had "generated enough discourse to approximate the ideas they [had]. . . ."[7]

Both Elbow and Perl stress the dangers of premature editing, not premature arranging. The premature editing they find harmful involves tinkering with sentences, trying to get them to conform to rules the writer has heard about or imagined. Because they do so much of this tinkering, many inexperienced writers never generate enough discourse to have anything to arrange. Linda Flower, who has worked with more experienced but still not accomplished writers, does speak specifically of the dangers of premature arranging. She distinguishes writer-based from reader-based prose. Writer-based prose is "the record and the working of [the writer's] own verbal thought."[8] According to Flower, a writer-based essay is usually organized in one of two ways, either as a narrative of the writer's discovery process or as a survey of the subject of the paper. Reader-based prose, on the other hand, is a "deliberate attempt to communicate something to a reader."[9] Its structure is not a record of the writer's discovery process or a survey of the data but an "issue-centered" arrangement designed with the needs of the reader in mind.

Flower argues that writer-based prose has some advantages for the inexperienced writer. Good writers, she says, can organize information for a reader while they are in the process of generating that information, but many inexperienced writers cannot. These less experienced writers will write more effectively, Flower suggests, if we allow them to start writing without the constraints imposed by a reader. After they have produced a writer-based text we can teach them how to transform it into a reader-based one. "By allowing the writer to temporarily separate the two complex but somewhat different tasks of generating information and forming networks," Flower argues, "each task may be performed more consciously and effectively."[10]

Others, however, argue against separating invention and arrangement. A. D. Van Nostrand, for example, has suggested a way of teaching the writing process diametrically opposed to the approach advocated by Flower. Flower says that, for many students, moving to reader-based prose *through* writer-based prose is easier than trying to produce reader-based prose from the start. Not so, says Van Nostrand.

It is easier and faster, he tells students, "to organize your information for someone else than it is to organize it for yourself."[11] It's easier to generate reader-based prose than writer-based prose because the writer "is trying to solve too many questions of priorities to be aware of the one thing the reader most needs to know, which is 'So What?' "[12] By concentrating on answering this one question, the writer limits his choices and makes the task of writing easier.

How is it that two scholars, who both claim to have derived their approach from research studies of how people write, have come up with completely different ways of teaching the writing process? Probably because they observed different kinds of writers. Flower became convinced of the advantages of writer-based prose after observing inexperienced writers. She recommends her approach for them—not for highly skilled writers. In a recent article, Flower and Hayes describe a research project they conducted which involved the comparing of protocols taken from both "novice" (college students) and "expert" (teachers of composition) writers working on the same assignment.[13] They found that the expert writers were able to skip the writer-based phase: they analyzed the assignment and developed a sophisticated notion of a reader before they started to write; then they wrote with this reader in mind. The novices, however, "never moved beyond the sketchy, conventional representation of audience and assignment with which they started."[14]

Van Nostrand developed his Contract Theory after "seven years of experimenting with the writing habits of persons in corporate management groups: persons who were daily writing formal discourse."[15] Although they may not have been expert writers, Van Nostrand's corporate managers were probably more skilled than Flower's students. Reader-based approaches that work well for them may work less well with students, who are younger and have had less experience producing "formal discourse." Furthermore, students often write about subjects that are new to them, not, as corporate managers do, about subjects that they are quite knowledgeable about—the work of their division, for example. Postponing considerations of audience may allow students to explore their subject in a leisurely but productive manner.

Like Van Nostrand, Mark L. Knapp and James C. McCroskey also argue against presenting invention and arrangement as separate processes. Although they discuss speeches, not essays, their essay has been reprinted in a popular anthology of articles on the teaching of writing, and one can assume that it has influenced composition teachers. Knapp and McCroskey argue that invention and arrangement are "complementary parts of the same process—the process of analyzing the audience and developing a speech to evoke a predetermined reaction from that audience."[16] In their view, "telling students to gather ideas and materials and then organize their speeches retards their rhetorical growth." It produces a "material-centered" rhetoric when what we want students to master is an "audience-centered" rhetoric.[17]

Although Knapp and McCroskey present their views as being opposed to those put forth in the classical rhetorics, actually they are not. The classical rhetoricians obviously emphasized planning a speech with one's audience in mind. Knapp and McCroskey simply make more explicit what is implicit, I think, in rhetorics such as Cicero's *De Inventione*. They argue that invention and arrangement are inseparable because the three major aspects of "dispositio"—selecting, arranging, and apportioning—should be at least partially completed during the invention stage. When one invents, they claim, one doesn't invent just any arguments but those arguments relevant to the issue being discussed. Thus selection begins during the invention stage. Arranging also is partially completed during invention because, Knapp and McCroskey argue, a good speaker is concerned with sequence when he invents: he tries to come up not with unrelated arguments but with arguments that will fit together like the spans of a bridge, moving the audience from its present position to the position the speaker is advocating. And finally, apportioning is also a part of invention, since a speaker who isn't concerned with proportion while inventing will go on inventing forever, producing more arguments than will ever be needed.

Frank D'Angelo offers a different argument to explain what he sees as the inseparability of invention and arrangement. Unlike Knapp and McCroskey, D'Angelo doesn't encourage students to be audience-sensitive during invention. His technique, as described in his freshman rhetoric *Process and Thought in Composition*,[18] is a subject-based not audience-based technique, and thus it would be more accurate to call it a prewriting not an invention technique. For D'Angelo it is the classical topics, not audience sensitivity, that make invention and arrangement "synonymous" processes.[19] Because the topics that we've inherited from classical rhetoric—comparison and contrast, classification, and exemplification, for instance—are "symbolic manifestations of underlying thought processes,"[20] they play a role in both invention and arrangement. Classical rhetoricians erred in associating them only with invention. Advocates of current traditional rhetoric, who label these patterns "methods of development," err in associating them only with arrangement.

How do the topics, or "patterns of thought" as D'Angeló prefers to call them, underlie both invention and arrangement? In the approach to composing that D'Angelo recommends in his textbook, a student first probes a subject by asking questions based on the topics. If the student is writing about an automobile, for example, a comparison/ contrast question might be asked (How is it different from or similar to other cars?), or a cause and effect question (What are the effects of the different features—seat belts, wipers, bumpers, etc.?).[21] These patterns that give rise to questions for invention are not just invention techniques, however. D'Angelo tells students that as "you are probing a subject to get ideas, you are also arranging these ideas, putting them into some kind of intelligible form."[22] If, for example, the student writing on cars asked the analysis question "What are its parts?" and generated the headings *wheels, power steering, engine,* and *transmission,* these would become the headings for the major sections of the final paper.

Although D'Angelo has presented a coherent theory of rhetoric, when I tried to apply his approach in the classroom I was disturbed by the results. My students did learn to ask pattern of thought questions and did learn to use the categories generated by these questions to arrange their papers. But they used them in a very perfunctory way, producing papers which were often well-organized but also dull and lifeless because they weren't focused on aspects of a subject that would interest an audience. Although D'Angelo periodically reminds students of the importance of audience and purpose, these features of the rhetorical situation aren't built into his system, and so students tend to ignore them.

D'Angelo's approach is in sharp contrast to the approach recommended by Linda Flower. Flower urges teachers to get students to stop after a period of composing and ask themselves whether they have produced a writer- or a reader-based paper. If their early draft has a writer-based arrangement, teachers are to help students turn it into a reader-based one. Although D'Angelo probably wouldn't object to this teaching strategy, it runs counter to his theory, which fuses invention and arrangement, making them virtually identical processes. The advice D'Angelo gives to students encourages subject-centered papers, papers which Flower calls "surveys of the data." D'Angelo asks students what pattern they might use to develop their paper on a car. It depends on the type of car, he explains: "If it has safety features or gas-saving features you would probably choose the [pattern] of *analysis.* If it has extra features or characteristics that its competitors do not have, you may decide to *compare* it to other cars."[23] By giving

such advice, D'Angelo encourages students to think of these patterns
not as means to achieve a rhetorical purpose but as ends in themselves.

Application of Multiple Techniques

Some theorists believe invention and arrangement are separate processes whereas others insist they are inseparable. Which conception
should guide the teacher of freshman composition? Under most circumstances there is great value in presenting them to students as
separate processes, separate in both time and focus. In other words, we
should encourage students to invent first and arrange later; and we
should present invention as primarily a writer- and subject-based
activity, as activity best pursued with some of the constraints of the
rhetorical situation—audience constraints, for example—temporarily
suspended. If we accept Richard Young's distinction and use invention for reader-based techniques and prewriting for writer-based ones,[24]
then I am arguing for the superiority of prewriting over invention.

Of course invention can occur as the student is arranging. Those
researching the composing process emphasize its recursive nature:
writers generate some discourse, start arranging it, which leads to
more insights, which leads to more discourse, which they then arrange.
Composing for most writers appears to be the repetition of such cycles,
but this recursiveness is not an argument against getting students to
see invention and arrangement as separate psychological processes.
Perl points out that the composing processes of some unskilled writers
are excessively recursive in that they move too quickly from generating
discourse to reformulating it and then back to generating again.
Presenting the two processes of generating and reformulating as separate activities may help students stretch out their cycles and establish a
more productive rhythm of composing.

While writer-based prewriting techniques are generally preferable,
reader-based techniques may be useful for some assignments. They
seem particularly useful for persuasive discourse, and this is undoubt-
edly why the classical rhetoricians and Knapp and McCroskey, who
focus on this mode, prefer them. Say, for example, students have been
told to write a paper addressed to some school official in which they
argue for some change in school policy. Writing assignments such as
this one which come with a built-in argumentative edge and a clearly
identified and familiar audience make it easier for the student to
produce reader-based prose from the start. Prewriting devices which
encourage students to postpone consideration of audience and purpose
may force students working on such assignments to adopt unnatural

composing strategies. In doing other assignments, however, students will have to discover their argumentative edge; it won't be given in the assignment. They also need to learn how to write for audiences less familiar and more universal than a school official or a single teacher. Prewriting devices which allow students to generate ideas free of audience constraints should work better for these more open assignments. After they have generated some material, they can stop, clarify their purpose, and then select and arrange with their readers in mind.

In advising students we should also consider their previous experience with writing. Many who recommend that invention and arrangement be presented as separate processes do so because they are searching for an antidote to composition programs that emphasize a-rhetorical drills and conformity to rigid standards of correctness. But I wonder if students who passed through other programs in elementary and secondary school—James Moffett's curriculum, for example—would need the antidote.[26] Compared to students raised on a steady diet of workshop drills, students who from the beginning of their writing careers become accustomed to working within rhetorical situations may be better able to produce reader-based prose when they get to college.

For those not so well-prepared there is another possibility. Besides heuristics, which are either audience-centered or writer/subject-centered, other heuristics have been proposed, which are both audience- and writer/subject-based, but don't force the writer to deal simultaneously with constraints imposed by both subject and audience. One such device is the tagmemic heuristic proposed by Young, Becker, and Pike.[27] In their approach the writer first probes his subject by asking questions that force him to consider it from various perspectives; then he probes his audience using the same set of questions. Having grown in understanding of both subject and audience, the writer chooses those aspects of his subject that are relevant—relevant because they are not already known by the audience and are therefore worth sharing. This approach may relate invention to certain aspects of arrangement—selection of relevant material, for example—in a way that will not overwhelm beginning writers. Most teachers find Young, Becker, and Pike's scheme too complicated to present to very unskilled writers, but the principle of using the same set of questions to probe both subject and audience is simple enough and could be embodied in less complex schemes.

Not everyone will accept my views of the relation of invention to arrangement, but it is an issue we have to consider. The new process-oriented textbooks on the market force us to consider it. In evaluating these textbooks, we should demand that they have more than the word "process" in the title and an introductory chapter on invention. We should insist that they present an overall view of the task of writing that is sensible and that does not contradict recent studies of the composing process. Although thanks to professors Emig,[28] Perl, and Flower we know much more about composing than we did ten years ago, much still remains a mystery. In addition, these researchers remind us that different writers compose in different ways and that the same writer may compose differently depending on the mode of discourse in which he or she is working. We should therefore be wary of textbooks that present only one way to discover ideas and only one way to relate invention and arrangement. In our zeal to teach writing as process, we should be aware that premature formulation of models of the composing process is as dangerous for us as premature editing appears to be for our students.

Notes

1. Richard Young, "Paradigms and Problems: Needed Research in Rhetorical Invention," in *Research on Composing,* ed. Charles R. Cooper and Lee Odell (Urbana, Ill.: NCTE, 1978), 29–47.

2. Edward P. J. Corbett, *Classical Rhetoric for the Modern Student* (New York: Oxford University Press, 1971).

3. D. Gordon Rohman, "Pre-Writing: The Stage of Discovery in the Writing Process," *College Composition and Communication* 16 (1965): 106–12.

4. Cicero, *De Inventione* 1. 7, trans. H. M. Hubbell (Cambridge, Mass.: Harvard University Press, 1949), 19.

5. Rohman, 108.

6. Peter Elbow, *Writing without Teachers* (New York: Oxford University Press, 1973).

7. Sondra Perl, "The Composing Processes of Unskilled College Writers," *Research in the Teaching of English* 13 (1979): 333.

8. Linda Flower, "Writer-Based Prose: A Cognitive Basis for Problems in Writing," *College English* 41 (1979): 19.

9. Ibid., 20.

10. Ibid., 36.

11. A. D. Van Nostrand, "A New Direction in Teaching Writing," *Educational Technology* 17 (September 1977): 28.

12. Ibid.

13. Linda Flower and John Hayes, "The Cognition of Discovery: Defining a Rhetorical Problem," *College Composition and Communication* 31 (1980): 21–32.

14. Ibid., 26.

15. Van Nostrand, 28.

16. Mark L. Knapp and James C. McCroskey, "The Siamese Twins: *Inventio* and *Dispositio*," in *Rhetoric and Composition: A Sourcebook for Teachers*, ed. Richard L. Graves (Rochelle Park, N.J.: Hayden Book Co., 1976), 327. This article first appeared in *Today's Speech* 14 (1966): 17–18, 44.

17. Ibid., 328.

18. Frank D'Angelo, *Process and Thought in Composition*, 2nd ed. (Cambridge, Mass.: Winthrop, 1980).

19. Frank D'Angelo, *A Conceptual Theory of Rhetoric* (Cambridge, Mass.: Winthrop, 1975), 107.

20. Ibid., 28.

21. Frank D'Angelo, *Process and Thought*, 44–54.

22. Ibid., 70.

23. Ibid., 73.

24. Richard Young, "Invention: A Topographical Survey," in *Teaching Composition: 10 Bibliographical Essays*, ed. Gary Tate (Fort Worth: Texas Christian University Press, 1976), 16–17.

25. Perl, 328.

26. James Moffett, *Teaching the Universe of Discourse* (Boston: Houghton Mifflin, 1968).

27. Richard Young, Alton Becker, and Kenneth Pike, *Rhetoric: Discovery and Change* (New York: Harcourt Brace Jovanovich, 1970).

28. Janet Emig, *The Composing Processes of Twelfth Graders* (Urbana Ill.: NCTE, 1971).

9 A Writer's Tool: Computing as a Mode of Inventing

Hugh Burns
United States Air Force Academy

After teaching composition for several years, I became convinced that I needed to teach more about invention, the rhetorical art of discovering what to say. In the opening of "Invention: A Topographical Survey," Richard Young describes the process this way:

> Every writer confronts the task of making sense of events in the world around him or within him—discovering ordering principles, evidence which justifies belief, information necessary for understanding—and of making what he wants to say understandable and believable to particular readers. He uses a method of invention when these processes are guided deliberately by heuristic procedures—that is, explicit plans for analyzing and searching which focus attention, guide reason, stimulate memory, and encourage intuition.[1]

Noble aims certainly: guiding reason, stimulating memory, and encouraging intuition. The question was *how* to reach these goals in the English composition classroom. I assumed then (and still do assume) that students frequently failed to write insightfully because they did not inquire carefully enough. Commonly students use these lines: "I don't know what to write about. What can I say about this topic anyway?" Substitute the range of topics we normally see in college composition courses and you have the problem, the challenge. Just what can you tell a student at this stage in the writing process? What could I do to spur each individual's invention process along?

While I could not hope to teach insight, I could prompt students to answer questions. I also could explain the question if the student didn't understand the basic idea or didn't know a definition. I could usually prompt a student to elaborate an answer. And I could encourage students by not rushing them and by giving them positive reinforcement if they answered the question sensibly. What I couldn't do—mentally or physically—was meet all eighty of my composition students seven times a semester for 30 to 60 minutes just to guide their initial inquiry. That's 560 conference hours teaching invention alone. Impossible. Sounded like a job for a machine. Maybe it was. Maybe the computer in the writing lab could do it. Eureka! There were enough terminals. Our university already had some CAI (Computer Assisted Instruction) in basic composition. Other advantages? The computer in the lab could also provide each student a printed copy of his or her interaction; I could not. More ideas came. I could do research; I could compare three popular heuristic strategies for their effectiveness with the computer controlling the experiment.

Every day I became more and more intrigued by the nature and the potential of such programs. It was soon quite clear to me that if we in the humanities must have a machine in our garden, we humanists had better create the tasks it should help us with: not a pedagogical bed of drill and practice sequences alone, but a creative, open-ended, problem-solving application of instructional computing. *Creative* in that the computer program encouraged surprises and wild connections. *Open-ended* in that the software wouldn't "know" all of the answers; it would only be programmed to move the inquiry in different directions. And *problem-solving* in that the program might sustain an investigation until some solutions were discovered.

Over the past few years, therefore, I've been designing, programming, and evaluating practical computer-assisted instruction for stimulating rhetorical invention in English composition. The basic idea is simple enough: a computer program asks questions, and a writer answers the questions. In terms of creativity theory, these computer programs generate content-free "matrices of thought"[2] by asking specific heuristic questions, and the writer responds with other matrices of thought based on the specific knowledge of a situational context. In other words, the computer program is responsible for the direction and the motivational sequence while the writer is responsible for the content of the inquiry. So what should happen? Arthur Koestler describes: "When two independent matrices of perception or reasoning interact with each other the result . . . is either a *collision* ending in laughter, or their *fusion* in a new intellectual synthesis, or their *confrontation* in an aesthetic experience."[3] This resulting interaction thus raises to the conscious level what writers *already know* about their subjects and makes them write down their ideas. The interaction also has an uncanny ability to produce questions that writers *don't know* the answers to yet. It is open-ended in that sense. Thus such dialogues, by generating some dissonance, prompt writers to articulate problems which the computer-cued interaction uncovers.

These programs have been called such names as "artificial inquiry," "electronic brainstorming," and even "Socratic Systems, Incorporated." Today, I'm happy to report that a computer can be programmed to do some, if not all, of these inventive things. This calculating engine has a place in our humanities garden as a prewriter's tool.

How do these programs work? What do they look like? Here's part of a "run" that one of my American literature students created to answer the particle, wave, and field questions from a tagmemic invention[4] program. Her responses are underlined.

```
        A COMPUTER-ASSISTED INVENTION PROGRAM:
               THE TAGMEMIC MATRIX

     HI. WELCOME TO CAI-PROMPTED EXPLORATION. PLEASE
TYPE IN YOUR
     FIRST NAME:
KAREN
     THANK YOU, KAREN. I HOPE I CAN BE OF SOME
ASSISTANCE TO YOU TODAY. IF WE TAKE EACH OTHER
SERIOUSLY, I KNOW YOU'LL THINK ABOUT YOUR TOPIC AS
YOU NEVER HAVE BEFORE.
     BEFORE WE BEGIN, KAREN, THERE'S AN OLD SAYING
ABOUT COMPUTER-ASSISTED INSTRUCTION. IT READS:
"GARBAGE IN, GARBAGE OUT!" IN OTHER WORDS, YOU AND I
MUST COOPERATE SO THAT YOU CAN GET A GOOD START ON
YOUR RESEARCH PAPER.
     (PRESS "RETURN" TO CONTINUE.)
     WOULD YOU LIKE TO REVIEW THE DIRECTIONS AND THE
COMMANDS? (YES OR NO?)
NO
     DO YOU WISH TO SEE A SHORT DESCRIPTION OF THE
TAGMEMIC MATRIX? (YES OR NO?)
YES

          THE TAGMEMIC MATRIX HEURISTIC:

     BRIEFLY, THE TAGMEMIC MATRIX ENCOURAGES A WRITER
TO THINK ABOUT A TOPIC FROM NINE PERSPECTIVES. FOR
THIS PROGRAM, HOWEVER, I HAVE SIMPLIFIED THIS A BIT.
THIS PROGRAM WILL ASK YOU QUESTIONS FROM ONLY THREE
PERSPECTIVES, WHICH YOU WILL RECALL FROM OUR CLASS
DISCUSSION.
```

1. PARTICLE-VIEWING A SUBJECT IN ITSELF (STATIC):
2. WAVE-VIEWING A SUBJECT AS IT CHANGES
   (DYNAMIC): AND
3. FIELD-VIEWING A SUBJECT'S RELATIONSHIP TO
   OTHER SUBJECTS (IN A SYSTEM).

NOW I MUST ASK YOU WHAT YOU ARE WRITING ABOUT, SO
WOULD YOU PLEASE TYPE IN YOUR SUBJECT. (I'M LOOKING
FOR ONE TO THREE WORDS, MAYBE FOUR.)

DREISER'S DRAMATIC TECHNIQUE

FINE, KAREN! WE'LL HAVE A GOOD TIME BRAIN-
STORMING DREISER'S DRAMATIC TECHNIQUE.

A COMMENT ABOUT PURPOSE:

WRITING WITHOUT A PURPOSE OR AIM, KAREN, IS QUITE
FRANKLY A WASTE OF TIME. DOING SO GENERATES VERBAL
FOG, DESTROYS WRITING EFFICIENCY, AND DEFEATS THE
ESSENCE OF COMMUNICATION. THEREFORE, THROUGHOUT THIS
EXPLORATION PROCESS, YOU WILL BE ASKED TO WRITE ABOUT
THE PURPOSE OF YOUR PAPER. SO NOW WOULD YOU BRIEFLY
DESCRIBE THE PURPOSE OF YOUR PAPER BY COMPLETING THIS
STATEMENT:

THE PURPOSE OF MY PAPER IS TO....
EXPLAIN HOW DREISER USES DETAILS TO GO BEYOND
MELODRAMA.

ANYTHING ELSE?
YES

WHAT?
AND TO SHOW HOW DETAILS OF CHARACTER ARE PART OF HIS
DRAMATIC STRUCTURE

FINE, KAREN, YOU AND I WILL TALK AGAIN ABOUT YOUR
PURPOSE. HERE WE GO. RELAX AND ENJOY THE
MIND-STRETCHING.

QUESTION 1
DESCRIBE HOW DREISER'S DRAMATIC TECHNIQUE
PHYSICALLY CHANGES.
PLEASE EXPLAIN!

I'M LOOKING FOR YOUR NOTIONS ABOUT THE
DEVELOPMENT OF DREISER'S DRAMATIC TECHNIQUE....

FOR EXAMPLE, IF I WERE WRITING ABOUT ANOTHER
SUBJECT, SAY HUMAN DEVELOPMENT, I WOULD WRITE ABOUT

GROWTH, THE CHANGES THAT ARE DUE TO MATURING. YOU
KNOW ADULT "PASSAGES" HAVE BEEN POPULAR FARE LATELY.
YOUR TURN, KAREN.
I WANT TO SHOW HOW SISTER CARRIE ALLOWED DREISER TO
GROW, TO CONFRONT COMMON VALUES. IT IS A MATURE WORK.
        GOOD, KAREN. ADD TO YOUR RESPONSE NOW.
HURSTWOOD GROWS THE OTHER WAY. THERE ARE NEGATIVE
PASSAGES, AREN'T THERE?
        YES, THAT SEEMS OKAY TO ME.
ME TOO.
        AH, SHORT AND SWEET. PLEASE ELABORATE A LITTLE.
WELL, CHARACTERS EITHER GET WORSE OR BETTER: THEY
EITHER PASS TO A BETTER UNDERSTANDING OR NOT.
        TERRIFIC, KAREN! ANYTHING ELSE?
SOMETIMES HIS DETAILS GET IN THE WAY OF HIS
ORGANIZATION AND HIS EFFECTIVENESS–BUT CONTINUE!
        OKAY. (ALL IDEAS ARE GOOD IDEAS: TYPE IN WHAT YOU
THINK!!!!)
        QUESTION 2–ONE OF MY FAVORITES–COMING UP.
        TAKE A MENTAL PHOTOGRAPH OF DREISER'S DRAMATIC
TECHNIQUE. DESCRIBE ONE IMPORTANT DETAIL.
I DON'T UNDERSTAND WHAT YOU WANT ME TO SAY
        CONCENTRATE NOW ON SEEING DREISER'S DRAMATIC
TECHNIQUE. WHAT FEATURE STANDS OUT THE MOST?
DESCRIBE. YOUR TURN, KAREN.
LIKE THE SETTINGS?
        YES, THAT SEEMS OKAY.
THE FACTORY VS THE HOTEL.
        THAT'S THE IDEA, KAREN. GIVE ME SOME MORE
INFORMATION.
I SEE HURSTWOOD AS A SCAB. THOUGH HE'S BEEN REDUCED,
HE STILL HAS SOME DIGNITY. BUT THE SETTINGS AREN'T
DIGNIFIED. THE STREET & &
        GO ON, KAREN.
THE STREETS ARE UGLY, DISMAL. CONTRAST.
        SUPER, KAREN! ANYTHING ELSE?
YES
        WHAT?
I SEE SUFFERING AND COMMITMENT DESPITE IT BECAUSE
HURSTWOOD HAS BOTH KINDS OF EXPERIENCE.
        THAT'S AN INTERESTING REASON. ANYTHING ELSE?

```
WHY DO YOU THINK THIS QUESTION IS ONE OF YOUR
FAVORITES?
     WHY NOT, KAREN? REMEMBER WE'RE EXPLORING FOR
ANSWERS.
HOW DO YOU SEE HURSTWOOD'S SUFFERING. IS IT A
PASSAGE?
     I CAN'T PRETEND TO KNOW HOW, BUT YOU'VE ASKED AN
IMPORTANT QUESTION. REMEMBER IT. DO YOU WISH TO
NARROW OR CHANGE YOUR TOPIC? MAYBE REVISE THE WAY IT
SOUNDS IN THESE QUESTIONS?
NO.
     OKAY, LET'S GO ON....
```

Karen worked for about forty minutes. She commented twice more on her purpose as the program continued to ask ten more tagmemic questions—questions about the static, dynamic, and distributive features of Theodore Dreiser's dramatic techniques. The program told her that she elaborated (that is, answered a question at least twice) 75 percent of the time. It also told her that she was asked four particle questions, six wave questions, and two field questions. Twice she explicitly asked for *wave* questions since she sensed that this specific, dynamic perspective was useful to her own inquiry. When she logged out, she left with eighteen pages of transcript. She was pleased.

The two other programs ask different questions. Had Karen logged on the Aristotle program, she would have been asked questions based on the twenty-eight enthymeme topics.[5] When Aristotle writes about invention, he is most concerned with enabling us to discover the most suitable argument for persuading an audience; thus most of his explanations are examples of how a topic may be applied in a specific situation. Karen, therefore, would have been asked questions such as:

Who might believe the good consequences of Dreiser's dramatic technique are bad?

Divide Dreiser's dramatic techniques into three subtopics.

What are some of the previous mistakes concerning Dreiser's dramatic technique?

What is inconsistent about Dreiser's dramatic technique?

Had Karen logged on the dramatistic pentad program, she would have been asked questions based on the identification of the scene, the act, the agent, the agency, and the purpose of Dreiser's dramatic technique. Since Kenneth Burke envisions the dramatistic pentad as a more dialectical than rhetorical instrument, he traces its exploratory appeal not to Aristotle's system of topics but to Aristotle's classification of causes.[6] Burke's rhetoric, therefore, differs from classical rhetoric in that his major concern is not persuasion but *identification*. Four pentad questions Karen might have been asked are:

> What impresses people about the setting for Dreiser's dramatic technique?
>
> What audience would most appreciate knowing more about Dreiser's dramatic technique?
>
> What is the ultimate goal of Dreiser's dramatic technique?
>
> How is Dreiser's dramatic technique like mercury?

We all know a rhetorical renaissance has recently emerged within the teaching of English composition, but most of us aren't as ready or as eager to admit that an electronic revolution has emerged as well. What such programs illustrate above all else is that rhetorical invention and computer technology are indeed compatible; combining heuristic "modes" and computer "media" can well serve the inquisitive writer. I'm only echoing English educators like Ellen Nold of Stanford University when I report such heresy:

> What is preventing humanists from using the computer for humanitarian purposes is merely their belief that they cannot use the machine. It is ironic that a group known to undertake calmly and surely the study of Latin, Greek, Russian, Chinese, Swahili, or Gaelic often balks at the much simpler task of learning the more logical, far less capricious, language of the machine.[7]

Stimulating invention in English composition through computer-assisted instruction is, I'm convinced, an effective, supplementary way to begin teaching the art of systematic inquiry. It's also a most appropriate introduction to the richness of heuristic strategies in general. Look for creative computing approaches to enrich what we humanists can do. We have a tool, but you and I *must use it well*. After all, if this machine is already here, shouldn't we humanists be the ones to till the garden we all labor in?

Notes

1. Richard Young, "Invention: A Topological Survey," in *Teaching Composition: Ten Bibliographical Essays*, ed. G. Tate (Fort Worth: Texas Christian University Press, 1976), 1.

2. Arthur Koestler, *The Act of Creation* (New York: Macmillan, 1964), 38.

3. Ibid., 45.

4. Richard Young, A. L. Becker, and K. L. Pike, *Rhetoric: Discovery and Change* (New York: Harcourt Brace Jovanovich, 1970).

5. These questions are adapted from Aristotle, *Rhetoric* 2.23.1937a17-1400b35. See *The Rhetoric and Poetics of Aristotle*, trans. W. R. Roberts and I. Bywater (New York: Modern Library, 1954).

6. Kenneth Burke, *A Grammar of Motives* (Berkeley: University of California Press, 1969), 228.

7. Ellen Nold, "Fear and Trembling: The Humanist Approaches the Computer," *College Composition and Communication* 26 (1975): 273.

10 Invention and the Writing Sequence

Leone Scanlon
Clark University

Many critics and teachers have recognized that uninviting assignments call forth THEMES, dead letters written by no one to no one: Macrorie's Engfish. Most of us have to plead guilty to having written some of those assignments and would admit the justice of the penalty: having to read the responses. No doubt, the classroom *is* an artificial situation that creates some of a writer's difficulties with invention, as well as with other parts of the composing process. Yet every Monday morning back we go to the classroom, wanting something other than Engfish. Pointing to our goal, Mina Shaughnessy wrote: "It is the business of a writing class to make writing more than an exercise. . . ." How might we translate that intention into reality, the exercise into writing?

In 1963 in his now-famous survey of composition courses, Kitzhaber noted, among many other faults in these courses, a lack of progression—that is, of the development of students' abilities by engaging them in increasingly complex activities.[1] The need for progression is a major reason for using a sequence of writing exercises. Generally, such a sequence moves from simpler to more complex activities; repeats tasks, since an activity must often be performed more than once in order to be learned; but repeats them at increasing levels of difficulty, creating a spiraling effect. In addition to offering students a rhetorical or cognitive sequence of writing tasks, however, we need to help them discover a passionate commitment to a subject. In its humblest sense, "passionate commitment" is a feeling that the writing matters because it is something one wants to say that is worth trying to share with others. Although it is useful at times for students to write purely as an exercise in craft, students will not be moved to write often or well if they never experience wanting to write for their own purposes. The formalistic approach to writing that predominates today encourages students to box their ideas in ready-made forms, to write by formula. A danger of heuristic procedures is that they may appear to be another set of these formulas. What James Britton terms "expressive writing," on the other hand, may articulate that inner speech that Vygotsky believed was a source of thinking.[2]

Some writing teachers argue that expressive writing should not be taught in a composition course because it is not the sort of writing students have to do in other courses. This argument completely misses Britton's point that expressive writing is not simply another mode of discourse along with transactional and poetic—although it may become a mode—but that it is the matrix for all forms of writing. If Britton is correct, expressive writing as a source of thinking, of invention, belongs not only in composition courses but in other courses as well.

Sequence of Exercises

A description of the curriculum I designed for my freshman writing course, a curriculum inspired by Britton's theory, may help to show how students can experience knowing personally, even as they move towards creating a more impersonal product—a ten-page research paper, presented according to MLA guidelines. The writing sequence consists of twenty-eight exercises on the nominal subject of play and work. Beginning with several narrative assignments calling for personal experiences, it moves to the observation of people playing and working, and to the examination of writing on those subjects by Studs Terkel, May Sarton, Karl Marx, and others. While moving beyond their own experience, the students are asked periodically to reexamine it in the light of their new observations. They explore the meaning of play and work in a variety of contexts and in a variety of ways from informal notebook reflections to lists, to one-sentence definitions, to parodies (enacting play, as well as defining it), to formal essays. My hope is that each exercise will not only be interesting in itself but will build a cumulative body of written experience upon which the writers may draw for each new assignment. They should come to see that expressive writing may be part of every writing task, whatever its final form.

Expressive Writing Exercises

Though presenting these assignments out of context is to lose the way in which the sequence builds a spiraling effect, I offer a selection, which preserves some of the play between exercises:

6. Two short pieces. Tell us about a particular experience you have had on a job that embodies what is difficult and demanding about the job.

And now the opposite, an experience that embodies what is most pleasurable about the job.

26. The Quakers say, "Work is love made visible." Here are some accounts of work to which that statement might be applied. (Here I quote three long accounts: those of a hockey player and a welder from Terkel's *Working* and May Sarton's description of her relationship with her friend and gardener, comparing their work making poems and gardens.) The assignment continues: Using these accounts and your own or your classmates', if you like, write an essay in which you consider in what circumstances the Quaker statement might be true, in what false.

27. Go back now to the Quaker definition of work and compare it with one of the dictionary definitions you found. How do the two statements differ? What sort of language do you find in each? Which tells *you* more? In what circumstances might one be appropriate and not the other? Tell us in a short commentary.

Exercise 6 is the last of three opening narrative exercises that are interspersed with exercises that I call, to myself, meta-exercises, ones that ask students to reflect upon a previous writing. Exercise 3, for example, following a narative on play, encourages the students to study the forms they have created to tell their stories and to discover that as writers they make choices (many students assume that the narrative order they choose is inevitable):

3. The writing you just did was focused on one event in time. Imagine that I asked you to place a frame around this event, separating it from the flow of time. How did you decide where to place your frame? Did you leave out some aspects of the event? Did you relate the events within the frame in the same order in which they happened? Why or why not? Reflect on these questions in your notebook.

In workshops focused on two or three students' narratives we describe the forms the students have chosen and discuss their effectiveness. Thus, while the students are writing their three narratives over a period of three-and-a-half weeks, they see a variety of approaches to narrating. When they have written the third narrative, I ask them to revise one, the one in which they are most interested, for which they have the most energy. The others may be revised or simply left in the portfolio as evidence of work done. Such a method lets students see how much material writers discard, and it lets them try out different approaches. One student wrote in the course evaluation that he "learned to be more daring and less conservative" in his writing.

Exercise 26, which comes near the end of the course after the research paper is complete, asks the students to interpret and reflect upon three rich and complex statements. In urging the students to draw upon their own and their classmates' earlier accounts of play and work, the assignment suggests that they permit their own texts to illuminate the published texts and *vice versa* and that they see how personal experience may be shaped to be accessible to others. Thus, this exercise attempts to make the students' own writing available to them for performing a more complex task, interpreting others' writings. Exercise 27 tries to help students see that writers choose the form and tone of definitions to suit their rhetorical purposes. It builds on earlier exercises that study dictionary definitions, as well as upon exercise 26.

Research Project Exercises

The course design also includes a research project, taking up most of the class's time between the eighth and twelfth weeks of the semester. The goal for this project is to let students discover that writing a research paper is not an exercise in stringing together quotations from a few books and articles, but a way of learning about the world; and that, as such, it may call for a variety of investigative procedures beyond library work. Moreover, it may engage the researcher's curiosity and enthusiasm. The writing is personal in the sense that the researcher is committed to the act of learning, even as she or he weighs the findings by whatever impersonal methods may seem appropriate and publishes them in the impersonal style that convention requires.

The first exercise in this project invites teams of two students to observe a person or group at play or work. The students are asked to take notes on their subject separately, after which they compare the notes to see if their points of view are similar. When we have discussed these findings in class and have begun to focus on particular questions about their subjects, the students are asked to interview one or more of the people they observed. Not until this point are the students directed to the library. Here is the exercise, numbered as it was in the original plan:

> 18. Now that you have some idea of what is involved in the action you are observing, your task is to begin to put it in a larger context. What questions about the action cannot be answered by

observing it? Is the action typical of a larger class of actions or is it idiosyncratic? After you have some questions, list the ways you might try to find the answers.

Sort out the questions you might answer by reading published materials. Then go to the library to see what you can find. Bring to class an annotated list of the books and pamphlets, the newspaper and journal articles you have decided will be useful to your study.

Your readings may raise questions or offer interpretations that you will have to answer or test by more observing or interviewing, so keep questioning the relationships between your information and your interpretations.

As the students continue their research in the library and in the field, they make progress reports in class and in conferences with me and write a series of informal papers intended to help them discover what they want to say, what its significance is, and what further work they may have to do. These papers ask them to respond to the following directions, among others: tell what is most significant about what you have seen; summarize your response to this question in one assertion; write freely for fifteen minutes about the most interesting and significant aspects of your topic. The repetition in these exercises proved necessary because, as teachers often find, it takes students a long time and many tries to discover what their "thesis" is. They are not accustomed to the notion that finding the thesis requires moving back and forth between their data and their hypothesis. Nor are they accustomed, as far as I can tell, to the notion that their subject should be significant to anyone in particular.

We should not be surprised at such student attitudes, since many textbooks seem to work on the *deus ex machina* model of invention. Students may be told that a good area for research is a controversial topic, or they may be given a list of topics to be narrowed. Then they are told to make their thesis *before* they start their research. For all one can tell from these texts, the thesis descends, fully articulated from heaven, or is, perhaps, carried by Groucho Marx's duck. Once the thesis has landed, one researches it, discovering both sides of the question. It would be surprising if this formal exercise suggested to students that research papers are written by people who think, who care about their work, and who want to communicate their results.

Although the research papers my students wrote in this course were often naive and sometimes awkward, they were clearer, better organized, more creative, and generally better researched than others I have received. Most important to me, many of the students got a sense of what research really is. Some excerpts from the students' course evaluations will show what I mean: "My research paper was the most interesting piece of work I ever wrote because it dealt with just interviews." Another: "The research paper taught me many ways to go about research and setting up the rough draft as well as final copy."

Other exercises, not to the point here, assist the students to organize, revise, and edit their papers. What is important is that by using a variety of research methods linking the library with the field and by engaging extensively in the inventive process through informal and expressive writing, students learn not just the formal requirements of a research paper but that research is a way of learning (or attempting to learn) what one *wants* to know.

Conclusion

The research project is the middle segment of my writing curriculum, part of a sequence of writing exercises that repeatedly engages students in expressive writing. That is, I believe, a more effective design for experiencing invention than the familiar linear model. That model, essentially formal and product-oriented, generally asks students to produce a series of genre papers: narration (*the* personal experience essay), description, analysis, and argument. The narrative essay produced, the class goes on to the descriptive essay with little chance to discover that writers usually do not decide to write descriptive essays but to share their vision of Walden Pond or Lenox Avenue.

A sequence of writing exercises may, on the other hand, engage students repeatedly in expressive writing for itself or as a way of discovering ideas that may later appear in an analytic, persuasive, or some other form. Since some of this writing is purposely informal, not calling for extensive editorial comment, the teacher can assign more frequent writing than the product-oriented teacher who feels compelled to comment elaborately on each paper. Thus, the students may have several opportunities to shape their essays.

The test of this sequenced approach will be whether these exercises produce theme-writing or whether some at least will invite students to write with both passion and decorum. The writing my students have done so far is no more correct than that of previous students, but it shows more evidence that they are working to discover forms appropriate to what they want to say and that they are experiencing more of the whole range of the writing process—the mess and the false starts, as well as the excitement of discovering and of sharing ideas.

One of the dangers of writing a sequence is that pleasure in creating the game may blind one to the effects on the players. Like all other writers, the writer of a sequence has to be generous in throwing out material. Teaching the sequence, one must be alert to the need for adjusting it. Above all, one must insure that the sequence allows students to say what matters to them.

Notes

1. Albert Kitzhaber, *Themes, Theories and Therapy: The Teaching of Writing in College* (New York: McGraw-Hill Co., 1973), 13.
2. James Britton, et al., *The Development of Writing Abilities (11-18)* (Urbana, Ill.: NCTE, 1978), 10-11 *passim.*

11 The Basic Reading and Writing Phenomenon: Writing as Evidence of Thinking

Karen M. Hjelmervik
University of Pittsburgh

Susan B. Merriman
University of Pittsburgh

The University of Pittsburgh is faced with many of the same student population problems that greet other large, urban universities each fall—a growing number of students who cannot read or write well enough to be academic students in the traditional sense. Their entrance test scores place them within the group of students who statistically look as though they will fail or drop out of college. Or these are the students who somehow muddle through school, being among the college graduates who are ill-equipped to read and write in their chosen fields of work. We often say that these are students who don't "think" very well, by which we mean they don't seem to be able to say anything that isn't oversimplified, underdeveloped, boring, or said better by someone else.

Basic Reading and Writing Course

In recognition of this kind of student, the University of Pittsburgh has designed a six-credit course called Basic Reading and Writing, for which incoming freshmen are now required to register if tests so indicate. The idea of the course is described by David Bartholomae in the 1979 Spring/Summer issue of *The Journal of Basic Reading*. In his article, Bartholomae talks about BRW students as those who have a hard time imagining themselves as a reader/writer/thinker, as students who are capable of dealing with academic tasks requiring these abilities. There is one central difference between the students we recognize as competent and those who are not: all the experiences of BRW students have taught them that they cannot be successful in controlling ideas either as interpreters of what they read or generators of what they write. Ideas are something which other, smarter people have. Our course is designed to accommodate their lack of experience in these processes.

There are two kinds of reading requirements. Students are required to read six books over the term: two fiction and four nonfiction. They also prepare a collection of their own autobiographies, which everyone reads. Second, each term we require students to select and read at least four other books for their own pleasure. We allow students one hour a week in class (later, we extend the time to nearly two hours) of sustained silent reading of books chosen by the students. For both the required and selected books, we ask for a written journal entry of at least one hour's writing time, which means that students produce ten to twelve entries over the course of the term.

There are also two kinds of writing requirements within the course. Students write at least one paper a week, including revision assignments. These assignments are sequenced so that students have experience in reporting and recording, narration, explication, and argument. In addition, the assignments all relate to a central concept, growth and change in American adolescence, which we spend the term defining, describing, and exploring. The longest paper in the sequence is the midterm autobiography mentioned earlier. Second, we ask students to write an inclass interpretive essay on a 4,000 word selection from each of the assigned books. The essays, which remain ungraded, focus on the students' comprehension of the authors' main ideas.

The students' immersion in these reading and writing activities has as its implicit aim the development of clear thinking. Our students cannot think clearly, however, until they develop some measure of confidence in their ability to carry on such mental processes. Because we want to put our students in a position to be successful as readers and writers in control of language, we structure the course so that they will experience success and therefore accumulate evidence that language will work for them. We ask them first to write about what they know best—themselves. We stress quantity of information in these first assignments. They repeatedly write and revise, getting a feel for the uses of "detail" and "illustration" and all those other terms that they have never really understood before. Meanwhile, they are reading and writing about the lives of other people who talk about themselves. After the sixth–eighth week, our students pass what we call the "threshhold of fluency": they are now able to generate a significant amount of writing (though it is primarily narrative at this point) on command. Skills which were previously beyond their reach—prewriting, gathering and organizing details, shaping an orderly sequence of events—are now within their grasp. They can no longer say they are not writers, and they can no longer tell themselves that they have nothing to say or that they have never really thought about something. The irrefutable evidence is in the papers they hold in their hands.

At about the eighth week, we begin the hard work of helping them understand what explanation means. At this point we let them know that it is no longer enough to say "Holden Caulfield is screwed up," or that "my first real job was a significant event in my life." We want to begin demonstrating that it is possible to conceive of Holden as representative in some respects of American adolescents, and to explain what implications that characterization may have for a general theory of growth and development in American adolescence. Then we ask them to make the connection to their own lives.

We have found the move from narration to generalization to be difficult, and yet here we have the opportunity to demonstrate to our students what ideas can look like on paper. We offer exercises and read fables as a way of demonstrating what inferences look like and how they are different from the data they generalize. As they struggle to explain and define what their experience means, our students at last begin to see the evidence, however ill-formed, however poorly phrased, that they are, indeed, thinking adults. In their writing, they can see ideas being born and nurtured, played with, modified and refined. From the middle of the term on, we spend our time helping students do these things, so that by the end of the term, they have written records of ideas they themselves have created.

In this way, then, the students come to see writing as thinking, and as a process in which they can participate effectively. Our greatest wish at the end of the term, in fact, is that our students see themselves as the readers, writers, and thinkers they imagined eveyone else to be.

One Student's Story

But before our wish can be realized, we separate out the differences between the processes so that students can understand them. First, we ask them what they know about writing, what they think of themselves as writers, and how they view the papers they have written. Sam is a typical BRW student in many ways; therefore, we can use his writing to represent that of our class population. Sam came to the University of Pittsburgh on an athletic scholarship, after four years in a high school where he excelled in sports, but barely achieved an academic record that would allow him to apply for college entrance. He screened into our course and attended it begrudgingly. During the first week, Sam came into class with all the preconceived notions BRW students have about themselves: he thought that other students were smart, that certainly he was not, and that he was in the course only because he had to be, although he acknowledged that he could probably use such a course. His language about himself, in other words, suggested that he was going to tolerate the course, not participate in it. He didn't really believe he could be helped. When he talked about what he read and how he wrote, he demonstrated his inexperience in dealing with ideas that went beyond the simple, the moralistic, or the easily summarized. He wanted to come to closure too quickly and thus avoid confronting the complexity of the material he was reading or thinking about.

Sam's First Paper

His first paper of the term demonstrates many of these problems. On the first day of class, all students are asked to read a chapter (a little more than 4,000 words) from Margaret Mead's autobiography, *Blackberry Winter,* and then write about the main ideas in that chapter. They have two hours to do all of this. On the last day of class, students are given the same task again, only they read a different chapter of the same book (also having a little more than 4,000 words).

Here is Sam's response to the pretest assignment:

> As I read through Ms. Mead's Blackberry Winter, I noticed that she pointed out the main problem of discrimination. When she said it was very similar to the discrimination of blacks she was very true. I fell the main reason for this was the sorrieties and fraternitys and the compitition and rivalries of both. Ms. Mead was brought up different from what she was about to experience because of her Intelligence and the way she was brought up she was able to handle it. When Ms. Mead said White Americans came to realize that what they offered Negro Americans was not so very different from this, she was right. Freshmen were not aloud to be spoken to until they were accepted by a sorriety bid. When Ms. Mead showed up at her bid for the sorriety not well dressed she was an amidiate outcast. Ms. Mead then found out at this point that she would have to work within her own limitation to be successful and to be accepted. She did this by not try in competed with the discriminative men in there fields, but competed with women in her own way to by accepted and successful. Even through the women were very discriminatory also. They didn't what there rivalys accepting Mrs. Mead because she had hidden talents.

> I feel this is discrimination at its best. Ms. Mead made the
> right move by transferring to a all girls college where it was more
> democratic. I feel Ms. Mead got the last laugh.

One of the first things that struck us when we read this paper is the
kind of obtrusive error characteristic of many basic writing students.
We include a direction for editing in the test question to see how
many students know what editing means. For Sam, it may have meant
he should quickly and silently reread his own paper from the first
sentence to the last. Or it may have meant nothing to him at all.
There are two equally difficult editing problems facing Sam: he must,
of course, correct his errors, but first he must be able to find them.
BRW students usually don't know how to correct things, even if they suspect
something is wrong. So, for example, a word like "fell" that ought to
have been "feel," or "fraternitys" that ought to have been "fraternities," or "through" that ought to have been "though" stand out
glaringly for many readers but go unrecognized by Sam. BRW errors
are even more glaring in sentences which are already syntactically
incorrect, or ideas that are only partially suggested, or information
which is inaccurate and connections which are nonexistent or silly.
For these students, error serves as confirmation that they can't write.

But error is only one consideration. Many of our students can
control spelling and sentence boundaries, but can't grasp the notion
of an idea or thesis and don't know how to write for an imagined
audience. For example, Sam senses that discrimination has something
to do with the things which Mead says blacks have experienced in this
century, and he tries to connect discrimination with the sorority and
fraternity system at DePauw, but the connections he draws are as
vague as his understanding of what she said. Somehow he wants to
talk about the "Negro Americans" who suffered, and the girls in
college who "were not aloud to be spoken to until they were accepted
by a sorriety bid." He wants to say something about how Mead
adjusted to the discrimination she experienced by working within
"her own limitation," but again, he can offer no definition of this
"limitation" or explain how that fits into the world of competing
men and women.

One of Sam's other problems is his confusion over the meanings of
the word "discrimination." In the first sentence, for example, he says
that "she pointed out the main problem of discrimination," although
we don't know what sort of discrimination he is talking about. Whatever it is, he compares it to discrimination against blacks. Later, the
word is used differently, when he says that Mead "did this [work to be
accepted] by not try in competed with the discriminative men in there
fields." He is probably trying to say that the men discriminated

against the women (or does he mean men against blacks?). When he adds that "the women were very discriminatory, too," he may mean that women as well as men discriminated against Mead, but he probably does not mean to suggest that women had discriminating tastes, as his wording here implies. He concludes that "this is discrimination at its best." His choice of the word "best" probably means that Mead's are good examples of the way people behave toward other people when they discriminate against them.

Sam's paper is, for many reasons, hard to read. In addition to error, omission of explanation, confusion of terms, and syntactical clumsiness, Sam has talked about only one small part of the chapter and ignored the part of the task which asked him to respond to the ideas in the chapter.

We think we understand the expectations and anxieties that put a student like Sam into a corner. First, he had a hard time reading the chapter in an hour. After having read it as slowly as he did, he couldn't remember most of what he had read. In fact, the issues of sororities and fraternities come rather late in the chapter, and quite possibly registered because there are fraternities and sororities at Pitt, too, and Sam didn't need to go outside of his own immediate experience to understand the terms involved. As an inexperienced reader, then, he didn't know how to sort information as he was reading and anticipate what might come next; instead, he spent his time reading the chapter line by line, nearly word for word, coming to the end of a page, forgetting what he'd read, going back again to the page he had just finished reading, struggling to get to the end. By the time he was ready to write, he must have had only the sketchiest memories of what he had read. Having no active strategies to sort that information, he had to rely on his street sense of what he thought he knew and could remember.

Being an inexperienced writer, moreover, he wouldn't know how to assemble coherently whatever information he had retained. Once into the writing task, Sam seems committed to an activity that controls him, rather than Sam's controlling the flow of each sentence. To get himself out of this dilemma, Sam pauses for the second and final paragraph, somehow recognizing that a conclusion of some sort is needed, some gesture that sounds as though he is offering his opinion on the essay's most significant point. He says that "Ms. Mead made the right move by transferring to a all girls college were it was more democratic. I feel Ms. Mead got the last laugh." We don't know where he gets the idea that this transfer of college will mean a more democratic life or why she got a "last laugh." Sam is relying on his notion of the way a paper ought to sound when it ends, not concluding with a general explanation of his own opinion. Sam, like other students who don't know what to do with a new learning situation, reverts to a strategy which is familiar to him, whether or not it has worked for him in the past.

There are other characteristics of these students which we observed in Sam's behavior as a reader and writer. For example, you cannot see from this typeset version the messy handwriting that slants left to right and also right to left, the multiple starts and scratchings-out which are not the results of editing, but the results of trying to say something and then cancelling it out before it has gone more than a few words. Nor can you see, as we did, the physical agitation, the restlessness, the pencil chewing and finger drumming, the eyes that could not focus for long periods of time either on the chapter to be read or the paper while it was being written. Reading and writing, for this typical BRW student, are difficult, agonizing processes, ones which he feels control him and get the best of him.

We learn a great deal about our BRW students from watching them and understanding how they generate this first paper. We see this paper as evidence of an inexperienced reader and writer trying to make sense out of a difficult assignment involving many difficult processes. We don't view the paper as evidence of stupidity or the absence of thinking. Though Sam's response is not pleasing academically, it is not an indictment of his intelligence.

Sam's Final Paper

Here is his response to the question given at the end of the term:

> I felt that Ms. Mead's chapter on college at Barnard was enlightening, but life in the 20's in our society was dismal. I feel the change in school from Depaul to Barnard was necessary for Mead becasue Barnard seem to be more of a free and radical school for girls. In 1920's women where looked down upon in our society, they did not have many rights. But at Barnard it seemed that the girls where more free, because they did not have to live in a sorority. At Barnard the girls lived in dormitory apartment houses.
>
> I feel Mead made the right choice about switching schools, because at Barnard she would be able to increase her intelligence in many areas. They where no longer true decendants of the group of girls who had lived in the coop, they belonged to the new generation of young women who felt extraordinarily free—free from the demand to marry unless they chose to do so. This liberal type attitude in girls at Barnard made the learning situations

better. It seemed that these group of girls wanted to bring about
change in the world.
I felt throughout this chapter Mead is undecided what she
really wants to do in life. She is influenced by a vareity of people
during her time at Barnard. Mead was a very bright intellegent
girl who was considering many different fields of study. At DePaul
she was an English major and she was considering that as her
study at Barnard. She also was interested in politics, antropology,
psychology and sociology. Ruth Benedict who was an assistant to
Professor Boas help Mead with her decision. One day at lunch,
when Mead was discussing with Ruth about her going into
sociology as Mead wanted to, Ruth told her that "Professor Boas
and I have nothing to offer but a opportunity to do work that
matters." This caused Mead to chose anthropology because it had
to be done now.
Ruth Benedict turned out to be a life long friend of Mead's up
until Ruth's death in 1948. Mead said Ruth read everything she
had ever written and Mead read all of Ruth's work also. Mead
ended up mastering many different fields of study like antropology, psychology, arts, English and politics. I felt Mead was able
to achieve all of this knowledge because of Ruth Benedict and the
school Barnard with its liberal values. Barnard was the type of
school that opens peoples' minds and enlightens there values of
each other.

Once again there is the issue of error to contend with. Sam spells
DePauw as "DePaul" and variety as "vareity." But error here is no
longer interfering repeatedly with meaning. Sentences are sensible
and paragraphs are coherent, though there is an error or two in
sentence boundaries.

Clearly, Sam has enough control of the subject to make a paper of
several paragraphs, each paragraph of several sentences. He is not
only able to refer to the chapter he read but has also been able to
recall some information from the first chapter (the reference to the
"coop," for example), even though it was not even mentioned in his
first paper. The ideas seem to connect from paragraph to paragraph.
The movement from the first paragraph, where he talks about Barnard as a more "free and radical" school for girls than DePauw had
been, is extended in the second paragraph, where he talks about
Barnard as a better "learning situation" for Mead. He says that she
had many interests, made many friends (he is now able to name them
specifically), and was finally able to make a career decision. By the
last paragraph, he has zeroed in on her indebtedness to her good
friend, acknowledging Mead's emphasis on friends as being central to
her development as a woman as well as an anthropologist. He ends
the paper with Mead's discussion of the need for friends in a liberal
school, a conclusion which refers back to the paper's beginning.

Sam doesn't try to center this paper on one word as he did on the word "discrimination" in his first paper. He seems in control of the orderly progression of observations. We see evidence of this coherence in such constructions as his "because" sentences, which demonstrate his understanding of cause/effect relationships. Sam is past the point where his writing is a reaction to a threat. Instead, his writing is a response to a question he believes he can control.

Our observations suggest that he now believes in himself as a reader and writer. His handwriting is guided and neat, slanting in only one direction and staying on the lines, and each word is clearly discernible. He had also written a rough draft which he attached to his final draft, copied neatly, and edited as carefully as he knew how. Moreover, for about half an hour, he read steadily, with no breaks and no physical agitation. He brought a dictionary with him, which he used while he wrote, and he was able to remember what he read so that he could go back to the chapter and refer directly to important points (for example, the reference to the people in Mead's life and the specific fields of interest she talked about). And he patiently read each of his sentences several times, looking for misspelled words (here he used his dictionary) and punctuation errors (here he would test the appropriateness of a comma). It was clear that Sam understood the processes of reading and writing well enough to get through both tasks, applying different strategies to each, recognizing them to be separate processes, yet sensing how one nurtured the other, feeling that he was master of the information he read and sorted and that he could write about it intelligently.

Though our inferences have been drawn from these pre/post examples, they do not tell us everything we need to know, or necessarily provide the best examples for understanding writing problems or the factors which promote successful writing. The test does not, for example, allow the kind of tinkering and revising that happens with most academic tasks. And individual papers are not as significant as the general growth over the course of a term in which students read about twelve to fifteen books and write about them, compose four inclass papers, and produce about twenty-five sequenced writing tasks. Perhaps less important even than what Sam could do in his final assignment is the fact that he believed he could do it.

Conclusion

Our course exists to help troubled readers and writers imagine they can become competent. As their confidence in themselves increases, they begin to control reading and writing so that they can first read well enough to talk about meaning and write enough to pass a threshhold of fluency which allows them to generate writing with confidence. Second, they learn to identify ideas in what they read, write, and talk about, distinguishing ideas from things like details, narration, summary, and moralizing. Then, they begin learning to generate and develop ideas that are not organized in the way narration is, but in other, not so easily understood, structures. And finally they learn to read what others have said about those ideas (here we are referring to the nonfiction books we mentioned early on) and imagine why authors say what they do. By the end of the term, then, students are exposed to a sequence of experiences in which they report and reflect on their own lives, on the lives of others immediately around them, and on their lives within the whole range of people their own age.

Writing, reading, and thinking nurture each other in this course so that students experience processes which they must master if they are to survive the demands that college makes. Our intention is to prepare our students with the skills necessary to academic survival. Our students, like Sam, are not stupid, inept, or devoid of ideas. They are, however, inexperienced in the very processes that would help them believe in themselves. By reading and writing, and talking about what they read and write, they learn to believe in their own abilities to think rationally.

12 Revising: The Writer's Need to Invent and Express Relationships

Sandra Schor
Queens College, CUNY

Although the primary purpose of the Queens English Project was not to elicit and study revision, the Project became a laboratory in which to study many ingredients of composing, revising among them. More and more composition teachers are encouraging their students to revise their writing. Workshop-like classrooms provide responses from fellow writers, and well-spaced assignment schedules allow the writer's own responses to ripen after continued rereadings. Yet nothing provides as cogent a redirection for rewriting as the comment from the teacher. In the light of our emphasis on structured writing in the work of the Queens Project, I thought it pertinent to ask how teachers influence the revisions their students make, particularly teachers who have given students frequent opportunity to practice writing in a few whole and impressive structures. Does practice in structured writing have an effect on revising? How can teachers of writing assist the writer to revise his or her paper effectively?

The Queens English Project

For this study I am drawing on the writing of a group of students who participated in the Queens English Project during 1978–80. Briefly, the Project has been an articulation project in English, bridging instruction in writing and reading between the last year of high school and the first year of college. Queens College and five feeder high schools[1] in the Borough of Queens, New York, collaborated under an award from the Fund for the Improvement of Post-Secondary Education.[2]

Initially, the Project had two key components: a cooperative seminar for teachers in a syllabus that emphasized structured writing,[3] and a tutoring program in which trained undergraduate tutors worked

113

with high school teachers and students. The Project emphasized several principles: first, writing in whole structures. Whole structures introduced the key arrangement in writing as alternations of abstract ideas with concrete support. Students wrote fables and parables, narrative anecdotes, family stories, and personal and literary essays. They arranged these to present an abstract or generalized thesis accompanied by concrete support that took a variety of forms: a dialogue (as in the case of the fable), an anecdotal narrative (as in the personal essay), or evidence from a work of literature (as in the literary essay).

A related principle was making copious concrete observations on a piece of writing and then drawing from them a few useful, critical inferences. Our teachers and tutors exercised students in this principle by applying it to both published and student writing. They limited their responses to descriptive observations of the writing, which were neither judgmental nor corrective insofar as that was possible. Rewriting was another important principle. Students knew at the outset that writing was in fact *rewriting*. They were to draw their own inferences about what and how to rewrite from the observations which their teacher made on their writing. Teachers did not instruct students in how or what to rewrite. By repeatedly offering students the set of observations made on a piece of writing, we expected our writers to infer for themselves what revisions they ought to undertake to improve the text. Since our emphasis was on structure, we also expected that in order to rewrite parts, they would first revise the whole, or at least consider the whole.

Project Emphasis on Revision

The students whose writing I incorporate below as samples are among the program's weakest writers. The papers in question were written as part of their college English 01 course, which they were required to take prior to the regular freshman writing sequence. Their teacher was Mindy Altman,[4] who doubled as an adjunct in the English department and as a member of the FIPSE team. Ms. Altman's comments on student papers are a model of restraint and descriptive accuracy.

For the most part, we found revision to be an unappealing and a complex task for our students. What is more to the point is how our emphasis on whole structures influenced the revision of essays—that is, (a) how teachers capitalized on the course's emphasis on structure in the comments they made on early drafts, and (b) to what extent students integrated their awareness of whole structure in actually revising the essays.

At best, students in the Queens project undertook substantive changes (that is, changes other than for neatness and correct usage): (1) to fill out the structure of the first draft by providing more detail and supplying information remarked on as absent by the teacher; (2) to avoid disturbing the existing structure by deleting "digressive" elements; and (3) to effect real structural change—that is, to reorder parts, to assert an abstract comment about a concrete event, to focus a paper on a purpose discovered through the writing of drafts, or to sharpen the focus on elements that appeared merely accidental or subordinate in preliminary drafts.

The work of Nancy Sommers[5] and the research study of eleventh grade writers in Virginia by Charles K. Stallard[6] both emphasize that students themselves see revision as a rewording activity, adding, dropping, or substituting single words as a major change they make. Rewording, however, is not the chief change made in the papers of our students who, you will remember, were routinely expected to infer the changes to be made from the observations of their teacher and peers.

The exasperating truth is that more time went to recopying for neatness and completeness than to any other single activity. Although nowhere in Ms. Altman's comments is there a hint of complaint about illegibility or sloppiness, the injunctions to be neat and to be legible carry the fervor of religion. Perhaps we can release students from the tyranny of the flawless copy by instructing them in how to make legible changes on a draft. Pencil-line insertions and cross-outs, numbered paragraphs, and clearly labeled substitutions are more instructive for conference study than completely resurfaced drafts that mask the process.

The second most frequent change corrected gross errors in mechanics, syntax, punctuation, and spelling. Since Ms. Altman's comments attended only to glaringly incorrect forms and punctuation, there are relatively few corrections. If we are to consider these errors a low-order concern in the revision of whole compositions, then teachers ought to reconsider the advisability of marking these weaknesses on a paper which first needs structural alteration or reconception. Delaying comment on mechanics in no way diminishes the importance of mechanical skills in the development of a young writer, but it does clearly demonstrate that ideas need to be sorted out first, that the bones of a paper need construction before we beautify the skin.

In a similar way, the third kind of change students in this class made also needs to be delayed. It constitutes, however, the leading substantive revision undertaken by students. Jerome S. Bruner has said we are in danger of becoming "slaves of the particular." And, consistently, the one teacher's comment to which students most effectively respond is the call to "be more specific." This is the single rhetorical change young writers produce with competence, though I am not convinced they see the rhetorical motives underlying these changes. Rather they are complying with a teacher's recognition that a structure needs filling out. The call for detail also supports some teachers' current interest in voice, in putting a personality on the page, that is conveyed by language rich in sensory detail.

Drafts and Teacher Comments: Essay 1

Draft 1a

A turning point in my life began on the twenty-fifth of June in the year of 1979. After 6 months of planning, I was finally taking the trip to Israel that I was dreaming and thinking about for a long time.

With all my baggage, my parents brought me to a building where they were having the orientation. Before I know it, I was saying good-bye and boarding the plane on the way to the land of milk-n-honey. My trip consisted of 6 weeks of new friends from all over the world. I had the best time of my life. I learned so much and experienced so many different things that at times I was actually speechless. I started picking up a new language and wanted to learn it as well as I could.

Upon returning home in August, I was welcomed by my family and friends. I had tears rolling down my eyes but a big smile on my face. I was so happy to have had the chance to go to Israel but I was so sad to leave there as well as leaving all my friends. I had story after story to tell everyone. The more I spoke about it, the more I realized how much I changed. I now know people who live different lives than that of mine.

I think that this trip did a lot for me. Its been one turning point that will stick out in my mind because of how much it meant to me.

Draft 1b

The turning point is something that changes the theme, subject or direction in a story, or any piece of literature. It's the highest point in a story. In life, people have a turning point as well. It's the highest point of their life where decisions are made. It is usually something that will affect their lives forever or for a long period of time. This could be a job, marriage or any event. Whatever the change might be, it will be a change, drastic or not.

A turning point in my life began on the twenty-fifth of June in the year of 1979. After 6 months of planning, I was finally taking the trip to Israel that I was dreaming and thinking about for a long time.

With all my baggage, my parents brought me to a building where they were having the orientation. . . . [The middle section of the paper is identical to version 1a.] . . . Upon returning home in August, I was welcomed by my family and friends. I had tears rolling down my eyes but a big smile on my face. I was so happy to have had the chance to go to Israel but I was so sad to leave there as well as leaving all my friends. I had story after story to tell everyone. The more I spoke about it, the more I realized how much I changed. My feelings, my actions as well as my attitude towards things changed. I now know people who live different lives then that of mine.

I think this trip did a lot for me. Its been a high point for me and it will effect the rest of my life. It's one turning point that meant a lot to me.

Teacher's Comment on 1b

Cindy, I notice that you begin with a paragraph which explains "turning point" abstractly and which generalizes about its role in literature and life. You mention literature first and then life; the main focus is a story taken from your life. Your story is about neither a job nor marriage; it falls under the category of "any event." The next paragraph tells us what kind of event: a trip. This trip was obviously very important to you. But if a turning point is that point where decisions are made and where changes occur, what decision did you make and how did you change? You start to tell us towards the end; how could you tell the reader more? Your feelings, actions, and attitudes changed from what to what? How did learning about others change you? Is this the most important point? I notice it is at the end of the essay. I would love to hear more about this trip some time.

Draft 1c

A turning point in a person's life, is the highest point. It is usually something that will affect their lives forever or for a long period of time. This could be a job, marriage, or even a change like moving, etc. Whatever the change might be, it will be a change, drastic or not.

A turning point in my life began on the twenty-fifth of June in the year of 1979. After 6 months of planning I was finally taking the trip to Israel that I was dreaming and thinking about for a long time.

With all my baggage, my parents brought me to the Rego Park Jewish Center. This was where the leaders of the trip were having an orientation to familiarize parents and the participants of the trip. Before I knew it, I was saying good-bye and boarding the plane on the way to the land of milk-n-honey. My trip consisted of 6 weeks of fun, learning, seeing and climbing. I also made a bunch of new friends from all over the world. I learned so much and experienced so many different things, that at times I was actually speechless. I started picking up a new language, Hebrew, and I wanted to learn it to the best of my ability.

Upon returning home in August, I was welcomed by my family and friends. I had tears rolling down my cheeks but a big smile on my face. I was so happy to have had the chance to go to Israel but I was so sad to leave there as well as leaving all my friends. I had story after story to tell everyone. The more I spoke about it, the more I realized how much I changed. My feelings, my actions as well as my attitude toward things. I was not as serious about things before my trip and I wasn't interested in the history of Israel until I came home. I now know people who live different lives then that of mine and I realized that everyone has special qualities. I learned from this because I got a chance to hear, see and learn about different people and their qualities. It gave me a special feeling that in six weeks I changed so much.

I think this trip did a lot for me. Its been a high point for me and it will effect the rest of my life. I had the best time of my life. It's one turning point that meant a lot to me.

Teacher's Comment on 1c

Cindy, you've included more here than in your previous version. You give more specifics about the beginning of the trip, and you begin to tell more about what you learned, for instance, about the people. But you could still be more specific. What did you learn about the people and their qualities? How do they live differently than you? In what ways have you been affected? How have you changed? You may focus on one specific incident (one of your many stories) and show from it what you learned and how you were affected. Come see me to discuss it.

On 1c, the second revision, in the paragraph beginning "With all my baggage," the student finally has changed "brought me to a building where they were having the orientation," to "the Rego Park Jewish Center. This was where the leaders of the trip were having an orientation to familiarize parents and the participants of the trip." These changes were made in response to the instructor's specific queries in the margin of draft 1b. I will return to this set of papers to talk about the teacher's and writer's common failure to achieve real structural change.

In the same way as Cindy has done, young writers will often change their papers to supply a specific detail in response to a reader's request for clarifying information, yet will entirely miss the larger purpose of the reader's comments. Phyllis, for example, retyped an entire essay for the sake of inserting a six-word phrase, "when I was 11 years old," into its third paragraph. Yet in her comments, Ms, Altman had reflected on the relationship of the parts of the essay to the whole in a way that brought into question the real point of the episode. Her suggestion that readers needed to know the writer's age at the time the episode took place was incidental to this broader purpose. Yet in Phyllis's revision, she responded only to the specific question about age and entirely ignored the more important discussion of the paper's focus which surrounded it.

Drafts and Teacher Comments: Essay 2

Another act of revision reflects a decision to delete digressive or unintegrated material. But digression is a novice's mishap. Certainly Kenneth Burke, Thoreau, and many great essayists have the ability to resist digression, but they also digress willfully, eloquently, and know how to relate digression to the main stream. Here are two versions of another essay, a tale of family bravado and regret:

Draft 2a

You should stick to what you believe in and never give in. Never let somebody do what you don't want them to do. My grandmother let somebody do something she didn't want him to do and almost lost somebody precious to her.

My grandmother had 4 children, all boys, of which my father was 3rd born. My grandmother also had a brother who was a butcher. When my grandmother gave birth to her first child, her brother, my great uncle, asked if he could perform the *briss*, the circumcision. He even had a kit for such a purpose. My grandmother flat-out refused him. When my grandmother had her second child, my great uncle again asked her if he could perform the *briss*. Again, my grandmother refused him. When my grandmother had her third child, my father, my great uncle again asked if he could perform the *briss*. This time my grandmother gave in. My great uncle cut off a little too much though and my father had to be taken to the hospital. My grandmother never forgave her brother for that. My father, though, became very close to his uncle, the butcher, as he became known.

My grandmother learned a very valuable lesson after that. She became one of the most stubborn women I knew.

Draft 2b

[This version of the paper is identical to 2a down to the middle of paragraph two.]

. . . He even had a kit for such a purpose. My grandmother correctly refused him. When my grandmother had her second child, my great uncle again asked if he could perform the *briss*. My grandmother stuck to her original decision and refused him again. When my grandmother had her third child, my father, my great uncle again asked if he could perform the *briss*. This time my grandmother gave in. My great uncle cut off a little too much though, and my father had to be taken to the hospital. My grandmother never forgave her brother for that and he became known as the butcher.

My grandmother learned a very valuable lesson after that. She always stuck to her original decision and never gave in to anybody. She became one of the most stubborn women I knew.

Teacher's Comment on 2b

Steve, I notice that the changes that you made put a greater emphasis on your grandmother. Her stubbornness isn't the lesson but is rather the result of the lesson. Although you focus on your grandmother from start to finish, it seems that the main action is performed by your uncle, and that it's his action that sticks with us rather than your grandmother's. What do you think?

The first draft, 2a, includes a throwaway sentence about the father's developing a close relationship to his uncle despite this nasty slice of history between them. In the final version, the writer has eliminated this sentence, probably feeling it a digression, and the teacher's final comment invites the writer to reevaluate the focus of the whole episode. It is possible that reconsidering the friendship of the two men might have allowed the writer to see another focus to this family story. The writer needed to ask why he included the information in the first draft and how he thought it related to the rest of the story. Perhaps alternative generalizations might deal with the strange attraction between victim and wrongdoer, particularly between family members who are forced to live out their lives almost within each other's embrace; or with the persistence of guilt; or the attempt to condone or pay back; all possible themes which do not come to light because the student sees the buried sentence as a digression without searching for whatever ties that interesting friendship to the rest of the writer's idea.

A reconsideration of a paper whose writer has attempted revisions of a first order of concern—that is, structural changes—might be instructive here. Look at 1a, b, and c. My guess is that the student noticed that she begins with a concrete narrative and that an abstract statement on the nature of a turning point is absent from her essay. The writer supplies the abstract comment in 1b, focusing on the decisiveness of a turning point and generalizing that change inevitably follows a turning point and can affect "any event."

But does what follows in 1b now carry out the promise clearly stated in the new opening paragraph and commented on by the teacher? It does not. As a reader of this essay, I expect the writer to show how her new knowledge bears on her own life. Attention needs to focus on the *language* of the assertion, on the *turn* of turning point. But turn from what to what? The details of learning a language, learning the history of another country, immersing oneself in other lifestyles and values in the context of this paper serve only insofar as they will be made to reflect on the *turn* in the writer's life.

But the writer doesn't know how to develop her essay in a way that conveys her life's changes. A writer who has this degree of difficulty in conceptualizing the point of her paper fails to apply the acts of invention necessary to conceptualizing. Let us look at this problem more closely. In isolating the components in her definition of turning point—that is, decisiveness, life-long effect, the high point it takes in a life, the changes the turning point sets off—the writer needs to analyze the complex experience of her trip to Israel for these attributes, to identify what is new in the experience and relate that to what she knows. Recognizing the new elements in a maze-like experience is an act of invention. Our students require practice in invention and accommodation that will habituate them to the writer's continuing need to relate new ideas with old—that is, to revise a first draft so that a second draft, whose relationships are more visibly signaled, evolves out of it.

Drafts and Teacher Comments: Essay 3

Now let us take one closing look at techniques writers use to revise effectively. Many of our writers understood the need for wholesale revision of structure and went after it in diverse ways. See for example essays 3a and 3b:

> *Draft 3a*
>
> There are different ways of remembering your childhood. Most of the time it is by looking at pictures or by having your parents telling you about it. Many times you vaguely remember. Sometimes you don't even believe what your parents tell you; you think they are just telling you a story, like a fairy tale or something.
>
> As a child I can recall many things that happened to me. Most of the things that happened to me, when I was young, come back to me in my dreams. For example I can recall when my brother and I were young we used to have pillow fights on my parents' bed. The pillow fell over the bed; I went to get it before my brother. I hit my forehead on the side of the bed, which is made of wood. I was bleeding a lot. I would have thought that it was only a dream, but I have a scar on my forehad from this incidence.
>
> Looking at pictures or someone telling you about your childhood aren't the only ways your childhood memories come back.

There is also another way, by your dreams. I would recall most of my childhood days as dreams, but they actually occurred because I have scars to prove some of them.

Teacher's Comment on 3a

Faith, I notice paragraphs 2 and 3 state that you remember your childhood through your dreams. The 1st paragraph doesn't mention dreams at all, but does mention other possibilities including "remembering vaguely." Paragraph 1 emphasizes ways of remembering. Paragraph 2 emphasizes dreams and names a particular incident. Paragraph 3 repeats the statements made in paragraphs 1 and 2. What is your most important point? Is it that it's important to remember your childhood? or that we dream about things that really happened? What's important about the particular incident you cite? I'd like to discuss this essay with you. Please make an appointment.

Writer's exploratory response to teacher's comment

Dreams are an important way in which I remember my childhood days. Usually these dreams come to me after I had thought about being young again. I know that my dreams are true because when I tell my mother about my dreams she tells me it was true. Dreams are sometimes considered as nightmares like mine are.

This dream which I mentioned was a nightmare because I was hurt. Any of my dreams which something . . . (unavailable).

Draft 3b

There are different ways of remembering your childhood days. One way is by your dreams. To me, dreaming is an important way in which I remember my childhood days. Usually I have these dreams after I see young children playing outside and see how cute they are. I have this feel of wanting to be young again. I know the dreams which I have are true because when I tell my mother about my dreams she tells me that it happened when I was young.

I can recall many things that happened to me. Most of the things that happened to me, when I was young, come back to me in my dreams. For example, I can recall when my brother and I were young we used to have pillow fights on my parents' bed. The pillow fell over the bed. I went to get it before my brother. I hit my forehead on the side of the bed, which is made of wood. I was bleeding a lot. I would have thought that it was only a dream, but my mother told me it was true. I also have a scar on my forehead from this incident.

Dreams could either be good or bad. In my case it was like a nightmare because I was hurt (not feelings) physically. Any dream in which I am hurt I consider a nightmare. This doesn't stop me from wanting to be young again. I always think it would probably turn out better the second time around because I wouldn't be as careless as I was the first time. I think that it is a real nice way to remember your childhood. In your dreams.

Teacher's Comment on 3b

Faith, you've done quite a job of rewriting this essay. You focus entirely on your dreams and the way in which they become a vehicle through which you remember your childhod. You start with a generalization and then state what causes you to dream. You move towards a specific dream. You explain your feelings, especially at the beginning and end. You've really put yourself into this. Nice work.

In 3b the writer completely restructures the paper to accommodate the discovery of her true purpose, that one way of remembering her childhood is by dreams. In response to the teacher's comments, this writer wrote several exploratory paragraphs in the space at the end of her first draft. These possibilities, once put into writing, break the perseveration of the original structure. By working in short forms, the writer has been able to reperceive her subject and redesign her essay. The writer of another essay hit upon a similar method to unlock his ideas by underlining key sentences in the first draft and expanding each into a paragraph. My feeling for some time has been that the first draft reflects our best spontaneous, unexplored ideas but leaves the relationships between them unexpressed or partially expressed, relationships that are at once worthy of further detection and mapping.

Other Considerations

If writing in whole structures cannot be counted on to elicit whole revisions,[7] what else can we do to extend our relatively myopic students' prospects for revision? Pursuing relationships between ideas is a creative act that completes the writer's work. Other devices I have tried in classes of advanced and beginning writers appear to direct students toward more substantial revision.

Metaphor or analogy, for example, is an analytical thought structure which, students discover, exposes and extends relationships by linking the unfamiliar to the familiar, identifying as many corresponding parts as possible. Writing analogies also assists writers to work from intuition to system, a track more inventive and hospitable to ideas than one that operates in the reverse. By contrast, establishing a fixed structure and filling it out, while it imprints structure everlastingly in the mind of the writer, operates from system to intuition;

one complaint of our high school teachers was that students often remained stuck in the system. Our college teachers, on the other hand, found that their more confident students moved very quickly to intuitive resources for invention.

Shifting to another point of view also requires student writers to reperceive their material or their problems. Shifting the time of an essay or the governing pronoun requires revision of a more profound kind, since an issue must be viewed from a wholly new perspective and perhaps within another time frame.

Finally, focusing on language is central to solving rhetorical problems. Conceptualizing in *language* makes the most of inexperienced students' myopia since it requires a close look at the language of the concept statement—such as in the essay on the turning point. Only language can help the writer track the new idea as it emerges in the act of revising and trace it to existing ideas locked in the language of the first draft.

Practicing a sequence of structured writing exercises, as we have been doing in the Queens English Project, becomes a program of considerable consequence in learning to write. High schools in the project report that New York State regents exams written by participating students were noticeably more coherent and better structured than those written by nonparticipants. But structured writing may not be enough to habituate students in the larger moves of revising. Revision requires strategies for reperceiving, a chance to place structural alterations ahead of the filling in of details or adjusting for correctness. It requires inventing new ideas and expressing their relationship to what already exists, often somewhat stranded, in the draft. On the teacher's part, teaching revising means understanding that a good revision has all the creative implications of a new piece of work.

Notes

1. Beach Channel, Flushing, Grover Cleveland, John Adams, and John Bowne High Schools.

2. Six Queens College faculty members were awarded the Fund for the Improvement of Post-Secondary Education. grant. They are: Janet Brown (Secondary Education), Judith Fishman (English), Betsy Kaufman (Secondary Education), Donald McQuade (English), Marie Ponsot (English), and Sandra Schor (English).

3. Marie Ponsot and Rosemary Deen, both of the Queens College English Department, introduce their seminal work on whole structures in their book for teachers, *Beat Not the Poor Desk* (Montclair, N.J.: Boynton Cook, 1982). Marie Ponsot led the teachers seminars in the project.

4. I am indebted to Ms. Altman not only for her cooperation in providing me with copies of revision sets of her students' work, but also for her intelligent adherence to the principles of the project during the fifteen weeks of her 01 class.

5. Nancy Sommers, "Revision Strategies of Student Writers and Experienced Adult Writers," *College Composition and Communication* 31 (December 1980): 378-388.

6. Charles K. Stallard, "An Analysis of the Writing Behavior of Good Student Writers," *Research in the Teaching of English* 8 (Fall 1974): 206-218.

7. Although I have included none of the students' fables in this study, I need to say a few words about them. In revising their fables, students generally rewrote the moral for elegance and conciseness. Those few students who rewrote the narratives of their fables changed diction, sharpened dialogue so that it advanced the plot and/or was more representative of stereotyped character, or included more details of setting. My judgment is that the aphoristic rewriting of the morals was highly effective; but it involved different, usually local, *rewriting* strategies; on the other hand, *revising* skills are necessary in redoing the whole fable structure: narrative and moral. What I observe in the rewriting of fables has been a general neglect of students to link the moral to the narrative and work reciprocally in a total, structural revision of the whole fable, this despite teacher observations precisely on the reciprocity—or lack of reciprocity—between moral and narrative.

13 The Development of Discursive Maturity in College Writers

Janice N. Hays
University of Colorado, Colorado Springs

The introduction to this volume alludes to recent studies[1] suggesting that college freshmen write poorly not because they make mechanical errors but because, in Susan Miller's words, they lack the ability "to compose original responses to generally interesting questions."[2] Charles Cooper and others believe that secondary education has given these students so little practice in writing persuasive or analytic discourse that they have internalized no "scheme" or "script" to "enable them to perceive, and thus fulfill, the requirements of well-formed persuasive discourse."[3] Miller, on the other hand, suspects that developmental factors are involved in students' inability to write competently when given an argumentative task. To test this hunch, she asked freshmen to compose an essay on one of psychologist Lawrence Kohlberg's "moral problems"—problems designed to measure a subject's level of ethical and moral (and thus, indirectly, cognitive) development on a scale ranging from "pre-conventional" to "post-conventional" reasoning. Miller concludes that her Ohio State freshmen functioned at a point midway between the conformity to traditional wisdom of Kohlberg's Stage Three and the "law-and-order" respect-for-authority orientation of Stage Four. In both these positions, students would be limited in their ability to question premises and to think analytically.[4]

As Miller readily admits, using Kohlberg's stages to assess writing development presents interpretive problems.[5] Yet researchers wishing to explore developmental factors in college-age writers must fall back upon some such scheme for lack of any other model. That is, although Piaget has chronicled the cognitive development of children and young adolescents, and Walter Loban and James Britton have studied the development of language and writing abilities in the same age groups,[6] we have no paradigm for what constitutes the normal development of writing abilities in young adults; yet psychologists suggest that it is during young adulthood that some of the most complex analytic competencies develop.

Given these realities, Cooper's suggestion that college freshmen write poorly because they have not been taught to do otherwise is the parsimonious explanation. Yet I suspect that many college composition teachers have had experiences similar to that which Miller describes: namely, discovering that students who have been performing well on their comparatively simple writing tasks suddenly do abysmally on assignments requiring more abstraction, more deductive reasoning, or "analytic competency,"[7] than they have until now attempted. That is, students experience great difficulty in negotiating the move from concrete and immediate to more abstract and universal writing, a difficulty suggesting that they may be struggling to achieve a new stage of cognitive development. Further, Piaget himself has suggested that the acquisition of formal-operational thinking is by no means automatic.[8] Rather, if young adults are to develop it, they must interact with an environment that demands such reasoning just as children, although possessing the potential for language, must be exposed to an environment in which language is used in order themselves to develop it.

College Level Cognitive Development

At least one researcher, William G. Perry, Jr., of Harvard, has conducted a longitudinal empirical study suggesting that the college experience may initiate new kinds of cognitive development, enabling students to "conceptualize about concepts," to engage in "meta-reasoning," and that this development occurs in a regular, identifiable sequence encompasssing nine positions, or stages.[9] There are, of course, individual variations in the time-table, but in general, entering college students perceive the world in dualistic terms of right-and-wrong, good-and-bad, and they assume that "Right Answers for everything exist in the Absolute, known to Authority, whose role is to mediate (teach) them"; the road to Knowledge and Goodness is paved with hard work and obedience.[10] Largely as a result of their exposure to the multiple perspectives of a liberal-arts education,[11] students move, during their four college years, to a stage in which they perceive "all knowledge and values (including authority's) as contextual and relativistic"; at the same time, they come to realize that the individual must, nevertheless, sort and evaluate information and attitudes, arriving at those positions that seem better rather than worse and making a commitment to them—in the full recognition that knowledge is contingent and all values relative.[12] (See figure 1.)

Position 1—Basic Duality

The student sees the world in polar terms of we-right-good vs. other-wrong-bad. Right Answers for everything exist in the Absolute, known to Authority, whose role is to mediate (teach) them. Knowledge and goodness are perceived as quantitative accretions of discrete rightnesses to be collected by hard work and obedience (paradigm: a spelling test).

Position 2—Multiplicity Pre-legitimate

The student perceives diversity of opinion and uncertainty, and accounts for them as unwarranted confusion in poorly qualified Authorities or as mere exercises set by Authority "so we can learn to find The Answer for ourselves."

Position 3—Multiplicity Subordinate

The student accepts diversity and uncertainty as legitimate but still *temporary* in areas where Authority "hasn't found The Answer yet." He [sic] supposes Authority grades him in these areas on "good expression" but remains puzzled as to standards.

Position 4—Multiplicity Correlate or Relativism Subordinate

(a) The student perceives legitimate uncertainty (and therefore diversity of opinion) to be extensive and raises it to the status of an unstructured epistemological realm of its own in which "anyone has a right to his own opinion," a realm which he sets over against Authority's realm where right-wrong still prevails, or (b) the student discovers qualitative contextual relativistic reasoning as a special case of "what They want" within Authority's realm.

Position 5—Relativism Correlate, Competing, or Diffuse

The student perceives all knowledge and values (including Authority's) as contextual and relativistic and subordinates dualistic right-wrong functions to the status of a special case, in context.

Position 6—Commitment Foreseen

The student apprehends the necessity of orienting himself in a relativistic world through some form of personal Commitment (as distinct from unquestioned or unconsidered commitment to simple belief in certainty).

Position 7—Initial Commitment

The student makes an initial Commitment in some area.

Position 8—Orientation in implications of Commitment

The student experiences the implications of Commitment, and explores the subjective and stylistic issues of responsibility.

Position 9—Developing Commitment

The student experiences the affirmation of identity among multiple responsibilities and realizes Commitment as an ongoing, unfolding activity through which he expresses his life style.

Figure 1: Perry's Scheme of Development—from foldout chart in *Forms of Intellectual and Ethical Development in the College Years* (New York: Holt, Rinehart & Winston, 1968).

In the course of this development, students execute a series of maneuvers in which they first try to assimilate the new perspectives they are confronting to the dualistic framework that they bring with them to college. This process occupies the first three positions in the scheme. Positions Four, Five, and Six are pivotal; in them students come fully to realize the multiplicity of experience and knowledge. Position Five marks a turning point; in it students can no longer assimilate new experience to the old framework and must instead completely modify their perceptions of reality. After a period during which they in effect throw up their hands and say, "Everyone has a right to his own opinions," students learn that they must think about their own thinking processes, and that although everything is relative, not everything is equally valid.[13]

The evolution that Perry traces moves from simple and concrete to complex, abstract thinking, the ability to "conceptualize about concepts."[14] And, according to Perry, as students confront coexisting and contradictory realities and see the need to reconcile them, they begin to develop Bruner's "analytic competency."[15] If Perry's scheme has validity, we should expect evidences of the same development to show up in the writing of college students, and if there is a similar identifiable sequence in the development of college students' writing abilities, this fact has profound implications for the sequences and methods with which we teach writing.

Discursive Development Patterns in Sample

During the spring of 1978, I gathered papers from most of the students enrolled in freshman writing seminars at Skidmore College in New York and from a smaller group of more advanced students. Using Perry's scheme, which I find more cogent and more reliable than Kohlberg's as a frame of reference, I will examine patterns of discursive development in these samples. For this purpose, I have selected twelve excerpts, each typical of the student's entire paper and also representative of numbers of student responses.

All papers were written upon one of two topics involving identical rhetorical situations. This topic asked students to imagine themselves speaking, as typical college students, on a panel at an adult educational forum on either abortion or marijuana. Writers were told that the panel included representatives from community agencies and groups, which varied according to the specific subject (for example, "a Catholic priest" appeared on the abortion panel). Writers were also instructed that their talks would be published in the local newspaper.

Although hardly an original subject, this assignment turned out to be a Rorschach indicator of the level of students' writing and rhetorical abilities. In general, less skilled writers failed to respond to the assignment's cues. Many of these writers gave only token acknowledgment (or none at all) to the fact that they were writing for an audience, nor did their arguments really address the multiple perspectives of panel-members, which, in a real-life situation, they would have had to take into account. The more advanced student writers were more adept at perceiving and responding to these cues in ways that I will comment upon later.

John

The first writer I will discuss appears to be as close to Perry's Position One, Basic Duality, as any I discovered. This student, "John," perceives the world with undeviating moral imperatives. In Perry's terms, he is embedded within this dualistic frame of reference, one in which something is either right or wrong, the clear implication being that "we," who are identified with Absolute Truth,[16] are right and "they"— the others—are wrong. John makes broad, unqualified statements:

> Once a life has been conceived, it should benefit to [sic] right to experience "living" and be given the chance to further the process of reproduction. This is the whole basis of our evolution. Thusly, abortion, whether committed under any circumstances, is sinful and unjust.[17]

John does not explain the basis for his judgment, nor does he qualify his position, for Absolute Truth admits of no qualification and concedes nothing.

Yet presumably one semester of college has had its effect, for this writer knows that he must consider contrary points of view and rebut them even though they are "wrong." Thus he focuses on "the so-called accident case" and details some of the reasons why a pregnant woman might want to have an abortion. However, at this juncture the discursive process breaks down. Rather than answer the point he has raised, John dismisses this contrary position with, "Upon examining these reasons, the result is there's absolutely no substantial one for taking that innocent life. If she needs help, it's there for her." John tries to use the forms of discourse but does not yet grasp their substance. Using the structure of cause/effect ("upon examining . . . the result is"), he resorts to fiat rather than argument and deduction. Yet according to Perry, it is the practice of such logical structures, carried on, at first, mechanically and imperfectly, that eventually leads to genuine structural change in students' perceptual frameworks.[18]

Rena

The next writer, Rena, has probably progressed along the developmental scale as far as Perry's Position Two. Unlike John, who seems not to perceive the existence of perspectives other than the right one (he refers to "the *so-called* accident case" [my italics]), Rena recognizes a multiplicity of viewpoints: "Many people in the society have differing opinions about abortion. Some people feel it is okay. Pro-life people believe that a woman having an abortion is killing a human being." However, she regards positions other than her own as alien, in effect saying that she is right and that others, even the Authorities, are needlessly confused:

> . . . If a woman has been raped or sexually abused or has been the victim of incest the woman should be able to decide on an abortion or not. There should be no legal hassles.
> . . . I feel the woman who has control over her body should be able to make her own moral decision of whether to have an abortion or not. There shouldn't be all this hassle with all these other feelings when it is the woman's own decision. . . .

Like John, Rena relies upon assertion instead of reasoned argument. Yet again, such a position is appropriate to a world in which the truth is known and those who think differently can be dismissed. Of course, Rena is responding to the terms of the assignment: she is giving *her* perspective on the subject. But it is an indication of her academic and discursive innocence that she does not buttress that perspective with supporting data, for she does not realize that anyone might question her opinion.

Julie

The next writer, Julie, has moved somewhat beyond this dualistic position, for she has learned that she must give *reasons* for her opinions, a posture characteristic of Perry's Position Four, in which students perceive that a multiplicity of viewpoints prevails and that one must therefore justify one's opinions. Thus Julie tells us why abortion "is beneficial to our society" although she does so at a very general level and without any supporting data:

> Abortion is beneficial to our society because it is a free opportunity for women to help lower the population explosion, prevent unwanted children from being born and prevent the unwanted consequences for the pregnant woman. Abortion was a great discovery that helped both men and women.
> Even though abortion has many good sides some people think that abortion is the murdering of babies. . . .

She employs not only a causal conjunction (*because*) but also a concessionary one (*even though*), this latter device revealing her perception that there is more than one side to at least this particular question.

Yet despite her attempt to utilize some structures of complex discourse, she still operates from within a fundamentally dualistic framework. Rather than genuinely respond to the contrary point that she has raised, she turns to simplistic slogans and to an absolute ("But in a country with freedom of choice like ours, there would be no freedom if we as women were told what we could and couldn't do with our bodies for everything we did") and finally resorts, like John and Rena, to edict: "Abortion isn't the murdering of babies, but the option of women to have a baby or not." Thus she aligns herself with Absolute Right (freedom of choice) against a misguided and wrong Authority (whoever would deny that freedom).[19]

In such papers, we see students struggling with the transition from one developmental position to the next. This writer still perceives a multiplicity of perspectives as alien intruders into a dualistic universe, and thus she cannot really enter into those perspectives in order to deal with them; they are simply too foreign to her. Yet for her they are of greater magnitude than they are for John and Rena, a magnitude requiring that holders of the Right Position provide explanations of and evidence for that position—if for no other reason than that the authorities who grade one's papers demand this kind of justification. Perry notes the irony that the most conformist students most easily acquire the structures of complex reasoning, for they dutifully practice them at the behest of their instructors, and this practice lays the foundation for the genuine structural transformation that later takes place.[20]

Tom

The next writer, Tom, has moved closer to relativism. To begin with, he realizes that in areas where more than one point of view may be legitimate, one's simple word is not enough; one must establish credibility. Hence his desire "to clearify [sic] that he has never used marijuana" (his is not a self-serving argument). Further, he knows that he must give reasons for his position, and he proceeds to do so, developing these reasons quite fully:

> I would like to clearify that I have never used marijuana during my 20 years of living. However, my position stands for the legalization of marijuana. . . . To begin with, today's society is one which is constantly discovering new drugs whether they help to

prevent or cause illness. It seems that everything that we put in
our system is harmful and will result in undesirable diseases. . . .
I believe that marijuana users should also be warned; however,
they should be able to make their own decisions.

However, at this point Tom slides back to an earlier, more simplistic
position. Assuming what we might characterize as sophomoric can-
tankerousness, he adopts a stance similar to Julie's:

> The Declaration of Independence states that all people are created
> equally and that this is a free country. The question is, is it?
> . . . it seems that the government is dictating what we can and
> cannot do. Instead of hiring policemen to chase after pushers they
> should be working to capture criminals. . . .

Authorities are doing their job all wrong whereas Tom is on the side
of The Right. Yet in his concluding statements, he again shows signs
of approaching genuine multiplicity; he writes:

> As for myself, I have decided not to use marijuana and I am sure
> that many other people will be alongside of me. I do not feel that
> I have the right to decide whether the fellow next to me should or
> should not smoke marijuana. That decision should be his and
> only his.

In effect, Tom is assuming a stance characteristic of Perry's Position
Four, in which, since the Absolute cannot be known, any opinion is
as good as any other, and one thus has no right to persuade others to
one's way of thinking.

Ken

In the next paper, we see another student, Ken, struggling with this
transition from dualism to multiplicity. Ken is genuinely aware of
opposing arguments about marijuana use and can concede some
validity to both viewpoints. Yet he cannot resolve these polarities and,
throughout most of the paper, adopts a strategy common to beginning
writers by sliding off into a long personal-narrative digression about a
film on drugs which he saw when he was younger. In the final
paragraph, though, he qualifies his assertions and then questions his
questions, a process that in more mature writers eventually leads to a
new synthesis:

> Marijuana has been successfully used in the treatment of certain
> diseases. Although it has also been proven "possibly to cause
> cancer," I have recently seen many signs on products that say
> "Warning: this product may be cancer causing." The problem
> with this statement is that people don't really know what is
> "cancer causing." In the marijuana it could be the pesticide used

to keep the bugs away. Until more research is done, this statement
is not a strong argument against the use of marijuana.

However, Ken is evidently too thoroughly adrift in multiplicity to
head for the shore of resolution. Rather than conclude his paper, he
merely stops, having never taken an identifiable position on the
subject he has discussed.

Jean

Jean is also struggling with her perception of the world as a focus of
various and competing perspectives. We can sense the *angst* in such
statements as, "The subject of the legalization of marijuana is a very
controversial subject. There are good points on both sides of the
subject that make it difficult to decide on which way to go." Yet
unable to sustain this uncertainty, Jean gives some unqualified reasons for her tentative position and then slides back to the reasoning of
Position Three, in which Authorities simply don't as yet have the
answers—and rather plaintively demands that they make up their
minds and end all this controversy!

Jack

The next writer, Jack, shows us an embryonic stage of the structural
revolution in which multiplicity is no longer just a specific case but
becomes a relativism that reflects the nature of reality itself.[21] It is
Perry's hypothesis that the structures of multiplicity assimilated to
duality in the earlier positions now provide the structure for the new
framework of relativism. Although he is far from comfortable with it,
Jack recognizes such relativism: "It is obvious that there are going to
be aura of opinions on the subject, *and presumably the opinions will
be well founded*" (my italics). He acknowledges viewpoints and contexts other than his own:

> There is such diversity among the people of this country, as far as
> religion and culture are concerned. Certainly there are going to be
> contrasting opinions, but let us understand, and realize, the dif-
> ferent points, policies, and dilemmas that are part of each section
> of people, religion, and government that we hear from.

Jack's paper displays a reasonableness of tone and a qualification
of terms missing from the earlier samples; most interesting, although
Jack is himself a Catholic, he maintains an objectivity and detachment
towards the Catholic position on abortion, recognizing that such
questions cannot be decided absolutely and that individuals must
make their own choices:

Since I am Catholic, I can only comment on their beliefs and
feelings towards abortion. As far as I know the Catholics absolutely prohibit the operation for anyone associated with the religion. . . . The main argument for the Catholics, besides that it is
a sin, is that the embryo is alive, thus making it murder. . . . The
opposing argument is, if you have the operation within a certain
period of time the embryo has no life, or brain. At any rate, the
religion aspect of this issue will probably never be solved. . . . I
feel that the operation should be left up to the discretion of the
people harboring the idea of an abortion. . . .

Denise

Denise, a second-semester sophomore, shows us a substantial forward
step developmentally, for she takes full responsibility for her own
position, anchoring it not in some legalistic framework of external
truth but in her own judgment and experience: "My reasoning behind
this outlook stems from knowing people who are frequent marijuana
users and also from limited exposure, but exposure nonetheless, to the
wide variety of 'drugs' available." Her posture characterizes Perry's
Stage Seven. We can also see developmental progress in Denise's
freeing of herself from adherence to authority: she does not hesitate to
admit her own experience with the drug scene, something none of the
younger writers has dared to do. Denise perceives gradations of better-
worse, a complexity missing from earlier samples. She also plays the
role that the assignment has given her more successfully than did the
writers of earlier papers: she responds to the hypothetical situation—
"I have been asked to state my views on marijuana and its usage and
will try to do so as candidly as possible"—and she maintains a tone
appropriate to a "representative" college student who wants to acquit
herself well:

It seems somewhat hypocritical to label the marijuana smoker a
criminal yet promote and applaud the rising executive who is
battling a serious drinking problem. There are so many ramifi-
cations concerning the drug scene that I just can't condone those
that are legal and condemn those which are not, on that worn
out, obsolete basis.
   The problem with *any* mood altering substance is not its use,
it is the abuse of that substance. There is nothing more offensive,
in my mind, about smoking an occasional joint than there is
about having a cocktail before dinner. Smoking dope is a very
pleasant way of unwinding and just relaxing. When the need to
smoke becomes chronic or the time one chooses inappropriate,
that is when marijuana becomes dangerous in those situations.
My point boils down to the old saying, everything in moderation.

Denise has thought about her audience (middle-aged, middle-class adults who would respect business executives and would see nothing wrong with cocktails before dinner) and has tried to relate her arguments to them. This ability accurately to project oneself into an imaginary situation in writing, to present ideas in ways that will be effective with one's audience, is virtually lacking in younger writers. Although some of the freshmen in my study tried to respond to the assignment's speaker-panel-audience situation, none of them was able to do so in any believable way. The ability to anticipate the oppositions' arguments is a characteristic of maturity that younger writers simply do not yet possess.[22]

Don

Don's paper also demonstrates a writer's ability to play a role. Even though Don personally opposes the legalizing of marijuana, he is able to detach himself from his own perspective, to assume the role of "average college student," and to present the viewpoint that he considers representative of such a student:

> . . . If you polled the average college student body, I think you would find the majority of the students in favor of legalizing marijuana, even those students who do not smoke themselves or have never even tried it. . . . Most college students feel that if alcohol and cigarettes can be legalized, then pot which in some way is less harmful because it has not been proven to *cause* lung cancer, only "black lung," and in most cases, better controlled than alcohol, why can't it be legalized also. . . . In my opinion all three should not be legalized because they do not do your body any long term good but if one is legalized all three should be legalized. . . .

Betty

With Betty's paper, composed at the end of this student writer's junior year, the awareness of context widens to include the historical as well as the contemporary: "Women of past ages knew ways to induce abortion, yet we often see their efforts restricted by religious and/or societal views, similar to arguments of today." Betty establishes the complexity of the issue and her own objectivity ("I have never been in the position of having to make the decision myself"). She takes a position (she favors abortion) but also qualifies it, emphasizing the individual's responsibility for her choices—an emphasis characteristic of Perry's Positions Seven and Eight, in which students accept the implications of commitment to beliefs and behavior in a relativistic world:[23]

> I don't advocate abortion as a means of birth control, not only
> because I feel it could be physically harmful if performed fre-
> quently, but also feel it is unnecessary if partners are taking
> responsibility for planning their parenthood. . . .

Sue

Sue's paper, written mid-way in her senior year, and Molly's, produced
shortly after the writer's graduation, are the most discursively mature
of the samples. Unlike their freshmen counterparts, Sue and Molly
perceive the assignment's directive to "inform your audience of your
views on the subject of marijuana [or abortion] and of your reasons
for those views" as requiring a well-supported argument. If one has a
view worth stating, one has a stake in it that makes it worth arguing.
Yet these are reasonable arguments that have about them the writers'
recognitions, on the one hand, that the entire field of knowledge is
relative and, on the other, that they can reason their way to a responsible position and express their identity by making such commitments.

Like Betty, Sue places the issue in a social and historical perspective
that indicates her awareness that attitudes and mores change with
time and circumstances:

> There was a time when only beatniks and hippies used the drug,
> people at the outer edges of society, but now marijuana is hardly
> the sensational or shocking drug that it was in the 40s or 50s, and
> its advocates include people from all walks of life. . . .

Sue emphasizes responsible choice, seeing the issue in terms of
the decisions that one wants to make about one's life. She expresses
her objections to marijuana use in a nonjudgmental way that even
includes some humor, developing her points with considerable
specificity:

> . . . It is an interesting experience to go into a room full of stoned
> people when one is completely straight. If the other people are in
> a fairly advanced phase of being high, they are quite disconcerting
> to watch. Typically, one sees several bodies slumped against the
> wall because "we're all feeling really mellow, man," and one
> hears such phrases as "Yeah," "You know," and "Wow." One
> probably will also see among the group several people frantically
> eating anything they can lay their hands on. I don't know if
> there's any scientific basis for the occurrence of "munchies," but I
> know that this horrible side effect of pot smoking does, indeed,
> exist. Once when I was high, I devoured an entire bag of puffed
> rice, something that is completely tasteless, which I won't touch
> at all if I'm straight! I'm sure there are some girls that have attri-
> buted the "freshman ten" weight gain to attacks of the munchies,
> and as for me, if I'm going to gain weight I'd just as soon do it by
> eating food I enjoy and will remember eating.

My main plea to pot smokers is this, then: at least think about pot in terms of what it does to your valuable time, and to others' as well. My saying that I don't like pot is hardly going to stop either a potential or an established marijuana smoker; he or she obviously is the only one who can accomplish that. And perhaps my words may act as an incentive to stop using marijuana—not because the drug is illegal or addictive or makes the user a despicable person but because it causes such a waste of valuable time, never, never a justifiable crime!

Sue states her position, one in which she clearly has some personal investment, and urges her hearers to consider it even as she also recognizes that she probably cannot modify anyone's behavior with her words.

Molly

Molly, who takes a position opposite to Sue's, establishes a context, identifying herself as part of the community that she is addressing; this posture represents the most mature stages on Perry's scale, stages in which students realize their own kinship with authority in the area of commitment. Molly utilizes the analogy between alcohol and marijuana to construct much of her argument, an analogy calculated to be effective with her audience and also one revealing her ability to relate one phenomenon to another in complex ways not possible for the sample's younger writers, who could only say, "Cigarettes are worse than marijuana, but *they* are legal":

Marijuana use in this country, as most of us are aware, is rapidly approaching the staggering dimensions of our most widely used drug, alcohol. And, like alcohol, it becomes a problem when it is used in excess or for destructive purposes. In the cases of both marijuana and alcohol use, a mature, well-adjusted, fairly sensible individual will encounter no problems with the drug of his/her choice and will derive pleasure from moderate usage. . . . Because I have discovered no significant differences in behavior between the users of these two drugs [alcohol and marijuana], . . . I see no reason for penalizing marijuana users. Therefore, I advocate the legalization of marijuana 100%.

Molly also goes further than any of the other writers studied in anticipating and genuinely addressing the objections her audience might make to her argument. In the earlier papers, we see students retreating from "letting in" or really considering opposite points of view: they allude to them only in order to topple them. By contrast, Molly concedes the validity of her hearers' possible concerns about marijuana's becoming accessible to children, and she deals with this question in a carefully reasoned way, admitting that some young

people will get into trouble with the drug but asserting that most
will, with maturity, achieve moderation:

> Perhaps some of you are afraid that legalization of this substance
> will be undesirable because it might encourage use by younger
> children. This comes to mind for it is an aspect of the problem
> which I have thought about carefully. Again, I stress the parallel
> behavior induced by pot and alcohol use alike. Youngsters will
> experiment with both these substances for a variety of reasons—it
> acts as a social lubricant, it is a status symbol, it is an assertion of
> independence. In most healthy cases, maturity curbs what may
> appear to be excessive use of either drug at an early age; the child
> comes to see the drug for what it really is. If anything, I think
> that legalization of marijuana may reduce its popularity among
> the very young. As it is now, part of the immature thrill to be had
> by using the drug is the knowledge that Mom and Dad would
> disapprove.

Thus she talks about calculated risks that involve degrees of better
and worse, an argument that does justice to the complexity of reality.
Yet even though she concedes these risks, Molly takes a position and
argues for it vigorously. But, like Sue, she also adopts a reasonable
and moderate tone that conveys her recognition of the issue's many
facets.

Conclusions

If we compare T-unit length, discourse structure, elaboration of argument, and sophistication of diction between the early and late papers
in this study, we find in the later papers a geometric increase in
complexity, an increase that seems regularly to occur in an identifiable
sequence: writers first construct "arguments" using flat, simplistic
and unsupported assertions. They next add to those assertions reasons
why they are so; that is, they justify them and in the process begin
slightly to qualify them and to acknowledge, although not really to
engage, other points of view. At the next stage of development, writers
display a reasonably full recognition of multiple perspectives and
some elaboration of these perspectives but lack the ability to deal with
and resolve their implications. Students in this stage either simply
state differing points of view or else fall back on earlier strategies:
arbitrary statement or fiat, simplistic appeal to common wisdom or to
some Absolute, and so on.

   In terms of Perry's scheme, the transition from Stage Four to Stage
Five, from multiplicity to relativism, appears to be the most difficult
shift for these student writers. Once they have made it, their writing
becomes more elaborated, more qualified, more concessionary, and yet

at the same time more committed to a position. Seemingly they now have confidence in their ability to work through complex realities and make judgments about them. These more mature writers can also enter into points of view other than their own and fully engage them, and they develop the ability to shape their discourse to an audience's needs.

Now all of this has important implications for teachers of college writing. First, we need not sink into the Slough of Despond when our freshman students do not write like mature adults, for we can reasonably hope that by the time they are seniors they will be considerably further along the road to discursive maturity. Nor, knowing their developmental limitations, should we make the mistake of giving freshmen and sophomores writing tasks that are more appropriate to graduate students. That way lies both failure and discouragement.

On the other hand, we cannot simply assume that the development of discursive maturity will occur automatically, much like the certain appearance of permanent after baby teeth. Perry's study suggests that it is the experience of a liberal arts education that produces this development[24]—and traditionally, a liberal arts curriculum stresses not only the presentation of diverse perspectives, of relativistic knowledge, but also the response to what is being learned *in writing:* through critical papers, essay exams, research papers, and so on. We badly need some comparative research to ascertain whether or not students studying technical and professional curricula rather than the liberal arts manifest the same development. Some work that I have done with older subjects (ages twenty-five to seventy-five) suggests that discursive maturity does not coincide simply with chronological age—that it results, rather, from exposure to an environment that requires its development. College students who have solidified their growth in one stage of development cannot function at a level several stages beyond that position, but they can be helped to accelerate development into the next stage by being introduced to "calculated incongruities"—facts and ideas that seem contradictory; having to reconcile and make sense of such conflicting realities will instigate movement towards a higher developmental level.[25] Knowing this, then, we need to design a college writing curriculum that will systematically confront students with tasks to develop their discursive and cognitive maturity.

If indeed such development can take place throughout the college years, and if Bruner is right that it is writing that fosters analytic competency,[26] it becomes crucial that students write in all their subject areas and not just in freshman composition. It may indicate something that the best of the older writers in my sample were all English majors and so had engaged in the extensive writing practice that helps develop discursive maturity. Thus I am really agreeing with Charles Cooper when he says that we need to teach students discourse schemes and require that they practice them. But I am also suggesting that these schemes must be sequenced to be appropriate to students' levels of development.

Finally, what are the concrete implications of this study for the teaching of writing? First, it suggests the immense value of requiring students to practice heuristic procedures that force them to view phenomena hierarchically and from multiple perspectives. Second, a developmental perspective dictates that we teach students discursive and syntactic structures appropriate to the discourse level just *above* the one they have achieved even though they will initially perform poorly at that level. For freshmen, this might mean requiring students to give reasons for their assertions and examples to illustrate those reasons, and then to develop these examples, in Christensen's terms, to a third or fourth level of generality.[27] At the high freshman or low sophomore level, we could require students accurately and fairly to summarize several opposing points of view on a given topic, to give reasons for and examples of each of those viewpoints, and then to choose the perspective they find most compelling and give reasons for their choice. We could then ask them also to argue just the opposite persective. Such sequencing of tasks could be designed for every stage of writing development up through the practice of mature discursive structures, such as the Toulmin model.[28] In the same way, we need to structure role-taking exercises and exercises in audience awareness and analysis that are appropriate to students' levels of development and the level just above.

Finally, a developmental perspective should remind us that our freshmen are not simply recalcitrant or stupid when they write in ways that seem to us puerile and simplistic. They really are struggling to achieve a new perspective on reality, and we need to acknowledge the difficulty of their struggle and support them as they engage in it, both assuring them that they will learn to jump these hurdles, encouraging them to continue to try, and challenging them by progressively setting those hurdles higher.

Notes

1. Also see Charles Cooper, Roger Cherry, Rita Gerber, Stefan Fleischer, and Barbara Copley, "Writing Abilities of Regularly-Admitted Freshmen at SUNY/Buffalo" (unpublished study, State University of New York at Buffalo,

1980), 82-83 *passim;* Susan Miller, "Rhetorical Maturity: Definition and Development," in *Reinventing the Rhetorical Tradition,* ed. Aviva Freedman and Ian Pringle (Conway, Ark.: L&S Books and Canadian Council of Teachers of English, 1980).

2. Miller, 120.

3. Cooper, 59.

4. Miller, 123-124.

5. John H. Flavell, *Cognitive Development* (Englewood Cliffs, N. J.: Prentice-Hall, 1977), 142-143.

6. See Barbel Inhelder and Jean Piaget, *The Early Growth of Logic in the Child* (New York: Norton, 1969) and *The Growth of Logical Thinking from Childhood to Adolescence* (New York: Basic Books, 1958); for a more complete bibliography of Piaget's work, see Mary Ann Spencer, *Understanding Piaget,* rev. ed. (New York: Harper & Row, 1980), 238-241; also see James Britton, et al., *The Development of Writing Abilities, 11-18* (1975; rept. Urbana, Ill.: NCTE, 1978); Walter Loban, *Language Development: Kindergarten through Grade Twelve* (Urbana, Ill.: NCTE, 1976).

7. J. S. Bruner, "Language as an Instrument of Thought," in *Problems of Language and Learning,* ed. Alan Davies (London: Heinemann, 1975), 70-80.

8. Flavell, 117.

9. William Perry, *Forms of Intellectual and Ethical Development in the College Years, a Scheme* (New York: Holt, Rinehart & Winston, 1968), 33 *passim.*

10. Perry, 9; Perry notes that few students arrive at college in quite this stage of innocence. For most, although not all, this is a precollege position.

11. Perry, 207; Perry defines a liberal arts institution as "a pluralistic institution where the teaching of the procedures of relativistic thought is to a large extent deliberate."

12. Perry, 3, 9-10 *passim.*

13. Perry, 95-176.

14. Perry, 33.

15. J. S. Bruner, "Language as an Instrument of Thought," in *Problems of Language and Learning,* ed. Alan Davies (London: Heinemann, 1975).

16. I am following Perry's example in capitalizing terms referring to entities that students elevate to the status of absolutes.

17. Except for regularizing spelling, I have left all errors in student papers intact; I have assigned fictitious names to student writers.

18. Perry, 207-212.

19. Perry, 91ff.

20. Perry, 95-96.

21. Perry, 207-212.

22. See John Flavell, P. T. Botkin, C. L. Fry, Jr., J. W. Wright, and P. E. Jarvis, *The Development of Role-Taking and Communication Skills in Children* (New York: Wiley, 1968).

23. Perry, 10.

24. Perry, 206-207.

25. Perry, 21.

26. See Bruner.

27. See Francis Christensen, "A Generative Rhetoric of the Sentence" and "A Generative Rhetoric of the Paragraph," in *Notes toward a New Rhetoric, Nine Essays for Teachers*, 2nd. ed., with Bonniejean Christensen (New York: Harper & Row, 1978), 23-44, 74-103.

28. For a discussion of the Toulmin model of discourse, see Charles Kneupper, "Teaching Argument: An Introduction to the Toulmin Model," *College Composition and Communication* 29 (October 1978): 237-241.

14 Building Thought on Paper with Adult Basic Writers

Elaine O. Lees
University of Pittsburgh

Written language is a constructed, construable representation of thought. It allows one to assemble (*construere*, heap together) representations of ideas; and it invites readers to assemble meanings from a text. Because it is a form of building (though not one that simply links prefabricated components according to blueprint-like plans), writing allows writers both to create the thing to be construed, and to revise and recreate that representation so that the thought construable from it changes. Good written "ideas" are as much the result of shaping as of discovery.

This notion and its implications frequently elude the Basic Writers I teach in the University of Pittsburgh's evening division. As David Bartholomae puts it, Basic Writing students' difficulty "is not so much that they don't know 'how to write' but that they don't know about writing."[1] In this case, they don't know the extent to which, and the peculiar way in which, writing involves construction. They assume that "good writers'" fundamental distinction is that they produce "good writing" from the very beginning and simply "polish" it later. They conceive of writing not as a building up and shaping of meanings but as a breadcrumb-trailing of thoughts which are what they are and land where they land as a writer travels through a set of pages.

The limitations of this view are often manifest in the way Basic Writers treat generalizations and conclusions. A study of Basic Writing students at Pitt showed that one distinguishing feature of their writing was an absence of generalization, an apparent inability to go beyond talk of specific incidents and experiences to conclusions based on them.[2] Given an assignment to "discuss a time when you were creative and then go on to explain, on the basis of the incident you have described, what creativity means," the students would compose more or less coherent narratives, but then would fail utterly to address the

145

question of what creativity meant, sometimes ending their papers before any such discussion had begun, more often settling into one-line formulations of common wisdom like "creativity is something we all possess" or "being creative is its own reward." Though deliberation, even painful deliberation, may have accompanied the writing of many of these papers, nothing in their conclusions represented adequately the movement of adult minds deliberating. The students were blind participants in a struggle with inherited language forms.[5]

To acquaint adult Basic Writing students with the nature of this struggle, particularly as it involves generalizing, I have worked out two series of assignments influenced by James Moffett's discussions of abstraction in *Teaching the Universe of Discourse*. Moffett outlines a hierarchy of abstraction in discourse, from what he sees as the lowest level, *recording* of "what is happening" at present, through an intermediate level of *reporting* or *narrating* "what happened," to higher levels of *generalizing* about "what happens" and, finally, *theorizing* or arguing "what will (or) may happen."[4] Moffett suggests organizing a curriculum by having it "recapitulate, in successive assignments, the abstractive stages across which all of us all the time symbolize raw phenomena and manipulate these symbolizations." Moffett asserts that at every stage of life we are "constantly processing new experience up through the cycle of sensations, memories, generalizations and theories."[5]

In designing courses for adult Basic Writers I have concentrated on making students conscious of their capacities to organize and reorganize knowledge in this way and of the role writing can play in the process. The courses present students with a single subject (or a pair of complementary subjects) to examine throughout the term.[6] The students' job is to find ways of constructing talk about this subject at what Moffett would call differing levels of abstraction.

Two Courses

The first course asks students to write all term about writing itself; the second retains writing as its real subject but employs a nominal subject as the focus of its assignments. In the first course, students are invited to report on and then generalize about themselves as writers, and finally to theorize about what the activity of writing involves for themselves and their classmates. Their weekly papers focus on composing itself—its processes, its satisfactions, its problems—and the responsibility for defining and analyzing these terms falls primarily on the students. If abstraction is, as Moffett says, a continuously evolving activity over a life-time, then perhaps one way adult Basic Writers may rid themselves of their restrictive notions about writing is to rework the generalizations and theories they have constructed about it. The first course invites students to perform such a reworking.

The second course employs a similar structure, but its nominal subject is Changing and Preserving. This course allows for discussion of writing but focuses its assignments on patterns of adjustment in adult life. Again, the reponsibility for defining and analyzing major terms falls primarily on the students, and again the sequence of assignments begins with students' reporting experiences of change and preservation, then moves to having them generalize about the activities of changing and preserving, and finally leads them to theorize about patterns of change and preservation as these activities are represented in the papers of the whole class.

Writing about Writing

Having presented this overview, let me explain the first of these courses more fully. Its initial assignments focus students' attention on what happens when they write. The course thus begins, in Moffett's terminology, at the level of reporting or narrating. In each of the first assignments students are asked to describe what happened on a specific occasion when they wrote: the circumstances that led them to write, the goals they had, the stages they and their papers went through. Assignment 1 begins by reminding students that as people who "must regularly prepare reports, essays, and papers" they have a right to consider themselves writers. Then the assignment asks them to describe one writing experience from their personal, vocational, or academic lives. The end of the assignment invites students to generalize from what they have described by drawing some conclusions about themselves as writers, based on the incidents they've written about in their papers.

Discussion of these initial papers demonstrates that writing is a construction, not a passive recording of "what happened" or "what was." It encourages students to examine the language in which they have narrated their experiences and to question the disparity between the textbook-like formulations they have very likely relied on to describe the activity of writing and the complex experience they have just had in constructing a paper. The problem lies, of course, in getting students to question where their ways of writing have come from and to see their accounts as constructions, not immutable givens. As a start, the student who writes that he "wrote down his thoughts" for a history paper and "polished them" may be asked what is involved in "writing down a thought" and what it means to say that a thought, once "written down," has been "polished." These questions, of course, are answerable in many ways and on many levels of sophistication; the point is that students are not likely to see that such ways and levels exist until they begin to see themselves as constructors and construers; they will argue instead that their papers "just tell what happened" and will underestimate their own roles as builders.

Continuing to probe this role, the next assignments ask students to narrate two other writing experiences: the first, a time when they wrote something that satisfied them, something they are glad even now that they wrote; the second, a time when they found writing particularly difficult. In these assignments, once again, students are invited to go beyond narration to generalization: in the first, they are asked to draw some conclusions about what makes writing satisfying to them; in the second, they are asked to give a name to the greatest difficulty they experience as writers and to explain why they think it is the hardest thing about writing for them.

Most student papers written for the first assignment in this pair follow a characteristic pattern, one that may be used to point out once again that writing is construction. The prototypal paper eagerly explains circumstances leading up to and following the composing of the satisfying piece of writing but is nearly silent about the writing itself, relying on stock descriptions like "I sat down at my table and the words just flowed from my pen." A class can examine together several such papers and then attempt to account for the fact that they say so little about the actual activity of writing. Someone usually offers the suggestion that "there really isn't much you can say about writing." The next question, then, becomes "What sorts of subjects *do* people have much they can say about?" and students' answers are usually "subjects they're interested in," or, "subjects they know well or study a lot." A teacher can point out that students are thus suggesting that what one can say about a subject is not so much a function of the subject—a thing "out there," a received thing—as it is a function of the writer's perception of the subject as problematic, as open to exploration and ordering through language. The class's fourth assignment, then, is to revise the paper by reconstructing its narrative, opening to question the original version's account of writing.

The papers about students' difficulties with writing also lead into an assignment to revise. This revision, however, focuses not on narratives but on generalizations, the sections of the papers in which students give a name to what they find difficult about writing. In revising, students must recast this section so that it states a new idea, an idea that enables writers to see something new about themselves and writing. Students are also asked to come to class prepared to say what they have learned, what they can say now about their writing problems that they couldn't before writing the final version of the paper.

Once again the purpose of the assignment is to dramatize a connection between writing and thinking, to enable students to realize that acts of naming and renaming may be seen as acts of learning and may affect the outcome of their writing efforts. Class discussions focus on the differences between naming one's writing problem "bad grammar" and naming it "worry about grammar," or on the different responses one may have to problems labeled "lack of time," "lack of interest," and "lack of planning." Such discussions encourage students to recognize that ways of addressing their problems as writers fall within their own control. More importantly, they draw attention to the fact that the revision of language can be more than a "polishing" process: the search for new words involves one in a search among new thoughts, among statements about the word; and in making such choices one creates one's possibilities.

Constructing Generalizations about Writing

When students have written their final versions of the satisfaction and difficulty papers, the papers are copied for the entire class and stapled together into two sets of packets, one containing all the class's papers about the times writing was satisfying, the other all the papers about writers' difficulties. All students then receive copies of these two packets to use as data for the next essays they will write: essays that require students to work on the levels that Moffett would label generalization and theory. In these assignments students identify trends in the packets of papers and, on the basis of the trends they have identified, construct theories about the satisfactions of writing and the problems that Basic Writers face. Because in these assignments, cut off from the task of narration, students often flounder, a good deal of the time in class is spent talking over what such assignments ask students to do. The class discusses the differences one may expect to find in pieces of writing that explain theories and those that narrate incidents, ways of structuring the former kinds of papers so that readers can understand what goes on in them and what they may expect from them, and the role individual narrative papers from the packet play as sources of evidence and illustration in the theory papers. And several class hours are devoted to evaluating students' rough drafts for these assignments, identifying strengths, weaknesses, and digressions, and suggesting ways that writers may revise. Students then revise the two theory papers into essays they believe suitably address academic audiences.

When one espouses a new theory, one possesses a new means of interpreting experience, or rather a new means of experiencing. To acknowledge theory's ordering power, the course's final assignment brings students full circle, to a reconsideration of their first papers. The students are asked to write again about the experience presented in their first papers, this time "in the light of" or "in terms of" one of their newly articulated theories. Then they are asked in class to explain what difference writing "in terms of" the theories has made, first, in the way their papers represent the experiences they had and, second, in the way they now perceive themselves as writers. These are difficult questions, but they are important ones for students who may never have considered themselves theoreticians before.

Such a sequence of assignments thus teaches adult learners the construction and interrelation of statements at various levels of generality: construction of generalizations about themselves from narratives of their experiences, and the construction of theories about the entire class from the statements of individual writers. Though I cannot claim that the generalization in the papers from these two courses attains great subtlety and complexity, the shuttling from particular to general, from evidence to conclusions based on it, offers students insight into some of the peculiarities of academic discourse. That this discourse, for a term, has been about themselves and that it has grown, in their own hands, from written narrative to written theory, further legitimates these adult learners' re-entry into the academic world. They have begun to do something academics do, to manipulate statements in ways that academics manipulate them. They have been involved in *making* ideas, not simply waiting for them to happen. They have had a chance to see that understanding of subjects like writing and change is not so much something one acquires as it is something each one, as a language user, possesses the power to create.

Notes

1. David Bartholomae, "Teaching Ourselves to Teach Basic Writing," *PCTE Bulletin* (April 1977): 19.

2. This study is discussed in David Bartholomae's "Teaching Basic Writing: An Alternative to Basic Skills," *Journal of Basic Writing* 2, no. 2 (1979): 106–7.

3. Lengthier discussions of this problem appear in David Bartholomae's "An 'I' for an I," *Composition and Teaching* (forthcoming) and Susan V. Wall's "A Sequence of Assignments for Basic Writing: Teaching to Problems 'Beyond the Sentence'" (presented at the 1980 Conference on College Composition and Communication; unpublished).

4. James Moffett, *Teaching the Universe of Discourse* (Boston: Houghton Mifflin, 1968), 47. I owe my introduction to Moffett's work and many of the germinal ideas for the courses discussed here to a seminar conducted by David Bartholomae and Anthony Petrosky at the University of Pittsburgh in 1978. I also have been influenced by the work of William E. Coles, Jr., at the University of Pittsburgh. See his *Teaching Composing* (Rochelle Park: Hayden, 1974); and *The Plural I: The Teaching of Writing* (New York: Holt, Rinehart and Winston, 1978).

5. Ibid., 25.

6. For this plan, I am indebted to William Coles and also to Paulo Freire's *Pedagogy of the Oppressed*, trans. Myra Bergman Ramos (New York: Seabury, 1970).

15 Integrating Instruction in Reading, Writing, and Reasoning

Marilyn S. Sternglass
Indiana University

In their search for the ways that the relationships between reading and writing can be exploited constructively in composition instruction, researchers have been examining the similarities between the two processes and their interactive effects. What further needs to be done is to find ways to foster cognitive growth at the same time that reading and writing skills are being enhanced. In particular, college students who are functioning below entry levels can benefit from carefully designed, sequenced activities, which will provide them with effective strategies for meeting the cognitive demands of college work.

Developmental Models

Research from a number of different disciplines forms the conceptual basis for this interactive instruction. What draws these areas of reading, writing, and reasoning together is the notion that all of these processes are based on developmental models. In reading, the psycholinguistic model relies on the idea that the prior knowledge of the reader (phonological, syntactic, and semantic) will determine the level of transaction taking place between the reader and the text. In Piaget's model of distinguishable intellectual stages, the level of cognitive development which the individual has achieved will determine his or her ability to comprehend and carry out specific processes and tasks. In composition theory, the writing process must take account of the maturational level of the writer and his or her ability to perceive and *construct* a meaningful topic, a purpose, an audience, and a mode appropriate to a particular writing task.

Current research in the psycholinguistic model of reading has alerted us to the importance of providing our students with links between their own experience and knowledge and the reading texts they use.[1] The concepts of prior knowledge and prediction must be carefully integrated into prereading activities so that students are prepared to read and respond to essays, narratives, and fictions. Students must be introduced to the conceptual framework of the reading materials with which they will be interacting through carefully constructed prereading activities that will relate their own knowledge base and background to the new information contained in the text. Through the presentation of concepts and key vocabulary items, instructors can provide their students with purposes for the reading and also prepare them for college level reading. As George Henry has pointed out, analysis and synthesis are useful in increasing reading comprehension. Henry has defined reading for concept development as "making one's way through printed and written language in such a manner as to seek out a number of relationships and to put this growing set of relations into a tentative structure."[2]

Piaget's model of conceptual growth through a series of stages provides the basis for the integration of concept formation activities into reading and writing tasks: "Piaget posits four distinguishable stages through which individuals pass as they develop from infancy to maturity: sensory-motor, pre-operational, concrete operational, and formal operational."[3] Although Piaget's work has suggested that young people move from concrete to formal operations at about the age of thirteen, in practice college teachers have observed that their students have great difficulty with formulation of abstractions and synthesizing statements. Andrea Lunsford has noted that basic writers are often "unable to practice analysis and synthesis and to apply successfully the principles thus derived to college tasks."[4] Joe W. McKinnon cites evidence that about 50 percent of students entering college cannot cope with abstract propositions and that this figure does not differ appreciably from college to college.[5]

The realization that students have had difficulty handling the abstract college-level tasks required of them has led various institutions of higher education to develop functional strategies for putting Piaget's theories to work in college classrooms. Such programs include ADAPT (Accent on Developing Abstract Processes of Thought) at the University of Nebraska, DOORS (Development of Operational Reading Skills) at Illinois Central College, STAR (Steps to Abstract Reasoning) at Metropolitan State College in Denver, the Cognitive Program at Essex County College in Newark, New Jersey, and SOAR (Stress on Analytical Reasoning) at Xavier University in Louisiana. R. D. Narveson has explained that in the ADAPT program the effort of teachers "interested in development must be to challenge students constantly to transform the objects of their knowledge in various ways.

A consequence is that we prefer classroom strategies calling for students to be active rather than passive. Students in ADAPT often complain that they do a lot of writing. They do write a lot. . . . In journals and formal papers, students are asked to formulate and reformulate their ideas about the material under study."[6] McKinnon has pointed out that college students are generally "not given the learning opportunties they need to develop logical thought with abstract propositions, because the college professor probably assumes that those mental abilities have already been developed. This assumption often leads the professor to create educational situations with which the student cannot cope and may contribute to the high attrition rates seen in today's institutions of higher education."[7]

From rhetoric and composition research has come the all too familiar observation that students do in fact create generalizations, but that they are often so empty as to encourage nothing but vague and undeveloped writing. In describing an epistemic approach to writing, Kenneth Dowst has argued that in "a writing class, indeed throughout a university, the principal interest of teachers and students is not in lower-level cognition—in an individual's perceptions and experiences, as such—but in the composing of sophisticated, abstract systems of discourse that select among and connect certain perceptions and experiences, connect them into patterns of relationships so as to produce meaningful guides to future study and future action."[8]

A Process of Integration

In order to write, writers need to have discovered something to say. As Jerome Bruner says, "discovery favors the well-prepared mind." Students can learn only by doing—and that doing must engage them in the cognitive processes which underlie the investigation of any topic for writing—that is, analysis and synthesis. The best way for students to engage themselves with these processes is through interacting with reading materials.[9] This interaction should be geared specifically to take advantage of the insights gained through the psycholinguistic model of reading: (1) that readers have some conceptual basis for relating the readings to their own experience; in other words, they must have a frame of reference so that they can relate new information to that which they already possess; (2) some purpose for reading the materials must be established; (3) readers should be prepared to make some predictions about what they will find in the readings so that they have some investment in the reading experience. It is best if these predictions are made *in writing*.

Following this specific preparation for the reading, the students read the material and evaluate their predictions. It is crucial that students not feel they are being tested for the correctness of their prediction, but rather that they examine the reasons why the author did or did not develop his/her ideas in the direction that the reader anticipated. In other words, these predictions should be examined to determine *why* they were or were not fulfilled.

At this moment in the process, students are ready to begin with more specific analyses of the reading materials themselves. But these analyses should not lead to absolute right and wrong answers about the text which has been read; rather, these analyses should be open-ended in design so that students can exchange ideas about the readings and become aware of different perspectives and interpretations of the text. One such task asks students to select a quotation that gets to the essence of the material read and then to provide a justification for their selection. Teaching students to distinguish among different types of summaries on restatement, descriptive, and analytic levels[10] can be helpful in moving them from earlier cognitive strategies to maturationally higher levels—that is, from concrete operations to formal operations. Creating such summaries in writing reinforces this development. In preparation for the movement from analysis to synthesis, students can analyze two or more readings in this manner and also react to the readings *in writing* from their own background and experience.

The next stage in the process is the most difficult for the students and the most important one: they must create an original synthesis based on the readings which they have just analyzed and on their own experiences. One way of doing this is to ask students what the readings have in common and what they share with the students' own experiences. The students can prepare their relationship statements at home before they come to class. At the beginning of the class they can work in small groups to make lists of possible synthesizing topics. With this preparation, they do not feel so threatened when called upon to share their ideas with the entire class group.

From their lists of synthesizing topics—and there are always many possibilities, not just one "correct" topic that could emerge from this process—each student selects a topic to develop in writing. The students then reconsider the material generated during the analyses and reexamine the readings in the light of the topics they have selected. They also work with their earlier written personal reactions to the readings. Only then does each student formulate a tentative thesis statement or paragraph.

These processes of analysis and synthesis give the students practice with both inductive and deductive operations, moving them back and forth between the two. The analyses of the discrete readings are deductive, the formulation of the synthesizing relationship inductive, the reanalysis of the readings for specific supporting evidence deductive, the formulation of the working thesis statement inductive, and so on. These operations continue as students examine the details they have generated and identify the major subareas that will organize their writing.

Students must be encouraged to identify relationships at every level of the process so that, for example, they use evidence from reading A, reading B, and their own experience to develop each major point in the paper, rather than writing separate paragraphs on the evidence from reading A, the evidence from reading B, and their own experiences. The integration of the evidence within each unit of support of their major thesis is an important aspect of the learning process.

Drawing then on the insights of the psycholinguistic model of reading, a process-centered approach to writing, and a cognitive model of reasoning utilizing analysis and synthesis, we can prepare students to master educational and professional tasks at ever-higher developmental levels.

Notes

1. Kenneth Goodman, "Reading: A Psycholinguistic Guessing Game," *Journal of the Reading Specialist* 4 (May 1967): 126–135; Frank Smith, *Understanding Reading* (New York: Holt, Rinehart and Winston, 1971, 1978).

2. George Henry, *Teaching Reading as Concept Development* (Newark, Del.: International Reading Association, 1974), 4.

3. C. Eric Lincoln, "From Concrete to Abstract Reasoning: SOAR Plots the Course," Report on Teaching #6, *Change Magazine* 10 (August 1978): 26.

4. Andrea Lunsford, "Cognitive Development and the Basic Writer," *College English* 41 (1979): 38–46.

5. Joe W. McKinnon, "The College Student and Formal Operations," in John W. Renner et al., *Research, Teaching and Learning with the Piaget Model* (Norman, Okla.: University of Oklahoma Press, 1976), 11.

6. R. D. Narveson, "Development and Learning: Complementary or Conflicting Aims in Humanities Education," *ADAPT Program Handbook* (Lincoln: University of Nebraska), 82–83.

7. Joe W. McKinnon, 11.

8. Kenneth Dowst, "The Epistemic Approach: Writing, Knowing, and Learning," in *Eight Approaches to Teaching Composition*, ed. by Timothy R. Donovan and Ben W. McClelland (Urbana, Ill.: NCTE, 1980), 65–85.

9. Marilyn S. Sternglass, *Reading, Writing and Reasoning* (New York: Macmillan, in press).

10. Daniel Kurland, "Prose I: Reflections on the Development of a 'Basic' Critical/Analytic Reading and Writing Course," in *Building the Bridges between Reading and Writing*, ed. Marilyn Sternglass and Douglas Butturff (Conway, Ark.: L & S Books, in press).

16 Writing and Reading as Collaborative or Social Acts

Kenneth A. Bruffee
Brooklyn College, CUNY

Understanding writing as process has been pedagogically important because it has shifted our focus from what students have written to the way they write. It has therefore improved the way we teach writing. But from my point of view, our work on the process of writing has another importance as well, a theoretical one. Watching how writers behave leads us to ask why they behave that way. Our rhetorical tradition does provide some answers to that question, but these answers do not accord with our growing understanding of the writing process. The tradition says, for example, that writers must behave in certain ways because their readers require it. The writer must infer the reader's interest, needs, tastes, and biases; analyze them; and then choose rhetorical tactics accordingly. Similarly, a reader must infer the writer's interests, needs, tastes, and biases from the "voice" projected in the writing; analyze them; and respond accordingly.

The traditional analysis of the behavior of writers and readers rests on assumptions about the nature of writing and reading, and also about the nature of knowledge, thought, and learning, that are no longer quite tenable. The tradition sees the writer as an individual who prepares a product designed to have a specific effect on another individual. That person in turn is obliged to read defensively, with conscious awareness of the writer's design. The relationship between writer and reader tends to be adversarial. At least two assumptions underlie this traditional conception of writing, and they are closely related. One assumption is that the relationship between writer and language, and between reader and language, is linear and mechanical, almost in the Newtonian sense. The second assumption is that the relationship between writer and reader is one-to-one. Of course the writer hopes to reach more than one reader, and the reader is likely to read more than one writer. But writers tend to regard readers, and readers tend to regard writers, not as a complexly interrelated community but as classified aggregates of individuals: policemen in this audience, senior citizens in that, Republican writers here, Democrats over there.

Traditionally, then, we assume writing and reading to be intrinsically individual, asocial activities. But studying the process of writing casts serious doubt on these traditional assumptions. To study the process of writing itself is to examine what is obviously a late and well advanced stage of our use of language in practical affairs. We begin very early in life to use language as we use it in writing. Understanding this early phase, the origins of the relationship between language and abstract intelligence, sheds a good deal of light on the more advanced phase that concerns us here, the process of writing.

The Origins of Practical and Abstract Intelligence

Fortunately, the study of our use of language in practical affairs early in life has already been undertaken—or at least begun. In *Mind in Society*, L. S. Vygotsky explores a period of language development that I take to be the very earliest stage in the long process that culminates in learning to write effectively. Based on others' research and his own, Vygotsky arrives at the following conclusion:

> The most significant moment in the course of intellectual development, which gives birth to the purely human forms of practical and abstract intelligence, occurs when speech and practical activity, two previously completely independent lines of development, converge. . . . As soon as speech and the use of signs are incorporated into any action, the action becomes transformed and organized along entirely new lines. . . . [Before] mastering [their] own behavior, [children begin] to master [their] . . . surroundings with the help of speech. . . . Children not only *act* in attempting to achieve a goal but also *speak*. As a rule this speech arises spontaneously and continues almost without interruption throughout the [effort]. It increases and is more persistent every time the situation becomes more complicated and the goal more difficult to attain. Attempts to block [the speech that accompanies effort] are either futile or lead [children] to "freeze up."[1]

Vygotsky's analysis of the way children use language could not contend seriously for our attention as teachers of adult and near-adult undergraduates if it could not be generalized beyond that crucial moment early in life when "speech and practical activity . . . converge." The example Vygotsky gives of this kind of language use, however, suggests that it might be so generalized. In that example, a four- or five-year-old child tries to obtain a piece of candy placed out of reach on a shelf. She eventually gets the candy by figuring out how to use a stool and a stick to advantage. The report of the experiment records her talking-through her solution to the problem as she figures it out.[2]

One thing we notice in ths example is that the child does not address her speech to the objects that concern her. As part of her effort to solve the problem, the child talks *about* the objects and *about* what she is doing with them. As for her audience, in the course of talking-through her work she sometimes addresses another person at hand, as a glance she casts at the experimenter at one point suggests. Most of the time, however, she addresses herself. Already, Vygotsky explains, this child's "socialized speech (which has previously been used to address an adult) is turned inward. Instead of appealing to the adult [she appeals] to [herself]."[3]

What is evidently happening in this example is that the child is using social speech (as opposed to "egocentric" speech) *instrumentally* to help get something done. Instrumental speech in turn makes what appears to be a solitary task in reality a collaborative one. Once we begin to use speech instrumentally, we work together, as Robert Frost puts it, whether we work together or apart. This is because language is a social instrument that "shapes" action by affecting our relations with other people: our "ability to control another person's behavior" through language "becomes a necessary part of [our] practical activity." Vygotsky means nothing invidious by the word "control" here. He means that effective work comes to involve, first, engaging other people's attention, interest, and feelings with the task we have undertaken; second, tapping their expertise in order to fill gaps in our own and to augment and complement our own capacity to do the job; and third, drawing on the values, metaphors, and institutional commitments of our community of knowledgeable peers to give meaning to our actions. It is in at least these three senses that the instrumental use of language gives practical intelligence its social or collaborative nature.

Vygotsky contends, furthermore, that as we mature, we learn to internalize this instrumental use of speech, until instrumental social speech becomes what we later experience as "thought." When the child in Vygotsky's example is a year or two older, she will "say" much the same sort of things as she works. She will talk-through her solution to a problem in much the same way. But she will not be likely, except under stress, to do so aloud. Thus, although our instrumental use of social speech beginning at four or five years of age may not seem to continue as we mature, in fact it does. It, so to speak, goes underground. Even as adults working silently and alone, because thought is internalized speech used instrumentally, we are in fact always engaged in a process that is intrinsically collaborative: we work together whether we work together or apart.

Instrumental Speech at High Levels of Cognitive Development

This view that in adulthood speech and action do continue to be "part of one and the same psychological function" is extrapolated from experimental work with children. We may reasonably ask if there is any evidence, drawn directly from the experience of adults but apart from thought, which we cannot see or examine directly, to support that extrapolation? Do adults actually use language instrumentally? Do they in any demonstrable instance work and learn collaboratively in the way the child in Vygotsky's experience worked and learned?

The answer appears to be yes. Instrumental speech turns out, in fact, to be a key element in Thomas Kuhn's description of conceptual growth in *The Structure of Scientific Revolutions*. Kuhn argues that central to change in scientific knowledge, whether it be the acquisition of scientific expertise by novice scientists or a paradigmatic revolution of Copernican magnitude, is the process of "acquiring from exemplars the ability to recognize a given situation as like some and unlike others that one has seen before."[4] This process is familiar to humanists as thinking in metaphor, or as thinking in generic or schematic structures.[5] The link between thinking with metaphors or exemplars and the social or collaborative nature of knowledge lies in the process by which a person acquires these "ways of seeing." We acquire them, Kuhn says, by education, through which "the ways of seeing . . . that have withstood the tests of group use [are transmitted] from generation to generation."[6]

This transmission is not accomplished, Kuhn argues, "by exclusively verbal means. Rather it comes as one is given words together with concrete examples of how they function in use; nature and words are learned together."[7] We learn "group-licensed ways of seeing" when someone else gives us words together with concrete examples of how they are used. Language and exemplars together are "tested and shared possessions of a successful group," an assenting community of knowledgeable peers. Those who give us those shared words and exemplars are members of the community we aspire to join.

Kuhn's contention that we join a community of knowledgeable peers by acquiring that community's language and exemplars is a corollary of Vygotsky's principle that at a crucial point in childhood the convergence of speech and practical activity "gives birth to the purely human forms of practical and abstract intelligence" through the instrumental use of language. Common to Kuhn and Vygotsky, then, is the view that knowledge, thought, and learning are intrinsically social or collaborative in at least two senses: they involve internalized speech, and they involve ways of seeing tested and shared by a community of knowledgeable peers.

Several of Kuhn's illustrations demonstrate the social or collaborative nature of the learning of adults and near adults. One of these illustrations explains the way novice scientists—physics students, say—solve textbook problems. They do so, he says, not by learning to apply theory and rules, but by discovering how to see a problem as like one they have done before. "Having seen the resemblance, grasped the analogy between two or more distinct problems, [they] can interrelate symbols and attach them to nature in the ways that have proved effective before. . . . The resultant ability to see a variety of situations as like each other" allows students to see subsequent work in a particular specialized field of science "in the same gestalt as other members" of that specialist group.

A second illustration demonstrates the collaborative or social nature of scientific knowledge over the span of several lifetimes. "The role of acquired similarity relations also shows clearly," Kuhn says, "in the history of science." Galileo, Huyghens, and Daniel Bernoulli each in his turn solved a problem in mechanics by seeing its similarity to a problem his predecessor had solved. Kuhn borrows Michael Polanyi's term "tacit knowledge" to describe what this series of successful discoveries depended on. "Tacit knowledge" in this case is thinking in metaphors or exemplars, the capacity novice scientists gain through doing textbook problems, the capacity to see that a problem is like one they have done before.

In these two illustrations, conceptual growth is accomplished by developing the capacity to think with metaphors or exemplars. In a third illustration, however, this capacity interferes with conceptual growth. When two members or factions of an assenting community of knowledgeable peers differ over incompatible premises on which their work is to proceed, they must, Kuhn says, debate the alternatives. Recourse in that debate, he insists, must be to techniques that are not "either straightforward, or comfortable, or parts of the scientists's normal arsenal."[8] That is, recourse must be to translation of incompatible terms and to "persuasion as a prelude to the possibility of proof." Kuhn specifies as follows:

If two men disagree, for example, about the relative fruitfulness
of their theories . . . neither can be convicted of a mistake. Nor is
either being unscientific. [Nothing inevitably leads] each individual . . . to the same decision. In this sense it is the community of
specialists rather than its individual members that makes the
effective decision. To understand why science develops as it does,
one need not unravel the details of biography and personality
that lead each individual to a particular choice, though that topic
has vast fascination. What one must understand, however, is the
manner in which a particular set of shared values interacts with
the particular experiences shared by a community of specialists to
ensure that most members of the group will ultimately find one
set of arguments rather than another decisive.[9]

The problem, Kuhn explains, is two-fold. The two scientists have
attached the same words to different objects, and to the same objects
in different ways; and the two scientists are also exercising differently
their learned capacity to recognize similarities. Scientists in a state of
conflict such as this cannot resolve their differences "simply by stipu-
lating the definitions of troublesome terms" or by "resort to a neutral
language which both use in the same way." They must have recourse
not only to language, but to language about language.

In short, they must not just talk. They must pointedly talk about
their talk. They must engage in a collaborative process in which they
make language instrumental to the task of repairing language. As
Kuhn puts it, they must "recognize each other as members of different
language communities and then become translators." His description
of how two scientists might do this is illuminating:

Taking the differences between their own intra- and inter-group
discourse as itself a subject for study, they can first attempt to
discover the terms and locutions that, used unproblematically
within each community, are nevertheless foci of trouble for inter-
group discussions. . . . Having isolated such areas of difficulty . . .
they can next resort to their shared everyday vocabularies in an
effort further to elucidate their troubles. Each may, that is, try to
discover what the other would see and say when presented with a
stimulus to which his own verbal response would be different. . . .
Each will have learned to translate the other's theory and its
consequences into his own language and simultaneously to
describe in his language the world to which that theory applies.[10]

I think it does not strain credulity to see in this demanding,
sophisticated, complex effort to choose between two incommensurate
scientific theories something of the child's talking-through her effort
to get the piece of candy with a stick and a stool. In both cases, as
Vygotsky puts it, "speech not only accompanies practical activity but

also plays a specific role in carrying it out. . . . Speech and action are part of one and the same complex psychological function, directed toward the solution of the problem at hand. The more complex the action demanded by the situation and the less direct its solution, the greater the importance played by speech in the operation as a whole."[11] The philosopher Richard Rorty confirms this view. In *Philosophy and the Mirror of Nature*, Rorty argues from Dewey, Heidegger, and Wittgenstein that knowledge in general is "the social justification of belief," and that justification is "a matter . . . of conversation, of social practice."[12] At every level of cognition beyond earliest infancy—beyond that "most significant moment in the course of intellectual development" when language becomes instrumental in work—social speech is inextricably involved in learning and in active thought.

Writing and Reading as Social or Collaborative Acts

Social speech, then, must be involved in what is sometimes the most daunting of all adult tasks, writing. Although writing is enormously complex, it is basically a form of speech. To write is in effect to "talk" to someone else in a focused and coherent way. This is of course a broad assumption, and not an entirely correct one. We know that, linguistically and rhetorically, writing is both a lot more and rather less. But if for the moment we allow the assumption that writing is basically focused, coherent speech; if we also assume that "the more complex the action demanded by the [task] and the less direct the solution, the greater the importance played by speech in the operation as a whole"; and if we assume that speech is "of such vital importance that, if not permitted to use it," I may not be able to "accomplish the given task" at all—if we do make these assumptions, then in order for me to write the essay I am writing just now, for example, I *must* talk about it. Like the child's effort to reach the candy and the scientists' attempt to choose between incommensurate theories, the practical task of writing is a process of collaborative learning. It requires us to use language in the service of thought and action. In this case, the thought and action involve language itself, so that socialized speech used instrumentally becomes talk about talk.

This necessity to talk-through the task of writing means that col·laborative learning, which is the institutionalized counterpart of the social or collaborative nature of knowledge and thought, is not merely a helpful pedagogical technique incidental to writing. It is essential to writing. This is the radical difference between the conception of writing I am arguing for here and the traditional conception of it. It is a radical, paradigmatic difference involving for most of us what Kuhn calls a "gestalt switch" in our conception of writing. Of course, much in the actual activity of writing remains the same. But the way we perceive and experience that activity differs radically because it appears in quite a new frame of reference. Conceived traditionally as an individualizing and adversarial relationship, writing viewed as a form of instrumental speech becomes a referential and interdependent one. Reader and writer become part of each other's sustaining environment. Like any other learning or problem-solving activity, writing becomes essentially and inextricably social or collaborative in nature.[13]

This conclusion has some interesting practical implications for the future of research on the process of writing. Kuhn himself points out some of these implications. He concludes his argument with the generalization that "scientific knowledge, like language, is intrinsically the common property of a group or else nothing at all. To understand it we shall need to know the special characteristics of groups that create and use it." But since much of what he says about the nature of scientific knowledge is "borrowed from other fields," specifically the humanities and social sciences, this definition of scientific knowledge applies to knowledge in those fields as well. Indeed, Kuhn stresses explicitly "the need for similar and, above all, comparative study of the corresponding communities" in every field, a study that would undertake to answer questions like these:

> How does one elect and how is one elected to membership in a particular community, scientific or not? What is the process and what are the stages of socialization to the group? What does the group collectively see as its goals; what deviations, individual or collective, will it tolerate; and how does it control the impermissible aberration? . . . there is no area in which more work is so badly needed.[14]

These are questions that the study of writing as a process must also begin to address. And as students of the humanities we must begin asking questions of this sort of the whole humanistic disciplinary matrix as well. We must begin to assume that humanistic knowledge, like scientific knowledge, is intrinsically the common property of a group or else nothing at all, and that to understand the humanities in general and the process of reading and writing in particular we must understand first the collaborative or social process of which they are a part.[15]

This venture will lead us almost inevitably to a great variety of new, challenging, and enlightening areas of research. Many of these have to do with language itself. We might ask, for example, since talking about writing is essential to writing and learning to write, whether writers need to learn how to talk about writing? If so, what would learning that entail? How does talk about talk differ from talk about anything else? Or does it? Does anything distinguish critical discourse about language from critical discourse about other things, such as competing scientific theories? Or if, as Richard Rorty has said, "what is special about language" is that it lets us "enter a community whose members exchange justifications of assertions, and other actions, with one another,"[16] how does learning to write affect a person's entrance into a community? How does writing enhance one's membership in whichever community one joins? Exactly what types of community does a writing teacher give students access to? Do we define the type of knowledge community students gain access to by the *way* we teach writing? If so, how? And how do we choose among the possible communities different types of writing give students access to, so as to decide how writing ought to be taught?

Another area of investigation would have to do with role and status in knowledge communities or collaborative learning communities. The child in Vygotsky's example, comfortable with the parental role of the experimenter, could easily address some of her tentative, working speech to such a person in authority. But would that also be true of adults? Or do adults (and near-adults, such as most undergraduates) need to talk-through a task (of writing or anything else) to peers instead? And if so, under those conditions what is a peer?

Finally, if we accept the notion that writing and reading are inherently social or collaborative acts, what do we do with the fact that we normally write and read alone? As it happens, this question is one of the few that has a relatively brief answer relevant in this context. What we do with that fact is to reexamine the value and purpose of the written word in light of a collaborative theory of knowledge and learning. The value and purpose of the written word from this point of view, in contrast with the more obviously social or collaborative acts of speaking and listening, is that it allows us to displace the acts of speech and listening. Writing and reading are displaced social or collaborative acts. They are practical means allowing us to overcome the limitations of time and distance that would otherwise inhibit the communication essential to accomplishing many of the most complex and sophisticated tasks we attempt.

As displaced social or collaborative acts, however, writing and reading require another faculty that we may not yet, as writing teachers, be attending to sufficiently. Displacement requires the active practical use of imagination. To become writers and readers, we must learn to carry on the collaborative, referential exchange essential to writing *in imagination*, recreating imaginatively the social environment in which writing plays a part. In order to learn to write, we must learn to become our own representatives of an assenting community of peers with whom we speak and to whom we listen in our heads. This audible or inward talking-through of our tasks as we do them with a community of knowledgeable peers is itself, in fact, what becomes eventually what we have been calling "the writing *process.*" The *product* of writing results when internalized instrumental social speech (talking-through) is reshaped, revised, and edited to become a composition, a term paper, a dissertation, or the essay I have been writing just now.

Notes

1. L. S. Vygotsky, *Mind in Society*, ed. Michael Cole, Vera John-Steiner, Sylvia Scribner, and Ellen Souberman (Cambridge, Mass.: Harvard University Press, 1978), 24–26.

2. Ibid., 25.

3. Ibid., 27.

4. Thomas S. Kuhn, *The Structure of Scientific Revolutions* (International Encyclopedia of Unified Science, vol. 2, no. 2), 2nd ed. (Chicago: University of Chicago Press, 1970), 192.

5. See the interesting notion of the genre guess in E. D. Hirsch, Jr., *Validity in Interpretation* (New Haven, Conn.: Yale University Press, 1967), 75–78.

6. This parallel is not quite straightforward. Perhaps to call "ways-of-seeing knowledge" (that is, knowledge that Kuhn insists is "embedded in the stimulus-to-sensation route") metaphoric knowledge is misleading or confusing. "Metaphoric" means that the similarity recognized is tacit (our access to it is indirect), whereas in Kuhn's "ways-of-seeing knowledge" what is tacit is the process by which we recognize similarity. See Kuhn, 195–96.

7. Ibid., 191.

8. Ibid., 201.

9. Ibid., 199–201.

10. Ibid., 202. Kuhn goes on to point out that translation alone is not enough for a knowledge revolution to occur. One or the other of the people involved must eventually undergo the sort of "gestalt switch" or "conversion experience" that occurs when we discover suddenly that we are "thinking and working in, not simply translating out of, a language that was previously foreign" (p. 204).

11. Vygotsky, 24–26.

12. Richard Rorty, *Philosophy and the Mirror of Nature*, (Princeton, N.J.: Princeton University Press, 1979), 170. See also Thomas Kuhn, "Second Thoughts on Paradigms," in *The Structure of Scientific Theories*, ed. Frederick Suppe (Urbana, Ill.: University of Illinois Press, 1974), 459–82; and Stanley E. Fish, *Is There A Text in This Class? The Authority of Interpretive Communities* (Cambridge, Mass.: Harvard University Press, 1980), 303–71.

13. For a brief discussion of how collaborative learning may be applied to teaching writing, see Kenneth A. Bruffee, *A Short Course in Writing*, 2nd ed. (Cambridge, Mass.: Winthrop, 1980), 103-21. See also Nan Elsasser and Vera P. John-Steiner, "An Interactionist Approach to Advancing Literacy," *Harvard Educational Review* 47 (1977); Barry M. Kroll, "Developmental Perspectives and the Teaching of Composition," *College English* 41 (March 1980): 741-52; and Elaine P. Maimon, "Talking to Strangers," *College Composition and Communication* 30 (December 1979): 364-69; and Bruffee, "Getting Started," in *Linguistics, Stylistics, and the Teaching of Composition* (Studies in Contemporary Language #2), ed. Donald A. McQuade (Akron, Ohio: University of Akron, 1979), 52-60.

14. Kuhn, 209-10.

15. Kuhn's ideas have sometimes been rather badly distorted by proponents of scientific humanism. One early effort to correct that distortion is Patricia Bizzell's "Thomas Kuhn, Scientism, and English Studies," *College English* 40 (March 1979): 764-91. See also Ronald Schroeder's interesting article, "Writing, Knowledge, and the Call for Objectivity," *College English* 40 (February 1979): 618-24.

16. Rorty, 185.

17. The argument in this article has much in common with Stanley E. Fish's position in *Is There A Text in This Class? The Authority of Interpretive Communities* (Cambridge, Mass.: Harvard University Press, 1980), 303-71. Fish's clear statement of this line of thought is extremely valuable. See also Kenneth A. Bruffee, "CLTV: Collaborative Learning Television," *Educational Communication and Technology* (Spring 1982); "Liberal Education and the Social Justification of Belief," *Liberal Education* (Summer 1982); and "The Structure of Knowledge and the Future of Liberal Education," *Liberal Education* (Fall 1981): 177-86. Also, Clifford Geertz, "The Growth of Culture and the Evolution of Mind" and "Ideology as a Cultural System," in *The Interpretation of Cultures* (New York: Basic Books, 1973); Michael Oakeshott, "The Voice of Poetry and the Conversation of Mankind," in *Rationalism and Politics* (New York: Basic Books, 1962), especially part 1, 197-204; and Lewis Thomas, *The Lives of a Cell* (New York: Bantam, 1975).

17 Reuniting Rhetoric: Theoretical and Pedagogical Considerations

Richard A. Katula
University of Rhode Island

Celest A. Martin
University of Rhode Island

James Kinneavy notes in his influential book, *A Theory of Discourse*, that in the early twentieth century, some radical readjustments took place in the field of rhetoric. Departments of Speech were created by those who felt that instruction in oral communication was being neglected by English departments. "In a sense," Kinneavy writes, "the speech people took rhetoric (the art of persuasion) with them; only now is it being invited back."[1]

In writing programs around the country (and in many speech departments), there is a resurgence of interest in reuniting rhetoric, not only in theory but also in pedagogy, and nowhere is it more natural to combine forces than in the communications classroom. Writing teachers have long recognized the value of "talking about" assigned essay topics as a way of generating ideas. For many teachers, talk-write strategies have provided a way to activate native competence, to get the writer started, or to encourage the student who is blocked.[2] But what is becoming more apparent today are the similarities in planned discourse, whether spoken or written, and the ways in which public speaking instruction facilitates the writing of a composition, and vice versa. A contemporary theory of rhetoric should serve the objectives of both speech and writing instruction. In this paper, we suggest one approach to integrating speech and writing, and demonstrate how we have applied this theory in our classroom during the past few years.

Towards an Integrative Model

Oral communication instruction today is characterized by its emphasis on effects. A speech is a social act, designed to achieve some social

171

end. The movement of a speech is toward judgment. This *Krisis,* or judgment, is the heart of the classical rhetorical theories which were, of course, written for oral communication situations such as the courtroom or the legislative chamber. Because of this focus on effects, the speech classroom places great emphasis on audience analysis, delivery style, and "conventional" structures designed to move an audience toward judgment and action.

A conventional structure, which is a series of steps that have evolved out of the social process of moving a discussion toward some end, tells a student *how to* think about an idea or issue. Oral communication instruction uses conventional structures such as the motivated sequence (see figure 1), a three to five step procedure which holds a hallowed place in the speech classroom somewhat equivalent to

I. Attention Step
  A. Purpose—Overcome the "ho-hum" attitude of listeners and direct their attention to the subject. *Excite their interest! Gain their respect and achieve good will.*
  B. Techniques—Startling statements, questions, illustrations, humorous anecdote, reference to the subject or the occasion. These are the standard methods. However, choose an attention step which shows some ingenuity and creativity and your audience will be appreciative. The manner or style in which you introduce a persuasive speech relates very specifically to the way in which your audience responds.
II. Need Step
  A. Purpose—Describe the problem so that the *listeners feel personally concerned* about the situation.
  B. Techniques—
    1. State the need—
      a. Point out what is wrong and how bad it is—or—
      b. Point out the danger which threatens the continuance of present good conditions.
    2. Illustration—Give one or more incidents which illustrate the need.
    3. Ramifications—Employ as many additional facts, examples, and quotations as are required to make the need convincing and impressive.
    4. Pointing out—Show its importance to the *individuals* in your audience.
III. Satisfaction Step
  A. Purpose—*Present the solution so that the listener will feel that your proposal is sound and sensible.*
  B. Techniques—
    1. Briefly state the belief or action which you propose. (Proposition)
    2. Explain it clearly, by defining terms.

Figure 1. Motivated Sequence. This three step plan for organizing a persuasive speech is taken from *Principles of Speech* by Alan H. Monroe. In each step the specific techniques and amount of detail used depend on the particular situation.

Sheridan Baker's 500 word argumentative essay. The typical assignments in a speech course center on the understanding and use of conventional structures, and are devoted mostly to the elucidation and/or advocacy of social issues.

Such a theoretical framework helps students to develop a heightened sense of audience, of self in relation to others, and of the conventions designed to move communication through problems to solutions in a comprehensive and judicious way. What is lacking in speech instruction is adequate concern for the composing process. Knowing whether one is trying to inform or persuade is only a little help in probing, structuring, or styling a speech. As Knoblauch has recently noted,

> The discrimination of "persuasive" and "referential" intentions is merely generic, yielding broad categories in which to group statements that share similar characteristics. . . . The sense of purpose that actually shapes strategy is something more concrete, more immediate, and less encompassing; it is not generic but operational.[3]

Writing instruction and research, on the other hand, have taken some leave of the effects orientation and have begun to focus more on the composing process, on those controlling decisions writers make when they determine what they want to do and how they want to do it. Writing instruction is concerned with the way thinking, talking, drafting, and polishing a piece of discourse are related, and how each of these stages adds to the final product. In Mina Shaughnessy's words,

> . . . the composition course should be the place where the writer not only writes but experiences in a conscious, orderly way the stages of the composing process itself. . . . The student who has been systematically isolated as a writer both from his own responses as a thinker and speaker and from the resources of others, not only needs these other voices, but needs to become conscious of his own.[4]

Writing, then, is a meditative and reflexive act. The conceptual patterns used come not from social conventions but, as Frank D'Angelo suggests, from a careful scrutiny of the logical and psychological ways by which we process the world around us.[5] Recently, however, a concern has been expressed that writing instruction in its present state often fails to give students a clear-cut sense of audience.[6] Students who produce a descriptive or definitional essay often do not understand why they are producing it. Ask these students to do a descriptive speech and they express frustration as they look for that natural audience focus which is inherent in the oral communication situation. There is, then, a significant distinction between what the speech and writing classrooms emphasize in the production of discourse: speech instruction stresses conventional structures and the ends of discourse, while writing instruction leans toward process and the means of producing discourse. The questions which confront us are: (1) On what theoretical ground is rhetoric to be reunited? and (2) How can oral and written instruction be integrated so that students learn both, and so that instruction in one mode facilitates instruction in the other?

Clearly, the theoretical model must combine both conventional and conceptual structures, since each adds an important dimension to our understanding of human communication. As Kenneth Burke has clearly implied in his *Rhetoric of Motives*, it matters not whether a form is universal (conceptual) or acquired through social processes (conventional) so long as we become aware of it as an organizing principle of discourse.[7] Our model, then, would include a complete range of forms from the most personal narrative to the most social debate. We would want to study all the logical, psychological, and social forms we are aware of: process, cause-effect, analysis, enumeration, didactic forms, argumentative forms, and so on. Our guiding principle should be an elucidation of the entire range of communication situations in which we find ourselves. Such a range of instruction would ensure an understanding of the composing process as well as a heightened sense of audience.

The theoretical model used to reunite rhetoric should begin with thinking, since critical thinking is common to all effective discourse. We must emphasize to our students that knowledge and communication about that knowledge come through thinking deeply about themselves and the world around them. The student who sees social value in the exchange of ideas, and who thinks deeply about ideas, generally produces a higher quality of discourse. Stock issue systems and other heuristics which have recently been published should be recognized as socially contrived models which tell us *how* to think about an idea, while topical systems such as D'Angelo's should be recognized as models of the abstract, underlying patterns which we naturally use when thinking about an idea. Once we undertand this distinction, we can help our students think more clearly about communication.

Speaking is a valuable aid in teaching writing. An extensive literature exists that reveals the value of speaking in the writing classroom as a way of increasing problem-solving ability,[8] but there are other reasons for combined instruction. Because of their focus, speech assignments help students develop an acute sense of audience. They learn through speech experiences what might be called "hearability," using language that is lively and memorable. In a speech class, students are required to answer questions from the audience for about as long as they actually speak, and through this exchange, plus instruction on managing the question-answer session, they learn to anticipate responses to communication. In a sense, they learn how to use the dialogue model, a model they can then more readily apply to writing situations.

Writing instruction, on the other hand, facilitates the teaching of speech. There is, as Keenan and Bennett point out, a distinction between unplanned and planned discourse.[9] In fact, each of us has at least three language codes: our casual code, used in conversation; a more formal code used for public speaking; and a written code, generally the most formal level of discourse. Public speaking style falls somewhere between interpersonal speech and formal writing. We want our students to allow their own distinctive communication styles to show through in their public speaking, but we also want them to move away from the excessive colloquialisms and the shorter thought units which characterize interpersonal speech. We call this public speaking style "you at your best," and students learn what that means when they are in a classroom which involves them in all three language codes.

Course in Oral and Written Communication

Since 1978, with the help of a grant from the Fund for the Improvement of Post-Secondary Education (FIPSE), we have been combining our instruction in oral and written communication. A description of our course and of our findings will illuminate the value of reuniting speech and writing instruction. Ours is a six-credit course which meets each day and is staffed with both speech and writing instructors. On Tuesday and Thursday we meet in a large lecture to discuss principles of discourse common to both speech and writing. On Monday, Wednesday, and Friday, we meet in small groups of approximately twenty to present speeches and share essays. There are, of course, many ways to vary this structure and achieve the same results.

Vocabulary

The vocabulary we introduce to our students during the first lectures is "point," "pattern," and "detail." The terminology is simple, yet it continually reminds the students of the three essential elements that structured discourse should possess. We prefer the term "point" to "thesis" because while occasionally we use these words synonymously, there are times when "point" is more accurate. For example, many narratives have no thesis, but since they tell "what happened," they do have a point.

The term "pattern" simply reminds the students that although the discourse may employ more than one pattern in its various sections or paragraphs, only one conceptual pattern should dominate the work as a whole. Sometimes, mastery of point and pattern develops before the skill of selecting only the appropriate details—and the right proportion of them—emerges. Peer comments are especially helpful in this area. When students ask questions after a speech or essay is presented, they direct the speaker/author to details that should have been included, or discussed more extensively.

Time-oriented Patterns

We begin our course with a personal narrative since it is a low anxiety speech that places great emphasis on audience involvement. Many students finish their narrative, relieved and red-faced, only to look around the room to see their classmates leaning forward expectantly. Shocked by the sight of these still eager faces, the student mumbles, "That's it," or, "Well, that's the end." In that moment, the concept of audience has become a reality for them. This is the moment to begin talking about communication as a social act which must be addressed to an audience.

Unsatisfied peer expectations of this sort often succeed where a semester of teacher comments fails. Students become aware that they have not made a point, that in some respect they have failed to fulfill audience desires. As classmates question them, the speakers realize that they have told a story without anticipating the needs of their listeners. After this first experience, students strive for the supreme compliment from their classmates: the phrase, "I felt as though I were right in the scene." Meanwhile, the students turn in their first essay, an examination of cause and effect. Many are careful to use the pattern, but forget to make a point. Some get caught up in narration, and as an afterthought include a cause-effect paragraph at the end. But the majority are at least conscious of using a pattern, and progress is evident.

After the first speech and essay, students attend a lecture on presentational style (delivery). They smile as they recognize their mistakes in various comic illustrations of what not to do in a speech. At this point, we introduce another feature of the course: guest speakers. Students come to distinguish effective presentational style from ineffective; they play the role of audience members and thus become aware of shifting audience constraints. Most important, students experience the boredom of a random and disorganized speech, and the empathy and excitement generated by a good one. They become anxious to create this excitement themselves.

Issue Analysis

From time-oriented patterns such as narration and cause-effect, we move to structures based upon spatial and topical relationships. The second speech is an issue analysis. The analyses are often imprecise, but improvement from the first essay is noticeable. The organization is tighter, and students are careful to choose a topic they think will be of interest to their audience. There is an observable weakness in the analysis papers in selection and depth of detail. But because students are becoming more critical listeners, they are able to provide their classmates with concrete suggestions. They learn to recognize the unsupported assertion. For example, if a student begins to analyze why rock concerts are unsafe without first providing evidence that they are, indeed, unsafe, another student will point this out.

Informative Speech

It is not until the third speech that our students experience an all-around feeling of elation—the feeling that this presentation works—for them and for us. This feeling is partially due to the nature of the next assignmnent: an informative speech, our first introduction to a conventional pattern. Students are asked to find something "new" on campus—some service available, some obscure office—with which their classmates would probably not be familiar. We strongly suggest to the students that they prepare this speech by interviewing someone on campus connected with a special service or office. The interview requires them to use their oral skills by developing and asking questions intelligently and thoughtfully, and to use their written skills by shaping into a pattern the answers they receive.

On the day the informative speeches are due, something magical happens. Instead of sitting silently as we ask for the first volunteer, the speakers assemble notes eagerly and are anxious to be first. They use the chalkboard, pass out handouts from their sources, and are pleased with themselves and with the attention accorded them by their classmates. At the end of each speech, classmates ask questions, eager for more information. The speakers enjoy becoming instant authorities and gaining credibility with their peers.

This speech marks a turning point in the semester. Students appear to have found their voice, a voice that speaks to a clearly defined audience. We observe that many students are becoming good writers in the sense that they are clearly representing their rhetorical problem as a complex speech act.[10]

Argument

The next essay, an argument, builds upon this new-found sense of audience. It is written to be taken seriously, to achieve the interest and acclaim the students received from their previous speech. The students exercise this care even though they won't be getting the same immediate feedback this time. Still, they want to maintain the credibility they have begun to achieve as communicators.

The argument, a conventional pattern, allows us to introduce stock issues as a heuristic. Stock issues are the questions which occur with frequency in the course of argumentation. Their function as a heuristic is to move an argument through the appropriate stages, or points of potential conflict.[11] The strength of the stock issues approach is that it creates an integral sense of audience within the discourse, providing students with a means of anticipating those questions an audience might raise.

One category of questions might concern the information needs of an audience: for example, "Is the speaker/writer giving me the information I need to make a decision on this issue?" Another category would reflect the audience's awareness of opposing viewpoints in the argument. The audience expects a credible speaker/writer to acknowledge the opposition and to deal with it, perhaps by analysis of the advantages and disadvantages of the solution being offered.

Exposure to the conventional forms and the stock issues approach combines with the sharpened awareness of audience to produce marked cognitive development in the students' expression of ideas. Many students enter the course armed with right/wrong, good/bad, either/or thought patterns; their viewpoints reflect a polarized world.[12] By the end of the course, they assess experiences and situations in much more relative terms. It is as though they are able to "skip over" some of the less sophisticated stages of cognitive development; fulfilling the needs of a live classroom audience strengthens the students' ability to construct an imaginary one. By the end of the semester, the students have engaged in at least eight patterns, both conceptual and conventional. They have learned to think carefully and critically about their experiences, and to translate these experiences into communication of intellectual and social value.

Evaluation

What remains is the evaluation of the students' work. As teachers, we have learned from each other as well as from the students. Teachers of writing were apprehensive about grading speeches. How much should delivery weigh? Charisma? And speech instructors had another set of questions. Should poor punctuation and spelling be overlooked in an otherwise well-written essay?

But in the end, similarities rather than differences have brought us together and created common grounds for evaluation. We have returned to our founding theory that formal discourse must possess those distinguishing characteristics that set it apart from much unplanned discourse: purpose, pattern, and appropriate selection of detail. To insure that we judge speeches and essays with equal attention, we record the speeches, play them back in our offices, and spend as much time writing comments and suggestions for their improvement as we do with the essays. Evaluating taped speeches allows us to focus more clearly on the concerns of well-planned discourse without the advantages or disadvantages that student personalities can create in the classroom.

We are, of course, continuing to evaluate our program. The response so far, however, has been overwhelmingly positive. Student evaluation forms brim with support because, as our students see it, they have learned to compose a speech or an essay according to a single system of construction. Faculty who have been involved have commented that team teaching brings out the best in them. Most importantly, we have progressed to the point where we can suggest institutional guidelines for effective communication to our colleagues in the professional schools and can suggest them with a sense of confidence in our terminology and a set of standards that are common to both speech and writing.

Notes

1. James L. Kinneavy, *A Theory of Discourse* (New York: W. W. Norton and Company, Inc., 1971), 13.

2. Terry Radcliffe, " 'Talk-Write' Composition: A Theoretical Model Proposing the Use of Speech to Improve Writing," *Research in the Teaching of English* 6 (1972): 187–199.

3. C. H. Knoblauch, "Intentionality in the Writing Process: A Case Study," *College Composition and Communication* 31 (May 1980): 154.

4. Mina Shaughnessy, *Errors and Expectations* (New York: Oxford University Press, 1977), 82.

5. Frank D'Angelo, *A Conceptual Theory of Rhetoric* (Cambridge, Mass.: Winthrop Publishers, 1975).

6. Fred R. Pfister and Joanne F. Petrick, "A Heuristic Model for Creating a Writer's Audience," *College Composition and Communication* 31 (May 1980): 213-220.

7. Kenneth Burke, *A Rhetoric of Motives* (Berkeley: University of California Press, 1969), 65.

8. B. Bloom and Lois Broder, "Problem Solving Processes of College Students," *The Learning Process*, ed. T. Harris and W. Schwahn (New York: Oxford University Press, 1961), 59-79.

9. Elinor D. Keenan, "Why Look at Unplanned and Planned Discourse," *Discourse Across Time and Space*, ed. T. Bennett and E. Keenan (Southern California Occasional Papers in Linguistics, No. 5, Dept. of Linguistics, University of Southern California, Los Angeles, Calif.), p. 56.

10. Linda Flower and John Hayes, "The Cognition of Discovery: Defining a Rhetorical Problem," *College Composition and Communication* 31 (February 1980): 21-32.

11. Richard Katula and Richard W. Roth, "A Stock Issues Approach to Writing Arguments," *College Composition and Communication* 31 (May 1980): 183-195.

12. William G. Perry, Jr., *Forms of Intellectual and Ethical Development in the College Years: A Scheme* (New York: Holt, Rinehart and Winston, 1970).

18 Writing and Thinking in a Postliterate Society

William V. Costanzo
Westchester Community College, New York

When our freshman composition students first set pen to paper, we are frequently distressed by the broad gulf between what they have to say and what they write. This breach is not simply a matter of interest or intelligence. Although those students who seem most thoughtful and articulate in class discussion sometimes appear dull and incoherent in their writing, we should not be surprised to find such discrepant performances since some young people are much more experienced and comfortable with talk than with the printed page. Many of the features which characterize good talk (a loose, rhapsodic structure, frequent repetition, stereotyped expressions, a superfluity of words for the sake of flow) are unacceptable in written form. As Walter Ong and others have pointed out, orality and literacy involve different forms of conceptualization, and the more we learn about these differences the better we will understand the problems encountered by our students when they face a given writing task.

The changes we observe over the years in student writing can be seen as evidence of a larger movement, a massive shift in our society from the primacy of print to the primacy of the new media of sight and sound. Some of us may point out that best sellers still sell millions of copies. But the fact that so many of these books are tied to movies and television serials is itself a sign of the times. For the great majority of Americans, the dominant vehicle of communication is no longer the printed word. According to a recent survey of the time spent by adults in this country with different media, 85 percent is devoted to television and radio whereas only 15 percent is given to newspapers and magazines. And the trend clearly favors the electronic media.[1] Looking down the road toward the anticipated boom in cable television, video cassettes, video disks, and the other glittering offspring of the new technology, we can expect that even more time will be diverted from the printed page

Much of what I have described may seem familiar, but how does our profession meet the challenge that we are becoming a "post-literate society"? It seems to me that we generally respond in two ways. Either we chide our students for deserting the written word and rally to a lusty battle cry of Back to Basics, or we ignore the threat completely and continue to teach in the manner we ourselves were taught. Not enough of us have paid attention to the nature of those media which we consider to be the enemies of print.

Alternative Responses

We need to see our present crisis, if that is what it is, from an historical perspective, not just in terms of technological achievements in communication, but also—and primarily—in light of the development of thought, the different modes of consciousness which are fostered by these changes in technology.

First, consider the organizing patterns that characterize preliterate forms of communication. Building on and beyond the work of scholars like Eric Havelock and Marshall McLuhan, Walter Ong has pursued his studies of Homeric poetry, classical rhetoric, and African talking drums to define what he calls the basic features of "primary orality," the chief mode of expression for cultures which have never known writing.[2] Ong finds that the speech of these cultures is "rhapsodic": that is, themes and formulas are stitched together in broad, familiar patterns. Such speech abounds in epithets, clichés, and other stereotyped expressions. It favors standard topics (*topoi*) and conventional characters. Language is valued as sound, infused with the rhythms of life, and such language favors an abundance of speech, a copious flow of words. Among Ong's important insights is his recognition that these qualities are not attempts to be poetic; they result directly from the practical requirements of an oral culture. When speech must be memorized, formulaic phrases like "the sturdy oak" and "wise old Nestor" serve as mnemonic devices. Fixed, familiar ways of organizing information aid in the retrieval process. Such discourse tends to have a conservative bias because it must embed new information in the matrix of preexisting knowledge.[3]

By contrast, literate cultures have less need of formulary speech. Standard pagination allows for indexes and other retrieval systems which are independent of recollection through memory. Readers don't require all those slogans, epithets, and ceremonial patterns of expression to help them process, store, and later recover information. In fact, written discourse is considerably less tolerant of stereotyped language. As teachers of writing, we criticize our students for resorting to clichés, for typecasting their characters, for not trying to convey their thoughts in fresh language. Their efforts to be copious we often condemn as "padding." Their rhapsodic habits of mind we interpret as signs of loose or lazy thinking.

From one perspective, we are right to do so. Most of these traits are unacceptable in written composition. But are we presenting the total picture if we imply that they are features of a sloppy mind or careless logic? Wouldn't it be more accurate, more sound pedagogically, to say that there are different modes of thinking, and that one of these is better suited for speech than for print? By exploring the distinctions between orality and literacy, the unpracticed writer who is nonetheless a good talker can begin to regard writing as a road not only to alternative forms of expression, but also to different modes of thought. Speech is inherently integrative, ritualistic, formulaic, conservative. Writing, on the other hand, fosters analytic thinking, discrimination, a separation of the mind from the thing perceived. Writers, working along with the instruments of their trade, can probe more deeply than speakers, whose minds must also entertain a visible audience. Since they must wait before their words evoke tangible responses, writers are encouraged to become detached, to follow longer lines of thought. However, since they know that what they write will be open to scrutiny, that the reader can reread with a careful, critical eye, they are obliged to strengthen the internal logic of their prose. This fact of written discourse—that it is subject to rereading—discourages certain forms of repetition. Instead, it promotes originality, the search for new ideas and forms, and it encourages subtlety, attention to nuance, irony, and fine gradation of thought.

By focusing our students' attention on the intellectual differences between speaking and writing, we can clarify and magnify their options. They can begin to recognize that certain features of intelligence are best developed through the written word and that certain other habits of mind are not necessarily invalid, but may be better suited to different forms of discourse.

So far, I have been comparing primary orality and literacy. But of course we don't live in a preliterate society, and even the most poorly read freshman has been influenced by forces unavailable to Homer or the Bantu tribesmen. Ong uses the term "secondary orality" to describe our age. Although he has devoted less attention to this phase than to earlier times, his choice of terms is most revealing. It is not difficult to see that our chief means of communication today have, in an important sense, returned us to previous modes of thinking.

Consider, for example, the structural features of most television programming. The shows are intrinsically formulaic; from game shows to the soaps, they thrive on predictable patterns of characterization and organization. The habits of most television viewers are therefore ceremonial rather than selective. They watch most programs by the clock instead of choosing individual shows for their content, and most programming follows a well-known seasonal ritual. Whether we watch sit-coms, talk shows, or commercials, the underlying principle is repetition rather than development of new ideas. Even when a fresh approach is aired, it is either quickly transformed into a successful formula or immediately scrapped. Television, then, is ritualistic rather than analytic, a loose collage of familiar themes and forms rather than a single-minded linear investigation of a subject. In some respects, the feature film is closer to the book in its sequential logic and its large-screen tolerance of subtle effects, but it rarely matches the printed page for exploring irony or abstract thought.

So if our students' papers seem to jump from one idea to another as if switching channels, if they leave out steps as if we were expected to supply them as a matter of ritual, if they are short on supportive details and long on clichés, it may be that the underlying consciousness is still geared to the cadences of casual conversation or the television tube.

Bridging the Gap

What can we as composition teachers do about this situation? One way of bridging the gap between the spoken and the written word is suggested by James Moffett, who contends that "speaking and writing are essentially just editing and abstracting some version of what at some moment one is thinking."[4] Drawing on the terminology of drama, he distinguishes between *soliloquy* or "inner thought"; *dialogue* or "thought exchanged with others"; and *monologue,* "a holding forth to others" or an extension of one's inner thoughts. Moffett emphasizes that "interaction is a more important learning process than imitation," that inner thought is shaped most strongly and directly by the influence of conversation. According to this view, we learn to think primarily by weaving the give and take of conversational exchange into the fabric of our meditations. What Moffett recommends, therefore, is a greater emphasis on scripts and dialogue in the English classroom.

Although Moffett does not propose this strategy in the context of Ong's history of consciousness, it seems to me that a gradual shift from dialogue to monologue is what we need to move inexperienced writers from an essentially oral disposition of mind to the more formal requirements of written composition. So instead of starting with an essay, such students might begin by developing a topic through Socratic dialogue. By imagining two speakers, they can explore ideas through a sequence of questions and answers, assertions and challenges, explanations and refinements that build on their familiarity with real-life oral discourse and force them to develop their thoughts along the more extended lines of logic that are expected in written discourse. The next step is to combine the two views into one, anticipating the reader's responses, "shifting to a higher level of abstraction," and embedding or conjoining related details grammatically into a single voice.[5] In this way, beginning writers learn not by imitating model texts, but by growing through an organic, exploratory process from familiar forms of thought into new cognitive domains.

A second approach addresses the challenge posed by the visual media. The first step in making a transition from seeing to writing is to identify the rhetorical principles common to both visual and written forms of composition. For example, many of the organizational patterns taught in writing courses through prose models—comparison and contrast, classification and division, process analysis, cause and effect—also can be found in television commercials. Consider the Volkswagen commercial which compares the wisdom of Mr. Jones (who buys a large American car) and of Mr. Krempler (who spends the same amount of money for a new refrigerator, a new oven, two new television sets, a stereo . . . and a brand new Volkswagen Beetle) and concludes that Mr. Jones now faces the age-old problem of keeping up with the Kremplers. This tidy sample of visual composition makes its point in a manner similar to Bruce Catton's widely anthologized comparison of Ulysses Grant and Robert E. Lee, but the technique is easier to see in the commercial. The Burger King advertisement which classifies its four specialty sandwiches with the aid of a split screen uses the same method of arrangement as James Barker's essay on "Four Types of President," but we recognize the structure of the ad more quickly. Granted, most commercials may seem silly and trite, but their brevity, simplicity, and ubiquity make them ideal for introducing basic concepts which can then be studied in more complex films and printed texts. Once students see the principle at work in a familiar setting, they are more likely to recognize it elsewhere and to put it into practice in their writing.

In addition to such organizing patterns, commercials and documentary films can illustrate a wide variety of persuasive strategies which might be more difficult to spot in a classic or contemporary essay. Need an example of "glittering generality"? Consider the Sun Bug commercial which announces a car "so good the gods decided to reward it." Looking for an instance of snob appeal? Watch Orson Welles explain how "Paul Masson will sell no wine before its time." Bandwagon? "Come on in to the Schaeffer circle." Association? Just think of "baseball, hot dogs, apple pie, and Chevrolet." Or, if you look closely, you will find all of these techniques and more in a single documentary film by Frederick Wiseman.

One obvious advantage of beginning with visual models is how well they lend themselves to class discussion. Many students are used to responding collectively to films, whereas their responses to written works have been more private, and therefore more difficult to share. Moreover, as shown in a recent study of audience responses to literature and film, when college students evaluate a literary text they tend to emphasize its content, whereas when assessing a film they are more apt to stress technique.[6]

How far can this analogy of film as composition be pushed? The limit seems to depend on the students' background and the teacher's ingenuity. For students with some knowledge of filmmaking, the basic steps of film production can be compared to the stages which a writer goes through to produce an essay. Like filmmakers, writers can achieve clarity by manipulating the variable features of their instrument, the English language. They can bring their subject into focus by getting close to it, by selecting the most precise analogy or adjective to express their "close up" observations. They can alter the reader's image of their subject by approaching it from a new angle or by setting it against a different background. Like filmmakers, who may first collect raw footage of subject before starting to make the final print, writers may gather impressions in a rough series of notes. At some point, both filmmakers and writers must choose a particular point of view; they must identify a purpose and an audience, and their decisions as editors follow suit. Filmmakers may then make a "rough cut" by selecting shots that fit their purposes and by organizing them into a logical sequence. Writers may use an outline or a rough draft to accomplish the same goals. Just as filmmakers match the action to achieve a sense of continuity and add visual transitions, such as fades and dissolves, writers add verbal transitions to clarify relationships and maintain a natural flow of ideas. And of course both must "revise" their composition, literally "see it again," until they feel confident that their message will come across to the audience as it was intended.

In this way filmmaking becomes a serviceable model of the composing process. The common flaws that we have all observed in home movies—panning too quickly from one item to another, overexposing the subject, careless framing, fuzzy focusing, and so on—can help us to troubleshoot the home-made essay. And for those who find the process of manipulating words to be more abstract and mysterious than manipulating images the analogy of movie making offers a concrete plan for moving step by step from their first impressions of a subject to a final draft.

What about the differences between the camera and the pen? A picture may be worth a thousand words of sheer description, but it takes a gallery of images to express a single abstract concept such as "essence" or "existence." Or, to take another example, fades and wipes may signal certain shifts in a scene, but they lack the logical precision of transitions like "therefore" or "however." It is important, then, to demonstrate how filming is *not* like writing, and how the simple act of transcribing a movie or television ad does not result automatically in an effective composition on the page. In my own classes, I have found it useful to compare short films and commercials to their bare scripts. My students are quick to notice how much of a film's message is communicated through images. The words from a lively ad for "Shout" detergent, for example, may seem bloodless and banal when stripped of their visual accompaniment. By contrast, the careful structure and supportive statistics of a "Dasher" ad help to make it more persuasive as a script than as a film, where organizational subtleties and verbal details are usually lost. In other words, by analyzing print and cinematic forms of the same composition, students can begin to appreciate the formal and intellectual requirements of written composition. They can see how we tolerate clichés and unsupported claims more readily as viewers than we do as readers. They can recognize how writing fosters a need for more varied syntax, a richer vocabulary, and more complex patterns of arrangement.

My own experience along these lines has convinced me of the value of using visual analogies to writing. Students do recognize the principles of composition in more familiar forms of communication, and if they are led through a balanced sequence of activities, they can make the difficult transition from their comfortable roles as speakers and viewers to the more demanding roles required of them as readers and writers.

The final purpose, then, of outlining the shape of thinking and writing in a postliterate society is not to abandon the written word. Rather, it is to understand the place of writing among other methods of communicating. The more we know about the unique modes of thought which are nurtured by print culture, the stronger is our case for teaching writing. And the more we learn about the popular culture of our students, the easier it will be to help them move into the medium that sustains most of the thinking in our academic world.

Notes

1. 1980 Survey by R. H. Bruskin Associates: "Percent Reached and Time Spent Yesterday In Minutes With Major Media."

2. Walter J. Ong, *Interfaces of the Word: Studies in the Evolution of Consciousness and Culture* (Ithaca, N.Y.: Cornell University Press, 1977), 8ff.

3. See also Ong's *Rhetoric, Romance, and Technology: Studies in the Interaction of Expression and Culture* (Ithaca, N.Y.: Cornell University Press, 1971).

4. James Moffett, *Drama: What Is Happening? The Use of Dramatic Activities in the Teaching of English* (Champaign, Ill.: NCTE, 1967), 10ff.

5. Moffett, 12.

6. Alan Weber, *The Responses of College Students to Film* (Doctoral dissertation, University of Illinois, 1974).

III The Writer as Interpreter

19 The Intelligent Eye and the Thinking Hand

Ann E. Berthoff
University of Massachusetts at Boston

Everything we deal with in composition theory is fundamentally and unavoidably philosophical. I believe that it is only by being philosophical that rhetoric can "take charge of the criticism of its own assumptions." That was the way I. A. Richards put it in 1936 in *The Philosophy of Rhetoric*, a book that can help rinse our minds of the effects of the positivist assumptions which are everywhere to be found in current rhetorical theory and are everywhere the chief cause of all our woe. Let me offer a polemical summary. Positivism is a philosophy with a fundamentally associationist epistemology. The positivist notion of critical inquiry is a naive misconception of scientific method—what is sometimes called "scientism." Positivists believe that empirical tests yield true facts and that's that. They find inimical the idea that theory and practice should be kept together. Underlying all positivist methods and models is a notion of language as, alternately, a set of slots into which we cram or pour our meanings, or as a veil which must be torn asunder to reveal reality directly, without the distorting mediation of form. (If that last sounds mystical, it's because if you scratch a positivist, you'll find a mystic: neither can tolerate the concept of mediation.) I believe that we should reject this false philosophy, root and branch; in so doing it is important to realize that we are in excellent company.

Philosophical Allies

We can count as allies, among others, Susanne K. Langer, William James, C. S. Peirce, and I. A. Richards. Langer, in the first volume of *Mind: An Essay on Human Feeling* (the very title is important) explains how it is that psychologists have developed no sound theories of mind: when they have seen that to ask "What is mind?" leads to a futile search for metaphysical quiddities, instead of reconceiving the critical questions which would yield working concepts, they have worshipped the "Idols of the Laboratory"—Physicalism, Mathematization, Objectivity, Methodology, and Jargon. Any teacher who has been intimidated by the false philosophy of positivism should read Langer's critique every morning before breakfast. In resisting the positivists, we will have another ally in William James, a great psychologist by virtue of being a great philosopher. (Alfred North Whitehead listed him as one of the four greatest of all times because of his understanding of the importance of experience.) James, in his typically lively *Talks to Teachers,* warns his audience not to expect insight into the nature of such aspects of thought as attention, memory, habit, and interest to be forthcoming from what he calls the "brass instrument" psychologists, those who measured such phenomena as the fatigue your finger suffered as you tapped it over three hundred and fifty-eight times. The new brass instrument psychologists, like the old, are concerned with what can be plotted and quantified, and that does not include the things we want to know about— the composing process or the writer's mind or modes of learning and their relationship to kinds of writing.

Our most important ally in rejecting positivism is C. S. Peirce, the philosopher who first conceptualized the structure and function of the sign. The inventor of semiotics (including the term itself) had an amused contempt for psychologists, who were, in the main, ignorant of logic. He scorned the notion that the study of meaning was of a kind with the study of natural phenomena. In one of his calmer moments, he declared: "Every attempt to import into psychics the conceptions proper to physics has only led those who made it astray."[1] And, to conclude this short list of allies, there is I. A. Richards who memorably wrote in *Speculative Instruments:* "The Linguistic Scientist . . . does not yet have a conception of the language which would make it respectable. He thinks of it as a code and has not yet learned that it is an organ—the supreme organ of the mind's self-ordering growth."[2] Note the "yet": Richards always included it in even the gloomiest of his assessments of the state of rhetoric. Our field continues to suffer incursions from those who have no intention of conceiving language as "the supreme organ of the mind's self-ordering growth," and I am not yet sure that we should emulate his patience.

The reason for impatience is simply that we might very well lose the advantage which the novel effort to think about mind could give us. Unless we think philosophically about thinking, what's likely to happen with *mind* is what has already happened with *process:* it will be used and manipulated within the framework of positivist assumptions and thus will not help us develop a pedagogy appropriate to teaching the composing process. To be able to use *mind* as a speculative instrument—Richards' term for an idea you can think *with*—we will have to become authentic philosophers—and quick.

If we are to avail ourselves of that incomparable resource, the minds of our students, we will have to know what we're looking for, to have some philosophically sound idea of the power the mind promises. I believe that for teachers of composition, such a philosophy of mind is best thought of as a theory of imagination. If we can reclaim imagination as the forming power of mind, we will have the theoretical wherewithal for teaching composition as a mode of thinking and a way of learning.

Reclaiming the Imagination

Reclaiming the imagination is necessary because the positivists have consigned it to something called "the affective domain," in contradistinction to "the cognitive domain." You can see the false philosophy at work there, importing conceptions appropriate to neurology and biochemistry into psychics: certainly, there are areas and domains in the brain, but to use the term *domain* about modes of mental operation is to create the same kind of confusion as when the word *code* is used to designate both linguistic operation and brain function. The false philosophy cannot account for imagination as a way of knowing or a means of making meaning because it understands imagination as ancillary or subordinate, not as fundamental and primordial. Coleridge here, as in so many other instances, is our best guide in developing a philosophy of rhetoric, defining the imagination as "the living power and prime agent of all human perception." Perception works by forming—finding forms, creating forms, interpreting forms. Rudolf Arnheim, in his superb book *Visual Thinking*, lists the operations involved in perception: "active exploration, selection, grasping of essentials, simplification, abstraction, analysis and synthesis, completion, correction, comparison, problem solving, as well as combining, separating, putting in context."[3] (Doesn't that sound like an excellent course in writing?)

To think of perception as *visual thinking* helps make the case for observation in the composition classroom, not for the sake of manufacturing spurious "specifics" and vivid detail about nothing much, but because perception is the mind in action. Thinking begins with perception; the point is nicely caught in the title of R. L. Gregory's book on perception: *The Intelligent Eye.* The "dialectical notebook"

I've described in *Forming / Thinking / Writing,*[4] one in which students record observations and observe their observations, affords students the experience of mastery, because it exercises powers we do not have to teach: the natural power of forming in *per*ception and the natural power of *con*ception, concept formation, which in so many ways is modeled on the activities of the "intelligent eye." Observation of observation becomes the model of thinking about thinking, of "interpreting our interpretations," of "arranging of techniques for arranging." The consciousness represented in such circular formulations is not *self* consciousness but an awareness of the dynamic relationship of the *what* and the *how;* of the reflexive character of language; of the dialectic of forming. The consciousness of consciousness which is encouraged by looking and looking again is at the heart of any critical method.

Once we give some thought to imagination, "the shaping power and prime agent of all human perception," we can see how it is that visualizing, making meaning by means of mental images, is the paradigm of all acts of mind: *imagining* is forming par excellence and it is therefore the emblem of the mind's power. Students who learn to look and look again, to observe and to observe their observations, are discovering powers they have not always known are related in any way to the business of writing. If we trust "the intelligent eye," we can teach our students to find in perception an ever-present model of the composing process; they will thereby be reclaiming their own imaginations.

Shaping is as important an emblem as visualizing of that forming which is the work of the acitve mind. The artist at work—especially the sculptor—is surely the very image of imagination as the creation of form, though artists often prefer to speak of their creative activity as a matter of finding form: Michelangelo famously spoke of liberating the form in the stone. The popular doctrine of art as, simply, the "expression" of "emotion" leaves out of account forming, shaping, and thus cannot contribute to a theory of imagination. As an antidote, let me quote a passage from the autobiography of Barbara Hepworth, the British sculptor: "My left hand is my thinking hand. The right is only a motor hand. This holds the hammer. The left hand, the thinking hand, must be relaxed, sensitive. The rhythms of thought pass through the fingers and grip of this hand into the stone." I like the echo in Susanne Langer's title, *Mind: An Essay on Human Feeling,* of Barbara Hepworth's phrases, "my thinking hand" and "rhythms of thought," and I leave it to you to consider the implications of the fact that neither the philosopher nor the artist considers it paradoxical to speak of thinking and feeling as a single activity of forming. (And I leave it to you to consider that both are women.)

Forming as Modes of Abstraction

That single activity of forming can be carried out in two modes, and no theory of imagination can be sound which does not recognize them both. What we call them is a matter of some interest since our pedagogy will be guided, sometimes surreptitiously, by what we take as the implications of the terms. I have been arguing that the positivist differentiation of cognitive and affective is wrongheaded and misleading: indeed, it is the root cause of the widespread failure to get from so-called personal writing to so-called expository writing, from informal to formal composition—even from so-called "pre-writing" to writing. This false differentiation creates an abyss which rhetoricians then spend their time trying to bridge by roping together topics and places and modes of discourse, by one or another methodological breeches buoy. A theory of imagination can help us solve the problem of the abyss by removing the problem: there is no abyss if composing is conceived of as forming and forming as proceeding by means of abstraction. I will conclude by suggesting how we can differentiate two modes of abstraction, but let me note briefly why it is that current rhetorical theory manifests no understanding of forming as abstraction.

That fact must be correlated, I have often thought, with the fact that though it's defunct elsewhere, General Semantics is alive and kicking in the midst of any assembly of rhetoricians. For General Semantics, abstraction is the opposite of reality: Cow[1], Cow[2], Cow[3], are real, but *cow* or *cows* are not real; they are words and they are "abstract." Now, General Semanticists have never understood that Laura, Linda, Louise—all cows of my acquaintance—are also abstract. The smellable, kickable, lovable, milkable cow is, of course, *there:* it is recalcitrant, in Kenneth Burke's sense of that term[5] and the dairy farmer's; it is part of the triadicity of the sign relationship, in Peirce's terms.[6] But this actual cow, this cow as *event*, as Whitehead would say, is known to us in the form provided by the intelligent eye—and the intelligent ear and the intelligent nose. That form—that percept—is a primordial abstraction. Abstraction is not the opposite of reality but our means of making meaning of reality in perception and in all that we do with symbolic forms.

Forming is a single activity of abstraction: once we have the genus, we can then develop the definition dialectically by recognizing the two kinds of abstraction. There is the *discursive* mode which proceeds by means of successive generalization and the *nondiscursive* or *presentational* mode which proceeds by means of "direct, intensive insight." These are Langer's terms; they derive from Cassirer and they are, I think, both flexible and trustworthy. The discursive mode is familiar because it is what rhetoric chiefly describes: generalization is at the heart of all discourse and of course it is central to concept formation. But it is not the only mode of abstraction: we do not dream or perceive or create works of art by generalizing. One of the chief reasons that composition theory is stymied is the dependence on a brass instrument manufactured by General Semantics, the Ladder of Abstraction. Rhetoricians continually use it to explain how we climb from the positive earth to the dangerous ether of concept. But it's that metaphoric ladder itself that's dangerous. We could rename it The Ladder of Degrees of Generality to avoid the misleading notion that all abstraction proceeds by means of generalizing, but the ladder metaphor is inappropriate even to the generalizing central to concept formation, because, as Vygotsky points out, conceptualizing is "a movement of thought constantly alternating in two directions": only Buster Keaton could handle that ladder!

When we see a chair, we do not do so by a process of conscious generalizing; when the artist creates or finds the form by means of which feelings and thoughts are to be re-presented, he or she does so not by generalizing but by symbolizing insight, by *imagining*. In perception and in art, forming is primarily nondiscursive, but the point should be made explicitly that both modes of abstraction function in all acts of mind. We can save the term *imagination* to name only the nondiscursive, but having reclaimed it, I think there is much to be said for using it as a speculative instrument to focus on what it means to say that composing is a process of making meaning. The emblems I've discussed—"the intelligent eye" and "the thinking hand"—are images of imagination in the larger sense, that is, as the forming power of mind.

Notes

1. *The Collected Papers of Charles Sanders Peirce*, ed. Charles Hartshorne and Paul Weiss (Cambridge, Mass.: Harvard University Press, 1931–58), 1. 255.

2. *Speculative Instruments* (New York: Harcourt, 1955), 9.

3. *Visual Thinking* (Berkeley: University of California Press, 1969), 13.

4. *Forming/Thinking/Writing: The Composing Imagination* (Montclair, N.J.: Boynton/Cook, 1978), 13ff.

5. Kenneth Burke, *Permanence and Change* (1935; rpt. New York: Bobbs-Merrill, 1965), 6.

6. *Speculative Instruments*, 21.

20 Interpreting and Composing: The Many Resources of Kind

James F. Slevin
Georgetown University

Two quotations to begin. The first is from a psychological study of the composing process by Linda Flower and John Hayes. The second is from the well-received chapter on intuition in William Irmscher's *Teaching Expository Writing*.

> This model of the rhetorical problem reflects the elements writers actively consider as they write. It accounts for the conscious representation [of audience, persona, effect] going on as writers compose. . . . But in understanding a writer's process we can't ignore that rich body of inarticulate information Polanyi would call our 'tacit knowledge.' We think that much of the information people have about rhetorical problems exists in the form of *stored problem representations*. Writers do no doubt have many such representations for familiar or conventional problems, such as writing a thank-you letter. Such a representation would contain not only a conventional definition of the situation, audience, and the writer's purpose, but might include quite detailed information about solutions, even down to appropriate tone and phrases.[1]

> The more we have experienced, read, and reflected, the more likely we are to have spontaneous and sound intuitions in new situations. Intuition derives from both living experiences and experiences with language. Ben Shahn makes the point succinctly: 'Intuition in art is actually the result of prolonged tuition.' Intuition begins with our responses to isolated incidents in experience and results in a cumulative and synthesized attitude or set of principles, internalized and structured, ready to affect our future experiences. It is a kind of personal programming.
> Becoming a mature writer means essentially transcending skills by developing intuitions. Amateur writers depend upon prescriptions and rules for guidelines that mature writers sense intuitively.[2]

Both passages point to a characteristic of mature writers that literary critics would generally discuss in different terms. Perhaps the title of Rosalie Colie's last book, *The Resources of Kind*, best captures this other way of talking about how writers learn from, and intuitively draw upon, the inner resources of "stored representations." Colie's terms, less well known or at least less frequently employed by teachers of writing, are these: "kinds," "species," "types of discourse," "*genres.*"[3]

These different vocabularies used in discussions of literature and rhetoric suggest the need for some integrating perspective, some way of thinking about writing that unites a community of scholars and teachers interested in this subject. My concern is to survey some recent studies of genre and to explore the usefulness of genre-theory to the teaching of writing and critical reading. I hope my survey will provide a partial solution to the problem of our profession: the separation of literary studies from composition programs in American schools and colleges.

Recent Studies of Genre

This problem was discussed recently by J. Hillis Miller in an address to an audience of department heads:

> The worst catastrophe that could befall the study of English literature would be to allow the programs in expository writing to become separate empires in the universities and colleges, wholly cut off from the departments of English and American literature. . . . This belief rests on a simple premise. Learning to write well cannot be separated from learning to read well. . . .[4]

Miller goes on to suggest a solution to this problem, one calling on the theory of deconstructive criticism: " 'Rhetorical study' is the key to this integration,"[5] he asserts, and he sees rhetoric as a two-fold inquiry which considers, on the one hand, the nature and methods of persuasion, and, on the other, the study of the way language works, especially figurative language. Admitting that he simplifies somewhat, Miller sees persuasion being studied by those concerned with expository writing, while figurative language remains the province of literary critics like himself. But how do we bring them together?

Relating Literary and Nonliterary Discourse Forms

It seems to me that the problem which Miller identifies is really at the center of a much larger problem, the relationship between literary and nonliterary forms of discourse. We need a theory that accounts for a relationship among all forms of writing, and that accounts as well for the nature of composing and interpreting within those forms. If we must now examine the relationship between writing and thinking, we need first to develop a systematic framework for discussing all discourse, and the complex activities of creating and understanding discourse, *as discourse*. This seems an immense challenge, but fortunately we are not the first to face it.

Rosalie Colie has studied at length the problems for *literary* theory arising with the expansion of forms of written discourse in the Renaissance. In particular, theorists were faced with the increasing inclusion of nonliterary forms within works of the most important writers. In the first stages of the Italian Renaissance, she reports, the work of the greatest writers comprehended both literary and nonliterary kinds:

> In prose forms and poetic—in discourse, dialogue, biography, geograpy, epistle, as well as comedy, pastoral narrative, eclogues, triumphs, verse epistles, etc.—[Petrarch and Boccaccio] labored to present new models for good literature to Europe as a whole and Florentines in particular, always in generic form.[6]

This tendency persists throughout the European Renaissance. In Erasmus's *Adagia*, Burton's *Anatomy of Melancholy*, and Rabelais's *Gargantua and Pantagruel*, "the principal kinds exploited are nonpoetic: they carry an early humanist preoccupation into a later age, insisting on elevating to belletristic status kinds which had slipped below the level of artistic attention."[7] Even later, Sir Thomas Browne "worked to reestablish thematic genres—archaeology, geography, history and the like—genres which would have seemed fully literary to Petrarch and Boccaccio, as well as to the humanists of the quattrocento; and to restore to them their lost status as literature."[8] Similar elevations to literary status occur throughout this period. Donne does it for devotional books; Montaigne, through his *essais*, does it to autobiographical forms. Louis Martz has shown how many poets did it for forms of meditation; the dialogue, the debate, and the treatise are similarly elevated.

It is a period, then, in which both writers and theorists see the relationship between literary and nonliterary forms as either the *elevation* or the *incorporation* of the nonliterary into the literary. On the level of theory, the approach to this problem occurs within *poetics*, or the study of literary genres, the interrelations of genres, and the system of literature constituted by the hierarchy of genres. Renaissance poetics arose, in other words, as a response to the pressure within the culture to account for the interconnections of an increasingly vast repertoire of genres; generally, the solution was to accommodate by increasing appropriately the range of what constituted *literature*.

A Poetics of Writing

In our own time, we confront the need to account once more for the significance of so-called nonliterary forms. The theoretical orientation that enables us to respond rigorously to the works our best writers are producing, to the wide interests of our best critics, and to the institutional crises that Hillis Miller has identified, is an orientation I will call a *poetics of writing.*

A poetics of writing will concern itself not with universals but will instead concentrate on actual historical genres. So we will discuss not "the lyric," but the sonnet, elegy, aubade; not "narrative," but the primary epic, the historical novel, the gothic novel, the philosophical tale; not "drama," but Greek tragedy, the comedy of manners, the mystery play; not argumentative/referential modes, but the autobiography, the journal, the sermon.

A poetics of discourse is relevant to the relationship between writing and thinking because it allows us to specify the ways in which all thinking that occurs within available forms of discourse is historical. When contemporary rhetoricians make the claim that students think by writing, they often speak as if this thinking is free from cultural and social constraints, that there is to be attained, finally, some unmediated correspondence between writing and the discovery of self or of reality, some connection unmediated by culture and class. But the written forms within which such thinking actually and necessarily occurs are part of a cultural inheritance; this inheritance constitutes a system, a system whose structure (described by poetics) will reflect social, philosophical, and ethical systems within the culture as a whole.

Social Basis of Discourse Forms

Courses in writing need to examine these cultural assumptions, to examine directly the historicity of writing as a mode of thinking. Students should be encouraged to participate in the creation of this new poetics; it is, after all, a study of the *langue* of discourse, and therefore a study of their *competence* as writers, a study of the nature of discursive competence. The understanding of this competence in social terms reminds us that competence is an effect of a social institution. Frederic Jameson's insight that "genres are essentially contracts between a writer and his readers" and that this "generic contract itself [is] a relationship between producers and public"[9] must be understood in light of Alistair Fowler's observation that "*no* genre has ever been open to all social groups. . . ."[10] Indeed, most genres are not available to most people, and this is a condition of the culture and a condition (in another sense) of many of the students who now seek higher education

My informal studies of this matter have uncovered a rather clear connection between class origins and the range of generic options. This point may be too evident; I make it only to correct the somewhat misleading emphasis of Flower and Hayes, who attribute excellence in writing to conscious considerations of the components of the communication triangle and not to the range of "stored representations" which students derive from past reading and writing. Their view suggests such success in writing is a function of talent and education, ignoring the social origins of these problems. I am suggesting, in other words, that a poetics, which studies "available forms," must deal honestly with "availability" as a function of class.

In this regard, we can begin our attempts to solve this problem by observing Mina Shaughnessy's most helpful suggestion:

> If we accept the idea of academic genres, of certain basic forms students are expected to produce and teachers have defined in their minds if not in their instructions, there is no good reason why models of these genres cannot be presented to students so that they can locate on the sliding scale of 'proof' just what constitutes adequate evidence for their purposes.[11]

How can we best follow up on Shaughnessy's recommendation—and develop it further? How are genres learned so that they enter into the repertoire of available forms for our students? If it is unlikely that any "rule following" will genuinely improve their work, how do we cultivate in our students "the resources of kind" upon which they can draw intuitively? These questions point to the second area of concern for a poetics of writing, the area of the composing process and the larger process of learning to write.

Writers use genres differently from the theorist. They are concerned not with the social origins of genres and genre-systems but with making choices in the act of composing. Nevertheless, it is because genres exist as historical institutions that they can serve such an important function in the writing process. Todorov explains this function in terms of the "institutionalization" of genres:

> In a society, the recurrence of certain discursive properties is institutionalized, and individual texts are produced and perceived in relation to the norm constituted by this codification. A genre, literary or otherwise, is nothing but this codification of discursive properties.[12]

Reading, Writing, and Genre

Most critics identify five sorts of properties or aspects of discourse that can be used to codify genres: (1) aspects of subject matter (character types, conventional plot devices, etc.); (2) aspects of meaning (thematic properties); (3) aspects of organization (the relation of the parts among themselves); (4) pragmatic aspects (the relation between speaker and implied or actual audience); (5) aspects of style and language. Though certain aspects will be used to differentiate one particular genre from another, each genre is characterized by the way it combines all of these properties. In other words, a genre is a social form which guides the writer's fusion of meaning, organization, tone, effect, style, and diction within a discourse. Any individual discourse manifests one version of the way this fusion can occur within a particular genre. This observation allows us to reconsider and incorporate the ideas from Flower/ Hayes and Irmscher with which we began. Mature readers and writers grasp the total "rhetorical situation" of an utterance through an intuitive recognition of the type of discourse they are interpreting or composing. Moreover, the use of historical genres in both interpreting and composing helps us to explain the relationship between these two activities, reading and writing, and how one reinforces the other when a student is learning to do either. I will take up this final point, first by looking at the role of genre in interpreting, then by looking at its role in composing.

The Role of Genre in Interpreting

Critics like E. D. Hirsch and Alistair Fowler see genre functioning to assist the re-cognition of the author's meaning, the original intention which, they assume, remains available to interpretation. But the uses of genre with which I am concerned are not Hirsch's; I am interested in the way genres help modern interpreters open themselves to the properties and total form of a particular work. From this perspective, we do not read to make decisions about genres; rather, out of our own historical circumstances, we use our former experiences of discourse, carried within us in the forms of generic categories, to enrich our understanding of the work's properties—its tone, effects, theme, organization—and the manner of their fusion. In other words, we put genres to use in interpretation in order to enrich the significance of the works we read and to enhance the power of those properties most important to us. Only such powerful readings have an impact on writing.

An imaginative understanding of a work originates in the act of remembering and applying generic properties. In the hermeneutical theories of Gadamer and Bultmann, such an understanding is inseparable from the relevance or application of the text to one's life, and I would add, especially one's life as a writer. This kind of interpretation proceeds through the generic schemata of one's own time, even if the work originated within a different set of generic assumptions. For example, Fielding composed *Joseph Andrews* as a mixed form (*satura*), seeing its structure in terms of the interaction of discrete genres: the essay, the biography, the interpolated romance, the dialogue, the pastoral; it even included such minor forms as the sermon, literary criticism, the georgic, and prayer. In our own time—at least until quite recently—this work was read through the generic schemata of the great nineteenth-century novels, and was understood as a single kind, the novel, centering on an omniscient narrator's development of characters and their relationships. This is the way in which the work seemed most relevant, remained read at all. It was also the way writers found the work most useful to their own composition, especially their efforts to develop lovable quixotic characters and self-conscious, commenting, comic narrators. They read *Joseph Andrews* as they wrote.

A rich reading of a work involves making a choice about genre, and such choices derive from our own historicity. Richard Ohmann's recent essay, "Politics and Genre in Non-fiction Prose," clearly illustrates this point; I select it from among many because he discusses works we might find in a number of different Freshman English courses. Ohmann examines here a form he tentatively names "mediated speech" or "discourse of plural authorship," a class which includes Terkel's *Working*, Seifer's *Nobody Speaks for Me*, Rosengarten's *All God's Dangers*, Blythe's *Akenfield*, and many others, right up to what he calls "the epitome of the genre, Boswell's *Life of Johnson*."[13] It seems to me that, at a time when the interview is emerging as a dominant form (even in television, where it constitutes most of nonfictional programming), and at a time when film and drama are forcing us to develop a clearer concept of multiple authorship, such a generic placing of Boswell's *Life* surely enhances its significance for many readers. It helps us to concentrate on properties nearer our own interests, and strengthens the power of such properties for our own efforts as writers. Through this generic undestanding, it becomes a more useful model, allowing us to school ourselves on it.

In making this point about going to school, I wish to conclude by recalling the role of imitating models in classical education. Models

were used with a strong sense of historical change; imitation was not,
simply because it could not be, duplication; nor was it imitation of a
single work. One studied the models as they were grouped within
one's own system of genres, and one studied not to reproduce but to
adapt procedures from the past to new circumstances. Rosalie Colie
has noted that, in the Renaissance, notions of genre and generic
systems held primary social importance for writers as members of a
profession:[14]

> Rhetorical education, always a model-following enterprise, in-
> creasingly stressed structures as well as styles to be imitated in the
> humane letters—epistles, orations, discourses, dialogues, histories,
> poems—always discoverable to the enthusiastic new man of letters
> *by kind.*[15]

For our own purposes, we might add to that list of genres Ohmann's
"discourse of plural authorship," in order to stress that such reading
of *The Life of Johnson* benefits primarily our own writing. Deciding
that Boswell's *Life* belongs to the genre of the interview or "collaborative discourse" gives power to particular features of that work,
enabling those features to guide the writers' forming of their own
work. It is a process of generalization (abstracting form so that we can
group works around "essential" unifying characteristics) and then a
process of applying these generalizations in the interpretation of other
texts. This is the key point. In making decisions about the genre of a
work, we internalize the properties or aspects that were used in creating
the classification. These properties become firmly embedded as intuitive resources; they become the tacit knowledge that we intuitively
draw on in the composing process. As such, they serve to guide our
shaping of discourse.

Claudio Guillen, in his essay "On the Uses of Literary Genres,"
beautifully illustrates this process:

> A genre, in this sense, is a problem-solving model on the level of
> form. A "radical of presentation" like, say, the narrative, is a
> challenge—but the kind of challenge that sets up a confrontation
> between the poet and the "matter" of his task. More problems are
> raised than solved by the writer's determination, vis-à-vis the
> blank page, to "tell a story." But let us suppose that he is facing a
> particular genre like the picaresque novel. Let us say—hastily—
> that the picaresque model can be described in the following way:
> it is the fictional confession of a liar. This is already a provocative
> notion. Besides, the writer knows that the picaresque tale begins
> not in *medias res* but with the narrator's birth, that it recounts in
> chronological order the orphaned hero's peregrinations from city
> to city, and that it usually ends—that is, it can end—with either
> the defeat or the conversion of the "inner" man who both narrates

and experiences the events. What is at stake now, it seems to me—what is being constructively suggested—is not the presentation but the informing drive . . . that makes the whole work possible. Within the process of writing, the "radicals" and the "universal" fulfill their function at a very early stage; details of rhetoric and style play essential but partial and variegated roles; and only the generic model is likely to be effective at the crucial moment of total configuration, construction, *composition*.[16]

These moments of composing intensify reading, slowing it down and giving it added dimensions of interest. One begins to search for the principle of the total form, the relevance of particular features to that form, the means used to achieve certain effects.

The Role of Genre in Composing

Writing courses can encourage and teach these combined processes of reading and writing through a genre-centered approach to classifying, interpreting, and composing texts. Such an approach is profoundly distorted when essays in composition readers are arranged according to mistaken principles of classification. In these textbooks, *either* organization (for example, comparison/contrast) *or* subject matter ("self and society") *or* purpose (persuasion) serves as the principle of grouping, not the complex *fusion* of features that is the basis for generic classification. These books fail because the selected essays are grouped in simplistic and artificial ways. As Earl Miner notes, generic classification is central to interpretation, where comprehension of the nature and richness of a text depends on how we group this new text with others we already know.[17]

The "model essays" used in composition readers, in contrast, are severed from the complexity of the rhetorical situation. Students are asked to imitate only a small portion—an isolated feature—of the prose model. As a result, the writing becomes simply the performance of that feature, so that imitation as a way of learning how to read actively and comprehensively—to analyze all the dimensions of a text—is not encouraged, is, in fact, discouraged. The very concept of a model is thereby narrowed, even trivialized, and students are unable really to practice imitation, since the texts they encounter in their reading outside the course do not conform to such simplified categories. Students are not, in other words, learning how to imitate. If those who propose such models believe in the value of imitation (occurring beyond the particular assignment and course), they are in no way cultivating that practice. We may be helping students to create a particular product; but we are not developing an awareness of the process of relating reading and writing.

Teaching with a Genre Focus

Teaching this process involves two goals. First, we need to promote something like a spirit of "larceny" in our students, the notion that what they read is filled with techniques they can take for themselves, the way good writers constantly store away strategies for later use. We need to promote the idea that reading itself can enable writing, can answer their needs as writers, can teach them to write. Second, we need to undertake in our classrooms social and cultural examinations of the genres we ask students to compose.

An experiment by Flower and Hayes can illustrate how we can realize the first of these goals. Flower and Hayes gave two groups of writers—experienced, highly competent writers and inexperienced, "basic" writers—the following assignment: "Write about your job for the readers of *Seventeen* magazine, 13–14 year old girls."[18] These writers then went about this task, while noting on tape their representations of the rhetorical situation and particular goals. No reading seems to have been involved, or even allowed. One classroom strategy would be to ask our students to try the asignment as is, writing such an essay without consulting any other texts. As students encounter difficulties—even when encouraged and helped to consider audience, purpose, style, and so on—we can begin introducing a sequence of articles from that magazine itself. (It is likely that experienced writers faced with this particular assignment would naturally go first to read *Seventeen*, particularly the type of article they are requested to write.) By finding and classifying texts of the type they are assigned to compose, students will begin to notice patterns, common ways of implying an audience, achieving effects, establishing a tone. Reading these texts with an eye to producing a text of this type concentrates attention on these very features. What is important in such assignments is to create situations in which students feel the need to read in this way and experience the benefits of doing so. Such a procedure builds the habit of reading-to-write by introducing students to a process that carries over into many other assignments they will be given, both in and out of school. This process is essential to the way students can continue to teach themselves to write through their reading, can continue to improve their writing by enabling their reading to teach them.

A particularly useful practice in this regard is to encourage students to parody genres. If satire ordinarily adjusts our perspective to improve our vision, parody might be the form that most effectively gets us to see complex technique. This is particularly true of generic parody, as teachers of epic poetry or modern experimental drama or picaresque novels or five-paragraph themes will readily acknowledge. Parody concentrates the mind on features of organization, style, effect, implied audience that we all too easily pass over. And the playfulness of parody frees the author from any responsibility except to "caricature" qualities that characterize the genre. Writing in this way intensifies awareness when reading and encourages the process of connecting reading to specific problems faced when writing.

In addition to cultivating such uses of genre, a second pedagogical goal will be to help students analyze critically any genres they are asked to produce. Richard Ohmann illustrates what a critical examination of a genre can achieve. His approach can and should be applied to any genre we teach. He begins his study of the "discourse of plural authorship" with the most important question, "asking why such a genre exists at all and where it came from . . ."[19] Linking its present form to social and historical origins, he goes on to connect and explain the genre's defining characteristics: (1) author-speaker-audience relationships; (2) theme; (3) effect; (4) tone. (1) In his view, the speakers of these texts, the people quoted or paraphrased by the authors, have none of the literacy skills or access to media available to author and audience. "This means that the genre is grounded in a rather specific power relationship: author and audience are relatively well off, educated, and possessed of the skills that go with power or at least with influence in our society. The speaker is generally inferior in power and status to both."[20] (2) Such a rhetorical relationship entails characteristic themes. "Almost every book of this genre is written as if to shatter some stereotype or class term. . . ."[21] The genre exists to individualize people that the educated audience ordinarily think of as "undifferentiated masses."[22] (3) Given audience and theme, these books necessarily share a common effect: "the book leaves the audience naked, defenseless. . . . [It] makes the audience question where *they* stand in the power dynamic."[23] A book in this genre thereby "invites the audience . . . to take a critical stance toward the society; it poses anger and action as the only alternatives to guilt or smug ignorance. And it does this whether the author intends it or not."[24] (4) All of these considerations affect decisions about the tone of such pieces, for audience, theme, and intrinsic effect "are generic problems for the author [who stands] in an ambiguous position vis-à-vis the audience. . . . Shall he emphasize his similarity to them, as Coles does . . . ? Shall he merely recede into the background, letting the speakers' words do the work? How much interpreting and shaping shall he do?"[25]

These are exactly the questions that students should consider while composing their own "discourses of plural authorship" (among the most common types of writing now assigned). The critical analysis serves not only to improve the rigor of the students' reading but also to heighten their awareness of all they are learning when learning to write, since learning to write can be seen as an historical and social "event." Such considerations of genre in classroom teaching are therefore process-oriented, though the process here is not what is ordinarily meant by the "writing process"; rather, it includes numerous activities (imitation, parody, critical reading, cultural analysis) that cultivate those intuitive resources we draw on during all stages of the writing process. The basic objective of all these activities is not simply or even primarily to get students to submit good "products," but to get them to learn a process—of reading in a certain way and of using their reading when they write. Students learn how to read for the qualities of a type or genre, and to see how such reading is important to their development as writers. They become aware of the process whereby they can gain writing competence by such generic reading.

The "Writer"/"Reader" Dialogue

As writers build, through this process, a larger repertoire of genres and the aspects of genres that seem especially important to them, as they store within them these cultural forms that interrelate features of meaning, subject matter, organization, language, tone, and effect, their writing matures. This maturing process, as Guillen notes, is inseparable from critical reading:

> If a writer or a critic has decided that a group of works does exist, on the basis of certain significant resemblances, what matters then is the effectiveness of such a resolution, and the ways in which it helps him to understand and emulate those works. . . . These are decisions, then, *about* artistic form, and the writer who is making them is well on his way to his goal: the process of composition may have begun.[26]

The process of composition includes a writer's "active dialogue with the generic models of his time and culture."[27] But what sort of dialogue is this? A dialogue between the writer and his own reading? Between "writer" and "reader" in each of us? A dialogue through which *both* activities are guided and deepened, our reading "speaking to" our writing, our writing "responding" in kind? The dialogue metaphor suggests how reading generically invites us to write in turn, just as our writing (most professional writers confirm this) invites us to read in a certain way. To express this insight, Guillen repeatedly uses figurative language, trying to capture not a still, spatial model but a *process:*

> A genre is an invitation to form
> Looking forward, [genre] becomes above all else—to revise slightly my earlier words—an invitation to the matching (dynamically speaking) of matter and form
> [Actively inviting the writer to form in this way, the genre] offers a challenge, a foil, a series of guidelines[28]

Inviting, offering, guiding, challenging: what lively words to use about such a deadly academic subject as "genre"! Perhaps we will be the less surprised when we recall that "genre" comes from the Latin verb for the act of begetting, generating offspring of the same kind; from the Latin noun for birth, *kin*(d). This is one sense of the term that we need to recover, to restore to its place in the way we understand "genre." The writer—any writer, even Mina Shaughnessy's "Basic Writer"—desires to build a meaning out of the materials of his or her life and culture; this desire faces an extraordinary challenge: to give order to the fragmented, to bring to language what is no more than an intention to signify, to make public and shareable what is private and unique. The resources of kind do not simply guide; they empower us to meet this challenge.

The study of genre has a privileged position in our discipline; it alone ties unique acts of composing and understanding to the cultural conditions of that process. Genre, as the center of both interpretive and composing strategies, *enables* reading and writing. Understanding interpretation and composition in terms of genre, we can develop new ways of building courses in the arts of discourse. We can also build a curriculum that manages to integrate all the forms of writing (revising period and author courses, expanding the range of genre courses) and that also manages to integrate the teaching of texts and the teaching of composition, since these will now be seen as components of one type of course. All this is so because genre is the single category that enables us to *connect* the discourse system with acts of composing; in this connection, our work is of a kind and our discipline is one.

Notes

1. Linda Flower and John R. Hayes, "The Cognition of Discovery: Defining a Rhetorical Problem," *College Composition and Communication* 31 (1980): 25.

2. William Irmscher, *Teaching Expository Writing* (New York: Holt, Rinehart and Winston, 1979), 33–34.

3. Rosalie Colie, *The Resources of Kind: Genre-Theory in the Renaissance,* ed. Barbara Lewalski (Berkeley and Los Angeles: University of California Press, 1973).

4. J. Hillis Miller, "The Function of Rhetorical Study at the Present Time," in *The State of the Discipline,* ed. Jasper Neel, *ADE Bulletin* 62 (1979): 12.

5. Ibid.

6. Colie, 14.

7. Ibid., 82.

8. Ibid., 86.

9. Frederic Jameson, "Magical Narratives: Romance as Genre," *New Literary History* 7 (1975): 135.

10. Alistair Fowler, "The Life and Death of Literary Forms," *New Literary History* 2 (1971): 208.

11. Mina Shaughnessy, *Errors and Expectations* (New York: Oxford University Press, 1977), 271.

12. Tzvetan Todorov, "The Origin of Genres," *New Literary History* 8 (1975): 162.

13. Richard Ohmann, "Politics and Genre in Nonfiction Prose," *New Literary History* 11 (1980): 238.

14. Colie, 8.

15. Ibid., 4.

16. Claudio Guillen, *Literature as System: Essays Toward The Theory of Literary History* (Princeton: Princeton University Press, 1971), 120.

17. Earl Miner, "On the Genesis and Development of Literary Systems," *Critical Inquiry* 5 (1978): 345–6.

18. Flower and Hayes, 23–24.

19. Ohmann, 238.

20. Ibid., 240.

21. Ibid., 241.

22. Ibid.

23. Ibid., 242.

24. Ibid., 243.

25. Ibid., 242–3.

26. Guillen, 131.

27. Ibid., 128.

28. Ibid., 109, 111, 119.

21 Re-Viewing Reading and Writing Assignments

Phyllis A. Roth
Skidmore College

Among the major difficulties faced by composition instructors during the past few years (in addition, of course, to the need to work with the writing of nontraditional college students) has been the nature of the traditional writing about reading courses.[1] Relatively successful in the sixties, discussion of model expository essays followed by writing about them by writing like them ceased, for many of us, to be an effective way to deal with the writing and reading needs of many students during the seventies and into the eighties. Indeed, numbers of composition instructors discovered that the reading and writing assignments got in each other's way, that classes spent too much time on one at the expense of the other—that, in fact, the course design was incoherent. This was certainly my experience, and, to judge from their course evaluations, that of my students in the mid-seventies. In attempting to redesign the curriculum of the traditional writing about reading course with the goal of reuniting reading and writing, I employed the research and theory of those "reinventing the rhetorical tradition"[2] and the thinking of several literary theorists whose work in reader response criticism and theory seems to me to parallel developments in the "new rhetoric."

Specifically, James Britton's argument that expressive writing, writing for the self which traces the mind's efforts to think through problems and concepts, is the matrix of all writing[3] can be usefully coordinated with the positions of several reader response theorists: specifically with Norman Holland's emphasis on the individual's "identity theme" as it is manifest in a personal reading style[4] and with Stanley Fish's concept of "interpretive communities" which influence (or, as Fish would have it, determine) the making of meaning.[5] By working from both theoretical perspectives, one can design a curriculum which employs expressive reading and writing as the core of any language experience and assignment and as the basis for further assignments which require of students a move from the more personal to the more public[6]: from what Linda Flower has called "writer-based prose," that which traces the mind's private meditations and sequence of thought, to "reader-based prose," writing whose information and organization are sensitive to the needs of its particular audience.[7]

Revision as Key to Writing about Reading

In the context of the writing about reading course, I like to refer to both writer- and reader-based and to reader- and audience-based reading. In my own thinking, the organizing principle of this course design in particular is the concept of revision as both re-writing and re-seeing. However, the rethinking I have given this course has transformed the assignments in all the courses I teach. And since I wish primarily to emphasize the key concept of revision rather than any particular course sequence, I will discuss assignments I have used in several courses, assignments adaptable to a number of additional courses, even beyond the English department.

In many of the courses I teach, an initial problem for students is seeing beneath or behind the glossy print of any writing, that of professionals or their own, to discover its nature as artifact, as something made. In the language of the new rhetoric, they fail to see the process engaged in by writers who must constantly manipulate, re-think, resee—revise.

In discussing their focus on surface and product with my students, I have come to believe, with Linda Flower, that students suffer from the mystique of the perfect first draft. Convinced that professional writers *just write that way*, they are looking, we can only assume, for some magical potion that will enable them to write that way too. And, worse, the old method of teaching composition, the method I used with a notable lack of success until a few years ago, reinforced this view: read a model, write an essay, have it returned with comments describing what was wrong, go on to the next model and essay assignment.

Thus, for these students, learning *to view* and *to do* reading and writing as continuous processes of revision is, I believe, the most crucial component of the courses I teach. For me as the instructor, an essential recognition has been that afforded by reader response theories: when we complain that students do not read the material, we are often incorrect. Except for those who actually do not read the words on the page, literally do not open the book, students are, in fact, reading—typically in a highly individual (in this model the word "idiosyncratic" is theoretically inconsistent) fashion, based primarily on personal associations. Such "reader-based reading," to extend Flower's terms, has yet to be revised in the context of the course as interpretive community. And each course, each instructor and group of students, structures a unique interpretive community. Theoretically, then, viewing reading and writing in light of the definition of revision developed here should enable us to design a coherent curriculum for the writing about reading classroom, whether that classroom is in the humanities, social science, or natural science building. Such a curriculum is based on the following principles:

1. both reading and writing derive from an expressive, or personal and individual, matrix[8];

2. this personal matrix is the key to involving students in their reading and writing assignments;

3. the central learning experience is revision, revision in rereading and rewriting, both acts entailing a reseeing within the context (a) of the interpretive community which constitutes the meaning(s) of the text, and (b) of the needs of the audience toward whom the reading and writing are directed;

4. the course design needs to emphasize revision as students and instructor discuss the readings, as students rewrite, and as the instructor and peers comment on student writing. In this process, it is most important for the instructor not to berate students for having failed to see, but to help them to resee.

Exercises for the Revision Curriculum

To consider the two elements of the revision curriculum—viewing and doing—separately, I would like first to sketch out a series of exercises employing either nonfiction essays or fiction. These exercises can assist students in viewing the writing of professionals as efforts at solving the same sorts of problems with which students themselves might be personally concerned or which they face in our classes. The first task is what I think of as fracturing the surface of the reading (either of their own papers or of essays by professionals), a surface which appears icy smooth to the student whose mind, as a result, frequently slides off it, unable to grasp the relation between structure and sense. Beginning with a narrative reading and writing assignment, I ask students to do one of two types of prewriting exercise, depending on the appropriateness to the material being read.

One exercise requires the student to list events in their order of appearance in the text, then to revise to replace in actual chronological order. For example, a story like Joyce Carol Oates's "How I Contemplated the World from the Detroit House of Correction and Started My Life Over," which is not structured chronologically, but which requires an understanding of "actual" chronology to be fully coherent, provides an excellent beginning. Moreover, it is a story toward which most students will have strong personal reactions which can generate a debate beginning in disagreement and resulting, ideally, in a reading created by the interpretive community of the classroom. To further emphasize the point about writers' handling of time sequence, I often ask each student in the class or several in groups to compose their lists of events for different stories or essays, all of which all the students have read, then to discuss together or in groups the different types of chronological manipulation and effects achieved in the pieces. This exercise enables students not only to consider the relationship among alternative strategies dependent upon purpose, but also to realize that professional writers must consider the same sorts of alternatives that the student does. Students are then in a better position both to analyze manipulation of chronology in other stories or essays and in their own writing to free themselves from the tyranny of actual chronology or the chronology of cerebration.

Another type of exercise useful early in a writing about reading course—regardless of the reading material—enables the students to differentiate between description and interpretation, a distinction that is often made so reluctantly by many of my students that I suspect the ability to do so represents some type of cognitive leap. The difficulty students have is manifest in their responding to an assignment that requires analysis of a text by simply retelling the story. In response, I designed an assignment which requires that students do, in fact, retell the story but also that they go on, in a separate section, to interpret the significance of the story in relation to the action they have described. This assignment, therefore, asks them to see, and then to re-see, to "reread" the text as it moves them from their initial and personal sense of what is happening to a more highly generalized and communal sense of what happens.[9] Such an assignment early in the course allows me to remind them in later analytic assignments that their task is not to give me a plot summary. Moreover, it enables them to perceive a variety of strategies authors employ for achieving significance. For example, in this assignment as it might be applied to *Frankenstein*, students are able to discover that Shelley employs the techniques of nested stories and of mythological and Biblical allusion to reveal parallels among characters and therefore to generalize about human nature.

Another type of assignment appropriate for a course in which the reading material is literary allows students to explore, through their own writing of a story, the differences among literary genres. I have asked students, for example, to rewrite a scene in *Antigone* as a short story—or as part of one. This writing is preparatory to the second part of the assignment in which students write a comparison of fiction and drama, using Sophocles' version of *Antigone* and their own story as the data for the comparison. This is not only an excellent assignment for encouraging students to appreciate literary achievement, but it also encourages them to take their writing seriously and to see themselves engaged in the same effort as other writers. They are, in other words, revising reading and writing.

A similar assignment, and one which I use in several of my literature courses, I owe to Charles Moran.[10] The assignment requires that the student write a passage, following explicit directions which actually describe such a passage in a text they are reading or will be reading. For example, what follows is a fifteen-minute writing assignment to begin a class discussion of characterization in *Middlemarch* for an upper division Victorian fiction course. The directions are modelled on Eliot's description of Lydgate in book 2, chapter 18.

> Describe a character confronting a dilemma that constitutes a choice between two alternatives, each of which has advantages and disadvantages. Write one paragraph in which you first describe the choice in the character's terms, then show the character asking questions about the alternatives, then show the character's decision and try to make a summary narrative statement about the dilemma and, if relevant, about the decision. Try, as much as possible, to use the character's voice as s/he deliberates about the dilemma.

This exercise enables students to experience on their own the problems and choices writers face as they try to achieve a given purpose. In a literature course, it does indeed fracture the surface of the text, forcing the students to become aware of the structural, syntactical, and lexical levels of the writing. I have written such assignments directed toward students' understanding of dialogue, of irony, and of setting. Moreover, this assignment is frequently useful as a sort of role-playing technique, requiring that students assume different personae and anticipate audience response.

A final type of assignment, one adaptable to a variety of situations and useful throughout a writing about reading course, involves a series of writings which lead ultimately to a research paper. In this type of assignment in particular, one can again dramatize for students the continuum from expressive to transactional writing. Beginning with a journal entry, students explore, for example, a difficult family relationship, one which they experience or perceive as a problem, one which they hope to resolve. Then, they write an initial narrative paper for me to evaluate, in which their purpose is to reveal through the description of a particular incident the difficulty of the relationship. The next step is to compare that narrative to several essays or stories (for example, "Barn Burning," "The Nightingales Sing," "The Garden Party") by professional writers in order to generalize about a type of familial relationship or problem. At this point, students are usually exceptionally eager to discover the causes of the dynamics or problem and they are, therefore, appropriately motivated to begin library work for a critical paper which entails research. While this entire assignment is lengthy, it results in several pieces of writing, each increasingly decentered from the personal but based on it. Indeed, each piece of writing represents a type of writing we typically wish to cover in such a course—narrative, comparison/contrast, cause/effect, and the research paper. Moreover, it teaches students two crucial lessons: what it means to resee a problem, to revise with a different purpose and often a different audience in mind (I have found it useful on occasion to ask students to shift audiences for different parts of this project); and why the professional writer is moved to write about an idea or experience from a certain perspective. Thus, assignments are all designed to enable students to revise both their reading and their writing, to move back and forth, with control, between the personal, based on their own experiences and interests, and the public or transactional modes of reading and writing.

To focus more specifically on revision of student writing, I require not only that students in the composition course revise most of their papers, but that they learn to internalize revision strategies, resolving difficulties in previous versions by the next assignment. This demands of me a clear and shared sense of my expectations for each paper, expectations which ask the student to handle only a manageable number of tasks at a time but to learn skills cumulatively through the course. I attempt to achieve this goal through a three-fold strategy consisting of carefully described assignments, structured peer critiquing, and rigorous instructor comments on all student papers. In all three cases, the emphasis is on writing as revision.

Evaluation Criteria, Peer Critiquing, and Comments

In the assignment sheets, in addition to the definition of the assignment and the reading for that assignment, I stipulate the prewriting work that is to be done. Next, I suggest ways of going about the process of writing which will, first, enable the students to get all their ideas out on paper and, second, to transform that "writer-based" prose into "reader-based" prose. This seems to me crucial, whether one writes the directions out for students and/or discusses them in class, for here too we need to dispel the mystique of the perfect first draft—because of this mystique, students either become paralyzed at the thought of a graded writing assignment and as a result lose their ideas, or they write all their thoughts out as they come to mind, and, believing this writing to be final, they then type it up, regarding rewording and checking spelling to be revision. Nancy Sommers calls this belief a "thesaurus philosophy of writing"; because of it students, unlike experienced writers, "understand the revision process as a rewording activity."[11] Finally, I will indicate the grading criteria on the assignment sheet—that is, what I expect to see in the version they submit to me. The hardest part for me, of course, is sticking just to those criteria, but doing so is necessary to get students to trust and internalize revision strategies.

Two further points about the grading criteria: I begin with the "grossest" level of writing at the beginning of the course, believing that the more dramatic achievements in overall organization and focus will provide the greatest incentive to students and will entail the truest "revision" right from the start. Then, with each succeeding assignment, the criteria include previous achievements as well as additional components of reader-based prose which have been discussed in class, such as paragraph coherence, subtopic sentences, transition words, sentence combining, etc. Highly structured direction sheets for each assignment (which I try to keep under one page in length) are extremely valuable in other courses as well, perhaps even more valuable to the student in a course in which there is no opportunity to submit multiple drafts.

The second element of this approach is peer-critiquing, an invaluable aid to students' sense of audience and of themselves as serious writers and critics of writing. Most of us have probably employed this technique, so I will only say that my critiquing sessions are highly structured, requiring students to evaluate each other's papers by the same criteria I am using. I have found Kenneth Bruffee's descriptive outline a helpful tool here.[12] I have also found that I must intervene repeatedly in the groups during the early weeks to ask students to refrain from commenting only on each other's spelling, a habit they have formed which probably suggests something about comments they have received in the past.

Finally, and perhaps most important, are the instructor's comments on papers. I say "most important," because when I have done what I think to be a good job, students do pay very close attention and let me know that various comments were particularly useful. In "Placing Revision in a Reinvented Rhetorical Tradition," Douglas Butturff and Nancy I. Sommers also emphasize the role of instructors' comments in enabling students to view the writing process as recursive and to do substantial rewriting.[13] In any course I teach, I attempt to do the following on all student papers, whichever version I am reading:

1. comment both marginally and at the end of the paper on what the student has done well;

2. restrict my criticisms to those criteria I have previously announced;

3. evaluate for the student where the paper falls on a continuum from extreme writer-based prose to beautifully reader-based prose (that is, did the student only discover a focus in the last paragraph, or does the last paragraph contradict the first, or is the paper a narrative of what the student thought first, second, next, etc.). I have found it extraordinarily useful to say to students, for example, "You're giving me a first draft—it's a necessary stage in the process but not a version you should be handing in." This is much more helpful both for the writing and for the ego than "this is a mess."

4. I suggest to the student (more or less explicitly, depending on my sense of the student's current capabilities) *how to go about* revising; that is, not just what the product should be but how to get there. More than anything, revision is what we want them to internalize, and we must therefore help them learn how to proceed. Frequently, I will summarize the paper as it is, in a sentence or two, enabling the student to see the whole paper as perhaps she or he has been unable to so far.

In looking over these comments as I grade the revision (students return the first versions with their revisions), I note with satisfaction that students frequently underline this section of my comments, often making notes of their own in the margin as additional reminders. To summarize, then, my sense is that I am now teaching a coherent, well-balanced course which will actually show students how to go about reading and writing, through viewing both as revising, and through ensuring that all major components of the course reinforce this process model of what actually happens as readers and writers reread and rewrite.

Notes

1. This essay is based both on a paper discussing the classroom uses of reader-response criticism and theories, delivered at the Skidmore Conference on "The Writer's Mind" and on a paper describing teaching revision, delivered at the March 1982 meeting of the Conference for College Composition and·Communication.

2. I am employing the title and am grateful for the collection edited by Aviva Freedman and Ian Pringle (Conway, Ark.: L&S Books, 1980).

3. James Britton, et al. *The Development of Writing Abilities (11–18)* (London: Macmillan Education, 1975).

4. See *5 Readers Reading* (New York: W. W. Norton & Co., 1975); "UNITY IDENTITY TEXT SELF," *PMLA* 90 (October 1975); "Identity: An Interrogation at the Border of Psychology," *Language and Style* 10 (Fall 1977): 199–209; "Literary Interpretation and Three Phases of Psychoanalysis," *Critical Inquiry* 3 (Winter 1976): 221–233. The work of David Bleich is also important. See the debate between Holland and Bleich in *New Literary History* 7 (Winter 1976). See also Bleich's *Readings and Feelings: An Introduction to Subjective Criticism* (Urbana, Ill.: NCTE, 1975) and *Subjective Criticism* (Baltimore: The Johns Hopkins University Press, 1978).

5. See "Normal Circumstances, Literal Language, Direct Speech Acts, the Ordinary, the Everyday, the Obvious, What Goes without Saying, and Other Special Cases," originally in *Critical Inquiry* 4 (Summer 1978): 625–644, now included in *Is There a Text in This Class?: The Authority of Interpretive Communities* (Cambridge, Mass.: Harvard University Press, 1980, 1982).

6. Others have seen the value of such a combination also. In "In Search of Meaning: Readers and Expressive Language" [in *Language Connections: Writing and Reading Across the Curriculum,* ed. Toby Fulwiler and Art Young (Urbana, Ill.: NCTE, 1982), 107–22], Bruce Petersen says that "readers, like writers, proceed from a personal matrix of experiences, facts, social conventions, and conceptual and moral development towards creating meaning from a text" (p. 108). Further Petersen argues that "one of our jobs as teachers is to assist students in moving beyond personal knowledge to knowledge shared by a community, one shaped by cultural values and traditions" (p. 119) and that we need, therefore, to employ the student's personal response in our teaching of communal values and traditions.

7. Linda Flower, *Problem-Solving Strategies for Writing* (New York: Harcourt Brace Jovanovich, 1981), 143ff.

8. More or less individual, since as Fish would argue, the student has already read the text, in the sense of having learned how to make meanings

through participation in a number of interpretive communities, including family, religion, nationality, and previous classrooms, before he or she enrolls in our courses.

9. In alluding here to differing levels of abstraction as well as to a private/ public continuum, I am also indebted to the work of James Moffett. See, in particular, *Teaching the Universe of Discourse* (Boston: Houghton Mifflin, 1968).

10. "Teaching Writing/Teaching Literature," *College Composition and Communication* 32 (February 1981), 21–29.

11. "Revision Strategies of Student Writers and Experienced Adult Writers," *College Composition and Communication* 31 (December 1980): 381. For Sommers, students' efforts to rewrite are "teacher-based, directed towards a teacher-reader who expects compliance with rules" (p. 383). Sandra Schor's research, described elsewhere in this volume, points to the same student beliefs and behavior.

12. Kenneth A. Bruffee, *A Short Course in Writing*, 2nd ed. (Cambridge, Mass.: Winthrop Publishers, 1980), 36–38.

13. In *Reinventing the Rhetorical Tradition*, 99–104.

22 Metaphor, Thinking, and the Composing Process

Donald McQuade
Queens College, CUNY

Early in February 1978, the University of Chicago, supported in part by a grant from the National Endowment for the Humanities, sponsored a symposium entitled "Metaphor: The Conceptual Leap." Included among the distinguished literary critics, theologians, art historians, psychologists, and philosophers who addressed that meeting were Wayne Booth, Ted Cohen, Donald Davidson, Paul de Man, Clifford Geertz, W. V. Quine, and Paul Ricoeur. Their work on metaphor— and especially Paul Ricoeur's—provides a basis for speculating about the cognitive and compositional implications of metaphor. The more I have read about metaphor, the more convinced I have become that it bears *structural* implications and possibilities for writing courses that extend far beyond metaphor's value as an aid to invention. I am now reasonably confident that encouraging students to work with metaphor can help them understand—perhaps more appreciably than has been previously recognized—the processes of both their own thinking and their own writing.

The paper Ricoeur read at this conference—an essay with the imposing title of "The Metaphorical Process as Cognition, Imagination, and Feeling"[1]—constitutes both a precis and an extension of his long-awaited and now highly acclaimed and controversial study *La Metaphore vive* (1975), translated into English in 1977 as *The Rule of Metaphor*.[2] In this seminal study, Paul Ricoeur analyzes the importance of metaphor in literary, linguistic, philosophical, and aesthetic theories from Aristotle to the structuralists. Along the way, Ricoeur also charts a rather provocative course for metaphor in contemporary rhetorical theory. He proposes to return metaphor to a more central position in the study of rhetoric, "to understand in a new way," as he says, "the very workings of tropes, and based on this, eventually to restate in new terms the question of the aim and purpose of rhetoric."[3]

Of all the many facets of his work, Ricoeur's studies of metaphor bear—in my judgment—the richest implications and prospects for the theory and practice of teaching composition. I would like to explore the nature of metaphor within the broad context of Ricoeur's work,[4] *specifically* examining how thinking about metaphor can help us to understand rhetoric and the composing process more fully and to teach them more effectively. A close look at the workings of metaphor may also help us get at some essential features of the process of thinking. Given the still highly speculative nature of this subject, I will consider only a few points about metaphor—those which carry at once the broadest theoretical interest and the greatest practical dividends for teachers of composition.

"Metaphor," from the Greek word meaning *transfer*, is a process by which we discover resemblance between different kinds of things or ideas. When we identify something as though it were like something else, when we experience or understand one kind of thing in terms of another, when we discover the similar in the dissimilar, we are using metaphor. Metaphor is often distinguished from simile, in that metaphor works by implicit comparison ("Her mind is a computer"), whereas simile makes the comparison explicit through the use of "like" or "as" ("Her mind is like a computer"). I am using "metaphor' to cover both kinds of rhetorical procedures.

Working with metaphor in composition classes can restore creative power and freedom to our students' language. Metaphor is, after all, perhaps the most exquisite and powerful form of liberation available to *any* writer. To redeem the integrity of metaphor, to restore to it the power of cognition, metaphor must at once be freed from the debilitated identity of being no more than a simple decorative feature of language. It must be returned to a more productive role as one of the most inventive aspects of rhetoric—as a frame for building meaning in writing.

Nearly all discussions of metaphor focus primarily on poetic and philosophical formulations. This does not preclude, however, the possibility of applying and extending what can be said about the metaphoric operations of poetry and philosophy to what may characteristically happen when a writer works with metaphor in more widely circulated forms of prose. Ricoeur phrases the question this way: "Might metaphor not be a poetical process extended to prose?" Ricoeur musters a somewhat promising but also rather cautious response: "I can say at least provisionally that the difference lies not in the process but in the end that is envisaged."[5] In poetry, metaphor refers back on itself. In prose, metaphor bears reference beyond itself, celebrating an idea rather than itself. But it is this similarity of *process* that should interest teachers of composition, and perhaps especially those of us who are searching for ways to apply the same kind of intellectual energy and rigorous research to understanding and teaching the composing process as we have reserved previously to exploring and writing about literature.

Ricoeur's Theory of Metaphor

Ricoeur devotes a substantial part of *The Rule of Metaphor* to an encyclopedic catalogue of the theories of metaphor from Aristotle to the present, documenting in the most convincing terms the historic decline of the status of rhetoric in general and metaphor in particular. Ricoeur reports, for example, that

> Greek rhetoric had an impressively large scope and a conspicuously more articulated internal organization than rhetoric in its dying days. As the art of persuasion, the aim of which was the mastery of public speech, rhetoric covered the three fields of argumentation, composition, and style. The reduction of all these to the third part, and of that to a simple taxonomy of figures of speech, doubtless explains why rhetoric lost its link to logic and philosophy itself, and why it became the erratic and futile discipline that died during the last century.[6]

If, in the centuries following Aristotle, rhetoric was reduced to little more than "the art of pleasing," metaphor was relegated to an even more lowly function—simple ornamentation. Rhetoric, Ricoeur notes, came to be associated exclusively with style, which in turn, "shrank to a classification of figures of speech, and then to a theory of tropes." Given what he saw as the lamentable state of rhetorical theory and, more particularly, of metaphor's place in it, Ricoeur announced the principal task of what he calls "a new rhetoric" to be first to "reopen the rhetorical regions that had been progressively closed." Yet, such a goal would not be so much to restore what he calls "the original domain of rhetoric"[7] as it would be to understand the workings of the metaphoric process itself as one way of coming to terms with cognition and imagination. To do so would be implicitly to give new purpose and bearing to the study of rhetoric. There again, Ricoeur proves helpful.

Ricoeur's most consistent effort has been to challenge the prevailing rhetorical theories of metaphor—both traditional and current—which identify the word as the basic unit of metaphoric reference, to free metaphor, as he says, from "the tyranny of the word."[8] Ricoeur proposes to shift what he calls "the centre of gravity of the theory of metaphor from the noun to the sentence or discourse."[9]

In effect, Ricoeur envisions metaphor as a system of predication rather than of denomination—of producing and shaping meaning rather than simply designating it. Take, for example, our experience of "rising prices." Metaphorically, we can refer to this experience as an entity through the noun "inflation." But after we have made this lexical substitution, the significance of our experience of "inflation" surfaces when we *extend* this metaphorical process. We can say, for example, that "inflation takes its toll when we shop" and "lowers our standard of living," or that "inflation" is something we can "deal with" or even "combat" if we have to.[10] In such instances, Ricoeur argues that, unlike the lexical impact of metonymy and synecdoche, the full weight of meaning in the metaphorical process emerges within the larger context of the sentence.[11] In this respect, Ricoeur amplifies Max Black's contention in *Models and Metaphors* that the word may be the "focus" of metaphoric activity, but the sentence provides its "frame."[12] Having meaning emerge metaphorically within the frame of a sentence makes metaphor a transactional phenomenon rather than simply a form of lexical substitution. As such, metaphor can create—through its interaction with the other elements of the sentence—a greater contextual richness than is possible with either metonymy or synecdoche.[13]

In his lecture at the Chicago conference on metaphor, Ricoeur completed his formulation of a semantics of metaphor, fusing it with a psychology of the imagination. He claims, in fact, that the theory of metaphor developed by Richards, Beardsley, Black, Berggren, and others "cannot achieve its own goal without including imagining and feeling, that is without assigning a *semantic* function to what seem to be mere *psychological* features and without, therefore, concerning itself with some accompanying factors extrinsic to the informative kernel of metaphor."[14] Ricoeur demonstrated in his Chicago lecture that metaphor may well be one very productive way to get untranslatable information down on paper. In this sense, metaphor produces more than association in thinking and writing; it highlights the assimilative powers of the mind. "To imagine," Ricoeur says, "is not to have a mental picture of something but to display relations in a depicting mode." "Seeing"—itself a metaphor for the process of imaging or imagining—becomes then, as Ricoeur notes, "the concrete milieu in which and through which we see similarities."[15] If this is true, then imagination should no longer be defined solely in terms of mental images but in terms of rhetorical sentences. As Richard Young, Alton Becker, and Kenneth Pike have so ably shown in their book,

Rhetoric: Discovery and Change, thinking and writing create a rela-
tional "field" of meaning.[16] Metaphor, in effect, is nuclear rather than
atomistic—an intellectual activity that connects rather than isolates
the distinctive features of our experience.

Metaphor assimilates what previously seemed incompatible. In this
sense, it is more appropriate to state that metaphor creates the likeness
rather than that metaphor simply gives verbal form to some preexis-
tent similarity. In this respect, metaphor involves a conceptual leap.
Imagination, accordingly, is for Ricoeur the ability "to produce new
kinds [of congruence] by assimilation and to produce them not *above*
the differences, as in the concept, but in spite of and through the
differences."[17] It is the context of the metaphoric tension between the
remote and the near that allows us, as Ricoeur suggests, to speak of
"the fundamental metaphoricity of thought to the extent that the
figure of speech we call 'metaphor' allows us a glance at the general
procedure by which we produce concepts."[18] And it is the energizing
tension in metaphor between the remote and the near, between the
abstract and the concrete, between the general and the particular, that
brings us—and potentially our students as well—closer to the realities
of thinking—and by extension, writing as well.

Uses of Metaphor in the Writing Process

Ricoeur's work on metaphor reveals several new prospects and
resources for composition theorists and teachers. As I have tried to
suggest, the metaphorical process, as Ricoeur has analyzed it, may
well serve as a model of the way we formulate concepts. "If metaphor
is a competence, a talent," Ricoeur writes, "then it is a talent of
thinking. Rhetoric is just the reflection and the translation of this
talent into a distinct body of knowledge."[19] As the research of Ricoeur
and others suggests, we can neither write nor think without metaphor.
Should we choose to work closely with metaphor in our composition
classes, we ought to encourage our students to remember that it is
much more than a cosmetic device; it is a powerful mental act that
underlies all discourse and pervades all rhetorical structures and
strategies. Metaphor does, of course, play a vital role in enlivening
and vivifying the surface of prose, but it can also function structurally
at much deeper levels of thinking and writing. By allowing writers
to form images and concepts of one thing in terms of another,
metaphor helps perceive new connections that can frequently lead
to unexpected insights.

Metaphor and Invention

At the most fundamental level of the writing process, working with metaphor is one very practical way to begin exploring a subject and bridging what can at times be the difficult gap between having an idea and getting an essay started. As such it also can play an important role in the heuristics of invention. Metaphor supplies writers with a set of associated terms and concepts to be drawn on throughout the composing process. Metaphor, in effect, trades on the "polysemic" elements of language: that is, the property of words to bear multiple meanings. But rather than encourage this openness in language, many teachers of expository writing try to minimize the polysemic elements of language far too early, to be too concerned with being too precise too soon. Working with metaphor's potential for multiplicity of meaning is an excellent way, I think, for students to get started. The polysemic elements of metaphor may be viewed as another form of connotation, but one which has a structure implicit in it. In composition classes, then, metaphor may well serve as a natural structural extension of working with connotation. As such, metaphor can serve not only as a compositional activator, as an exercise in invention, but also as a way to discover the structural implications of any form of composing.

Consider, for example, the polysemic elements embedded in comparing an argument to a battle. Although these are obviously two quite distinct concepts, one can be understood—and even structured— in terms of the other. If we were to pursue the connotations—the associative implications—of the word "battle," we would discover, for example, that we could talk about "attacking" the weak points in our "opponent's" position. We could also charge that a particular claim is "indefensible"; we could "gain ground" in an argument, and the like. But note also that each of these points could serve the writer as the basis for structuring an entire essay.

The Controlling Metaphor

Metaphor can also be extremely valuable in pointing out directions for thinking at the outset of writing. It can exert a continuing presence by helping to guide writers to their compositional destinations. Some of the resemblances that naturally surface as writers begin to think about a subject, or that automatically come together as they link up operational words, may—if they take the time to track out the movements of their preliminary thoughts—activate a broader and thicker set of connections than they may have at first supposed their subjects were capable of suggesting. Take, for example, an assignment on advertising's influence on American life. In compiling a set of associations for the word "advertising," students could easily come up with a list of the goods and services promoted through advertising—"food," "clothes," "drugs," "cars," "cigarettes," and so on. If they decide to focus on automobile advertising, they could come up with such additional terms as "expense," "independence," "fun," "status," "mobility," and the like. They might also notice that of these terms the word "mobility" is a particularly promising metaphor that could help them explore their subject: a great deal of automobile advertising appeals to the consumer's desire for both physical mobility (travel) and social mobility (status). They could open their essay on just such a note: "Americans like to think of themselves as a highly mobile people—both on the road and in society—and no popular art confirms this national characteristic more emphatically than advertisements for automobiles." Should students decide to limit themselves to one of the key resemblances and shape their composition around it, they will have discovered the pleasures of working with controlling metaphor, a resourceful feature of rhetoric that has remained negected for far too long in writing courses.

Metaphor not only textures the sentence anyone writes, but it also thickens writing by embedding an idea in a three part structure: A is to B with respect to C. Students who work with metaphor usually strengthen the substance of their sentences: they can demonstrate that they know A, that they know B, and that they know the relationship between A and B. To say, for example, that an argument (A) is like a journey (B) is to recognize that they share numerous characteristics (C, C_1, C_2, etc.). We "set out" on both; we "move to the next point" in each; we can "cover a great deal of ground" in both; we can get "lost" in each, and so on.

Metaphor is also a very useful form of redescription. It enables writers to reconsider a subject from a different angle. As such, working with metaphor can be an invaluable aid to revision. It can empower students to re-see their idea freshly—and in novel terms, in terms that bear structural implications. Suppose, for example, that a student has completed a first draft on Poe's influence on the development of the American short story. In revising the draft, the student might decide that Poe's theory can be described metaphorically as a plant. The terms that gravitate around this metaphor ("seeds," "planted," "fertile," "off-shot," "fruition," etc.) could help the student reexamine both the substance of what has been said and the design for saying it.

Contextual Meaning

Studying metaphor in writing classes, moreover, is perhaps one of the most accessible ways to chart the mind's move from describing to evaluating experience. And since, if Ricoeur is right, metaphor involves contextual rather than simply lexical shifts in meaning, young writers are more likely to be more attentive to the broader stretches and resonances of meaning—to meaning as it emerges in rhetorical situations—in sentences and paragraphs rather than primarily in individual words. In effect, metaphor is a wonderful way to teach meaning in context.

There is another special benefit of working with metaphor in composition classes—it provides even the least experienced writer an immediate sense of success. Everyone can and does make metaphors. And by studying metaphor, young writers have easier access to understanding the writing process, to coming to terms with the distinctive qualities and operations of their own minds.

Conclusion

Metaphor can play a critical role throughout the entire process of composition. It can stimulate, screen, and direct writers' preliminary thinking, help guide their selection of material, control their particular emphasis, and, in general, furnish them with a uniform frame of reference within which individual observations, ideas, and snippets of information about a subject can be enhanced and consolidated. Metaphor can be a particularly valuable resource for helping writers generate productive thoughts and construct well integrated compositions. In sum, metaphor can not only actualize but stabilize the nascent meaning of a composition.

Ricoeur reminds us that we have yet to explore fully what Max Black calls "the emerging character" of metaphor, its capacity to bear "specially constructed systems of implications."[20] This is perhaps the most distinctive cognitive and compositional feature of metaphor, but one, as Ricoeur suggests, that may be dependent on the apparent "failure" of the metaphor's literal meaning. Metaphor in this sense serves once again as a cognitive paradigm—metaphor is used, as Ricoeur says, "to break the hold of an inadequate interpretation."[21] In effect, metaphor helps writers to move beyond the limits of a single interpretation and to examine the full range of implications embedded in the writer's original idea. In the case of the essay on Poe, then, the plant metaphor enables the student to see the subject in entirely new terms, and with the prospect of both a new interpretation and a new organization more clearly in sight. Metaphor creates a new order at the expense of another one. Thus the very nature of the metaphoric process facilitates what Ricoeur sees as the essential transition from semantics to hermeneutics.

The operational significance of the new thinking about metaphor, synthesized as it is in the writings of Paul Ricoeur and others, has only begun to surface in either textbooks or theoretical studies devoted to composition.[22] Both still seem bound up in the traditional belief that metaphor is, as Plato charged, a cosmetic art. My purpose here has been to call some attention to the potential of metaphor and to place it in the context of our work in composition not only as an opportunity for spontaneous creativity for ourselves and our students but also as an occasion when the power of eloquence and the logic of probability meet. I would also like to think that along the way I have helped to open the implications of Ricoeur's work for further studies of the rhetorical structures embedded in metaphor. It is, after all, the structures of rhetoric that make such discussions possible in the first place.

Notes

1. Published originally in *Critical Inquiry* 5 (Autumn 1978) and reprinted in *On Metaphor*, ed. Sheldon Sacks (Chicago: University of Chicago Press, 1979), 141-157.

2. *La Métaphor vive* (Paris: Editions du Seuil, 1975); *The Rule of Metaphor: Multi-Disciplinary Studies of the Creation of Meaning in Language*, trans. Robert Czerny, with Kathleen McLaughlin and John Costello, S.J. (Toronto: University of Toronto Press, 1977).

3. Ibid., 45.

4. For a full listing of Ricoeur's numerous articles and book-length studies (through 1974), see Dirk F. Vansina, "Bibliographie de Paul Ricoeur," *Revue philosophique de Louvain* 60 (1962): 394-413; 66 (1968): 85-101; and 71 (1974): 156-181. For a more recent list of Ricoeur's work, see *The Philosophy of Paul Ricoeur*, ed. Charles E. Reagan and David Stewart (Boston: Beacon Press, 1978), 255-256.

5. *The Rule of Metaphor*, 35.

6. Ibid., 28.

7. Ibid., 45.

8. See, for example, "Creativity in Language: Word, Polysemy, Metaphor," trans. David Pellhauer, *Philosophy Today* 17 (1973): 97-111; "Metaphor and the Main Problem of Hermeneutics," *New Literary History* 6 (1974-75): 95-110. Both essays are reprinted in *The Philosophy of Paul Ricoeur*, cited above. See also "The Metaphorical Process as Cognition, Imagination, and Feeling," in *On Metaphor*, 141-46; and *The Rule of Metaphor*, 13-24.

9. *The Rule of Metaphor*, 15.

10. This example—as well as a few that will follow—are adapted from an excellent study by George Lakoff and Mark Johnson, *Metaphors We Live By* (Chicago: University of Chicago Press, 1980), especially chapter 6, "Ontological Metaphors." I am also grateful to Robert Atwan for several examples.

11. See especially, "Creativity in Language," *passim*, and "The Decline of Rhetoric: Tropology," in *The Rule of Metaphor*, 44–64.

12. Max Black, *Models and Metaphors: Studies in Language and Philosophy* (Ithaca, N.Y.: Cornell University Press, 1962), 25–47.

13. Here Ricoeur's thinking about metaphor follows the auspicious lead set by, among others, I. A. Richards, Monroe Beardsley, Douglas Berggren, and Max Black, all of whom demonstrated that the figurative uses of words—and metaphors in particular—do convey enough *new information* to make them much more significant aspects of thinking and writing than earlier theorists had allowed. See I. A. Richards, *The Philosophy of Rhetoric* (London: Oxford University Press, 1936); Monroe C. Beardsley, *Aesthetics* (New York: Harcourt, Brace and World, 1958) and "The Metaphorical Twist," *Philosophy and Phenomenological Research* 22 (1962): 293–307; Douglas Berggren, "The Use and Abuse of Metaphor," *Review of Metaphysics* 16 (December 1962): 237–258; 16 (March, 1963): 450–472; Max Black, *Models and Metaphors*.

14. "The Metaphorical Process as Cognition, Imagination, and Feeling," in *On Metaphor*, 141–142.

15. Ibid., 148.

16. Richard Young, Alton L. Becker, and Kenneth Pike, *Rhetoric: Discovery and Change* (New York: Harcourt, Brace Jovanovich, 1970).

17. "The Metaphorical Process as Cognition, Imagination, and Feeling," in *On Metaphor*, 146.

18. Ibid., 147. See also, Hans-Georg Gadamer, *Truth and Method*, trans. Garrett Bardon and John Cumming (New York: Seabury Press, 1975).

19. *The Rule of Metaphor*, 80.

20. *Models and Metaphors*, 43.

21. *The Rule of Metaphor*, 302.

22. See Donald McQuade and Robert Atwan, ed., *Thinking in Writing*, 2nd ed. (New York: Alfred A. Knopf, 1983).

23 The Other Speaking: Allegory and Lacan

Robert Viscusi
Brooklyn College, CUNY

Everyone has heard, and many have said, "I don't know what I want to say until I see it." In writing, there springs up quickly a dialogue between writer and the text being written, so that it is characteristic for us to generate a third line by reading over lines one and two. Those lines which have already been set down acquire, while the writing continues, a provisional authority. They become what-I-see-of-what-I-want-to-say. But, no longer merely what-I-want-to-say, they become what-is-said and what-is-written. They are no longer the writer's voice but something other, something removed to the plane of what may be desired or imitated or obeyed.

The process of making one's own voice other *is* the process of writing. From this basic observation, I want to draw a speculation—that the process of writing involves of necessity a degree of allegory. ἄλλos-ἀγορία means, literally, other-speaking. We usually take this to mean "speaking otherwise than one seems to," but the very notion of allegory suggests the unaccountable authority that almost anything which is written immediately acquires—even, and perhaps especially, in the view of the person writing it. Allegory means other-speaking—the, or some, other speaking—and, because one finds in the written word the utterance of an other or of an Other, one discovers also in that word entirely new dimensions and meanings. Our encounter with these meanings constitutes much of what happens when we write, and it will be useful to compare two ways of thinking about these meanings, one familiar and one relatively novel.

Dante's Fourfold Hermeneutic

In the well-worn medieval approach to the reading of scripture, the possible meanings of a text fall into four categories: literal, allegorical, tropological or moral, and anagogical. The method is forever summarized in a famous distich:

Littera gesta docet, quid credas allegoria,
Moralis quid agas, quo tendas anagogia.[1]

The literal tells you what happened, the allegory what you believe, the moral what you do, the anagogy whither you go. In practice, this means that for the allegorizing reader the simplest narrative can carry the burthen of not only the bard who speaks but also of the architect of belief and of the arbiter of justice and, indeed, of the Father in Heaven. While this branch of hermeneutics has a long and elaborate history, its implications for the *writer* have never appeared so clearly as they do in Dante's letter to Can Grande della Scala:

> ... it is one sense which we get through the letter, and another which we get through the thing the letter signifies; and the first is called literal, but the second allegorical or mystic. And this mode of treatment, for its better manifestation, may be considered in this verse: "When Israel came out of Egypt, and the house of Jacob from a people of strange speech, Judaea became his sanctification, Israel his power." For if we inspect the letter alone the departure of the children of Israel from Egypt in the time of Moses is presented to us. If the allegory, our redemption wrought by Christ; if the moral sense, the conversion of the soul from the grief and misery of sin to the state of grace is presented to us; if the anagogical, the departure of the holy soul from the slavery of this corruption to the liberty of eternal glory is presented to us. And although these mystic senses have each their special denominations, they may all in general be called allegorical, since they differ from the literal and historical; for allegory is derived from *alleon*, in Greek, which means the same as the Latin *alienum* or *diversum*.[2]

Dante hears, as it were, in the Psalm, not one voice but serried choirs of voices. So vast an array of comment, hovering massively above every word, might seem convenient enough for the reader of texts but paralyzing for the writer. Far from being oppressed or stifled, however, by the other-speaking (or the Other speaking) in his poem, Dante seems positively liberated by it. He appears, in truth, to float and to rise upon its desirability, its imitability, and its authority, arriving at last at a vision which even the most skeptical reader must recognize as having dimensions that somehow exceed the range of mere conscious intent. That is, in *Paradiso*, Dante writes with all the numinous force of the other and the Other who speak in his lines.

Lacan's Drama of the Unconscious

This authority brings us to the second and more novel method I want to use in thinking about the meanings of the words spoken by the other in allegory. According to Lacan, we find our utterance, initially no less than continuously, in our relationship to the other.[3] Lacanian theory posits three others. The first is the Mother, the second the Father, and the third is the Name-of-the-Father, also called the Law. Now these others are not persons at all, but relationships. The Mother is the primordial other, from whom the infant does not experience any separate existence in the beginning: in knowing the separation, the infant knows for the first time of the being of the other, feels for the first time the anguish of desire. In his alienation from her, he also experiences alienation from himself, whom he had identified with her, and at the same stage he identifies her with his own image in the mirror, which becomes, along with the Mother-imago, the image for him of a desired and unattainable unity; in this same movement is constructed the unconscious, the place of the other, whose voice, belonging to his own alienated and distorted mirror-self, is the voice of the subject he can neither any longer be nor any longer resist, the voice of the desired other. The second other is the Father, who interrupts the Oedipal idyll between mother and son. As the mother has become what the child wishes to *have*, so the Father now becomes what the child wants to *be*. In the effort to imitate this possessor of the mother, the child, according to Lacan, comes to know that inauthenticity called narcissism: he becomes preoccupied with his own body as the image of the father's; the voice of this imaginary man or pattern is the voice of the second alienated self. The third other, the Name-of-the-Father, is the symbolic order of relationships itself. The child only comes to know this order when, and to the degree that, he accepts the emptiness of his own specular image and of his own attempt to supplant the father. For the symbolic order *is* that acceptance. It is the acceptance of symbolic castration as the price of entry to the particular symbolic order of relationships which is the family: by giving up possession of the mother, by giving up the attempt to supplant the phallos of the father, the child receives the symbolic guarantee of its own phallic maturity—the promise to a boy of his own wife, the promise to a girl of her own child. According to Lacan, all three of these others can speak in the analyzand. But the first other (the specular image) and the second other (the narcissist) can speak only empty words. Full speech, in Lacan's metaphor, only comes from the discourse of the third, the Other he writes with a capital letter, the discourse of the Name-of-the-Father, or the Law. The Other whose speech is full occupies an authoritative, even a final position in Lacanian theory, because its fullness grows from its complete subsumption of anterior others.

To put it another way, we begin to arrive at the sense of the final Other soon after we begin to attempt to speak. The logic of desire

impels us through the shadow relationships of the specular image
and the narcissist self as necessary cornerstones, as it were, to the
acceptance of the real order of relationships—for that order is the only
home, it would seem, which we can find once we lose the place of the
whole subject in separation from the mother. In Joel Fineman's
lapidary summary,

> The famous Lacanian barring of the subject—the loss of being
> that comes from re-presenting oneself in language as a meaning,
> correlative with the formation of the unconscious and the onset of
> desire, the construction of the Oedipal subject, and the acquisi-
> tion of a place in the cultural order through the recognition of
> the Name of the Father—is what makes the psyche a critical
> allegory of itself, and what justifies psychoanalysis as the allegory
> of that allegory.[4]

That is, Lacanian theory presents us with the notion that simply in
acquiring language, we institute the other-speaking which both
deludes us and makes us what we are; the steps in the process are what
Lacan isolates in the discourse of the Other in analysis, and which we
experience as writers in dialogue with our own evolving texts, our
own other-speaking.

Dante and Lacan: Parallels

To understand what happens in that exchange, it will be interesting
to make explicit a series of parallels, which some of my readers must
already have been noting, between Lacan's drama of the unconscious
and Dante's account of the fourfold hermeneutic. The literal level in
Dante corresponds to the barred subject in Lacan—the speaking subject whose very act of utterance—because it gives voice to the imagined
desire of the desired other—is an act of ventriloquism. I say that the
literal level in Dante corresponds to the barred subject because it, too,
is an act of ventriloquism, channeling into utterance the passions of
dramas located elsewhere but speaking through this letter in *allegoria*,
other-speaking. At the first stage of allegoresis in Dante, as in all
Christian hermeneutics, we encounter the story of the redemption of
mankind by Christ. When Dante, or Nicholas Lyranus, speaks precisely, this other-speech is what he means by *allegory*. For this is the
other-story which Christians use to reshape and recover all of history,
particularly all of Jewish history. Now the story of Christ is the narrative, at least in Roman Catholic myth, of the mother-son idyll.
Beginning with the fatherless conception, it proceeds through the
virgin birth, the wedding at Cana, the tragic union of the *pietà*, and

the triumphant union of Christ the Bridegroom with Mother Church His Bride. At this same stage in Lacanian allegoresis (if, after Fineman, I may adopt such a term), we find the first other, the specular image, which speaks the desire of the desired mother. As the first stage in both these paradigms is maternal, so is the second paternal. Lacan's second other is the narcissist self who desires to supplant the father by imitation. The Christian allegorist, at the second stage of interpretation, encounters the tropological or moral meaning, the admonitive application of the literal narrative: because Israel left Egypt, we must leave our sinfulness. Moral action of this kind bears a precise resemblance to the father-imitation of the narcissist self: this is action by pattern and formula, not the organic or inevitable result of one's being what he is. The third other in Lacan is the Other, the Name of the Father, or Law, whose speech is full because it entirely comprehends the relationships that the earlier others conceal and distort. At the third state of Christian allegoresis, the anagogical level, we perceive the direct relationship between the individual, the self of writer or reader, and Ultimate Reality, which is the Father in Heaven, Blessed be His Name. It is significant that this level, properly understood, like Lacan's Name-of-the-Father, subsumes and comprehends intermediate levels, so that *it alone* finally constitutes a full understanding of the other-speaking in the literal (this is what Dante means by pointing out that the three allegorical levels are really one). That is, anagogy, like the speech of the Other, is full speech, and its obliteration (barring of the literal) of the first level is, finally, merely the literal fully understood as the ventriloquism that it is. In this final level, the ventriloquist, the order of things as they are, reveals itself.

The Palace of Allegory/the "History of God"

What are we to make of these parallels? The coincidence of schemata, of course, proves nothing, though Lacan has both friends and enemies who will find a use for it What interests us here, as we contemplate the title of this volume, is what "the writer's mind" *does;* for both schemata show, in some detail, that the writer needs as the speaker needs, to be the conveyor of language rather than its creator.

As we consider the question of *genre*, we must acknowledge that Lacan has made it evident that allegory pursues our utterance, that it is the very essence of utterance. And, indeed, both schemata suggest that not only allegory, but the drama of allegory, is lurking in every utterance: the family *agon* plays itself out, speaks on all stages, thunders in every denunciation, caresses in even the most public consolings, for it is the shape of all we know and the force of all that speaks in us. But both the ancient scheme and the modern one turn us towards that very *shape*—that order of orders which is not so much what we know as what we are in the act of encountering it. This final turning is the moment of anagogy or the recognition of the Name-of-the-Father, the Law. In understanding that nature of this moment—rather than in any of the moments it subsumes—we glimpse why it was that allegoresis could set Dante free as it did, and we may find a claim to a similar freedom of our own.

For we identify the moment of anagogy as the moment when the very nature of my deed (written or otherwise) encounters that absolute Other which contains the possibilities of all others. For Dante freedom is absolute surrender to this Other. *"E'n la sua voluntade è nostra pace."* (*Paradiso,* III, 85) "In his will is our peace." Indeed, of our felicity there rests so much in the will of this Other that the whole of Dante's pursuit in the *Commedia* is precisely to locate that will: the drama of the poem rests upon an understanding that even to find this Other's place is an all-encompassing undertaking. But the drama, nonetheless, for many readers retains the scandal of its vulgarizers' assumptions that it could be captured in its own schema. So it will be helpful to address the question from another corner of history. Here, speaking with his usual aplomb, is Jacques Derrida:

> . . . God is of my own creation, my double who slipped into the difference that separates me from my origin, that is into the nothing that opens my history. What is called the presence of God is but the forgetting of this nothing, the eluding of elusion, which is not an accident but the very movement of elusion. . . .[5]

"This history of God," he adds, "is thus the history of the work as excrement."

Such an understanding, located at the moment of anagogy, relieves both schemata of their tendencies to turn into icons of their own accuracy. The work is that which falls away, as the "history of God" is no more than the map or scheme of our hunt along the traces of what has fallen away. Narcissist-tropological, specular-allegorical, and even speaking-poetic human action does not, cannot, from this perspective, advertise itself as anything more than a "history" of a relationship. But in this moment itself, in this recognition of Law and/or arrival at the place of *"la sua voluntade,"* we discover something else.

"God" *is* the name we give to the desire to find not nothing in "the nothing that opens my history." We give this name, it is worth emphasizing, to the *desire* and the willingness to act, entirely uninsured, upon the utter necessity of that desire. Thus, "Eloi, Eloi, Lama sabachthani," (Matt. 27:46) "My God, my God, why hast thou for-

saken me?" is not only the last of the last words of Christ, but is also
the very way in which the Christian prays along his journey. To leap
into the nothing before him is the nature of his love. His only reason
is that Christ has done it before him, as he may read. He may, indeed,
see that Christ himself not only utters the text but is *read* by it, for the
words themselves are David's (Ps. 22:1). All that he perceives is a path
of action. But this "forgetting of nothing," to turn Derrida's sentence
around, is "the presence of God."

Thus, finally, we attain freedom as writers when we, in the same
moment, accept and admire and deride and forget the allegory we
leave behind us in our progress. For this is no more and no less than
the "history of God." Because it is no less than that, we never discover
in it anything short of the full architecture that rereading and rever-
beration erect: this is the palace of allegory, a Solomon's temple
wherein both our nature and our duty admonish us to do reverence
and to admit wonder. But because this palace is no more than the
"history of God," we turn from it; inevitably, its interminable intri-
cacies oppress and weary and provoke us to laughter; and it is the
health of our minds that they refuse to retain its imponderable mass,
but "forgetting this nothing" they turn to the desert before us. There,
behind, are the sentences one and two; what-is-written, glittering in
the sunlight like the armies of the Pharaoh. Here, before, doubt and
desert and fathomless sea. Sentence three.

Notes

1. Nicholas of Lyre, *Patrologia Latina*, cited in William F. Lynch, *Christ
and Apollo* (1960; rpt. New York: Mentor-Omega, 1963), 229.
2. *The Latin Works of Dante Alighieri* (London: Temple Classics, 1934),
347–348.
3. What follows here does not offer itself as an account of Lacanian theory
as a whole or even in large part but is rather a reading of the "Schema R"
which Lacan employs in the article "On a Question Preliminary to Any
Possible Treatment of Psychosis," in *Ecrits: A Selection*, trans. Alan Sheridan
(New York: Norton, 1977), 197; this scheme is also discussed by Anthony
Wilden in his notes to his translation of Jacques Lacan, *The Language of the
Self* (1968; rpt. New York: Delta, 1975), 293–298.
4. Joel Fineman, "The Structure of Allegorical Desire," *October* 12 (Spring
1980): 62. In this exemplary essay, Fineman places Lacan's enterprise clearly
in the history of the development of structuralist thought.
5. Jacques Derrida, "La Parole Soufflée," *Writing and Difference*, trans.
Alan Bass (Chicago: University of Chicago Press, 1978), 182. While Derrida's
deconstruction of the "author of the Seminar on 'The Purloined Letter'" in
"The Purveyor of Truth," *Yale French Studies* 52 (1975): 31–113, has become
a necessary citation in any discussion of Lacan, the relationship among the

texts of Derrida and Lacan and Poe is anything but clear. And, while the question is too large to receive more than a mention here, the evidence of the present discussion suggests that Derrida saves Lacan from the worst dangers implicit in his approach, recovering the splendors of allegory by insisting upon their belatedness and by tracing the metahistory that brings them into existence, always returning our attention to the "nothing" and the "forgetting of nothing."

6. Lacan himself writes, "For I can only just prove to the Other that he exists, not, of course, with the proofs for the existence of God, with which over the centuries he has been killed off, but by loving him, a solution introduced by the Christian *kerygma*." "The Subversion of the Subject and the Dialectic of Desire in the Freudian Unconscious," *Ecrits*, 317

24 The Writer's Mind: Recent Research and Unanswered Questions

Richard L. Larson
Herbert H. Lehman College, CUNY

Some of the most productive recent work on composition is that which has tried to get at what writers do when they write—that which has tried to discover something of how writers' minds often work when writers are engaged in the act of writing. I recognize that attempts to study the workings of writers' minds invite severe criticism from many perspectives. But even the controversy over investigators' techniques and emphases in research has shed fresh light on important problems faced by teachers of writing and has substantially redirected the strategies of many teachers. In the course of my discussion I will mention the names of many authors and many essays (as well as a few books and monographs), trying all the time to avoid the two perils that threaten bibliographic essays: saying so little about a contribution that the reader is left uninformed, and saying so much that the relative importance of the contribution is distorted and the bibliographic essay is, in the reader's view, unnecessarily protracted.

Work that explores the activities of the writer's mind constitutes one of the broad categories into which research, theorizing, and speculation about rhetoric and composition today can be divided. To put the research on the writer's mind into perspective, I mention briefly some of the other broad categories. One might identify first the various efforts to develop a taxonomy of discourse and assign specimens of completed discourse to different classes, efforts typified by the work of James Kinneavy (in *A Theory of Discourse* [Englewood Cliffs, New Jersey: Prentice-Hall, 1971] and in his earlier brief article, "The Basic Aims of Discourse," *College Composition and Communication* (*CCC*), 20 [December 1969], 297-304), that of James Moffett (particularly in "I, You, and It," *CCC*, 16 [December 1965], 243-56), and also that of James Britton and his colleagues at the University of London in *The Development of Writing Abilities, 11-18* (London: Macmillan Education, 1975), who found it necessary, in order to analyze fully samples of writing by students at different ages, to identify categories into which various pieces could be placed.

A second category might include studies looking toward development of "heuristics"—strategies for locating and developing ideas one might want to discuss in writing. The best known of recent heuristics (besides that of Aristotle—made accessible by, among others, Edward P. J. Corbett in *Classical Rhetoric for the Modern Student* [New York: Oxford University Press, 1971]), include a plan based upon the "pentad" of Kenneth Burke, as most visibly elaborated by William Irmscher in *The Holt Guide to English* (New York: Holt, Rinehart, and Winston, 1972); a plan derived from the "tagmemic theory" of Kenneth Pike, made most accessible in Richard Young, Alton Becker, and Kenneth Pike, *Rhetoric: Discovery and Change* (New York: Harcourt Brace Jovanovich, 1970), and slightly simplified in Charles W. Kneupper, "Revising the Tagmemic Heuristic: Theoretical and Pedagogical Considerations," *CCC*, 31 [May 1980], 160–68; and, possibly, my own "Discovery Through Questioning: A Plan for Teaching Rhetorical Invention," *College English*, 30 [November 1968], 126–34.

A third category might include studies purporting to explain the "rhetoric" of the sentence. Such studies would include those in Francis Christensen's *Notes toward a New Rhetoric* (New York: Harper and Row, 1967), which incorporates his "A Generative Rhetoric of the Sentence" (*CCC*, 14 [October 1963], 155–61) and "A Generative Rhetoric of the Paragraph" (*CCC*, 16 [October 1965], 144–56), and the prominent recent work on sentence-combining, such as that of Frank O'Hare in *Sentence-Combining: Improving Student Writing without Formal Grammar Instruction* (Urbana, Ill.: National Council of Teachers of English, 1973) and Donald Daiker, Andrew Kerek, and Max Morenberg, of whose studies "Sentence-Combining at the College Level" (*Research in the Teaching of English*, 12 [October 1978], 245–56) is a good example.

A fourth category, sparsely populated indeed, might include studies of relations between discourse, context, and audience. Wayne Booth's famous essay, "The Rhetorical Stance" (*CCC*, 14 [October 1963], 139–45), is one example that might fit the category, as are Lloyd Bitzer's "The Rhetorical Situation" (*Philosophy and Rhetoric*, 1 [January 1960], 1–14) and Fred Pfister and Joanne Petrick, "A Heuristic Model for Creating a Writer's Audience" (*CCC*, 31 [May 1980], 213–220). A final category might include studies of error in writing; the category was created almost single-handedly by Mina Shaughnessy in *Errors and Expectations* (New York: Oxford University Press, 1977) and also includes, prominently, David Bartholomae's "The Study of Error" (*CCC*, 31 [October 1980], 253–69). Other observers might discover still other categories, possibly including one for studies looking at form in nonfiction writing. But such categories would be found, I think, as thinly populated as the least populous of the five categories I've named.

I do not in any way seek, of course, to undervalue the contributions to our understanding of rhetoric and composition made by the articles and books that I have identified (and many that I have not identified) in the five categories. Some of the work cited there, notably that of Britton and Shaughnessy, is unquestionably central to our field. But in none of these categories, as I see them, is the work cited hewing out new trails that other scholars seem eager to follow toward visible achievements. Efforts to categorize discourse encourage the counter-argument that discourse resists easy categorizaton and that searching for neat categories is simply misleading. Searches for heuristics that can aid the discovery of ideas have produced few models since that of Burke and of Young, Becker, and Pike. Studies of "generative rhetoric" have pretty much stopped with Christensen's work, and although sentence-combining has won devoted followers and appears to have the support of research studies (such as that reported by Daiker, Kerek, and Morenberg), it has raised substantial questions in the minds of astute observers such as Lester Faigley (in "Names in Search of a Concept: Maturity, Fluency, Complexity, and Growth in Written Syntax," *CCC*, 31 [October 1980], 291–299). Sentence-combining, as Marion Crowhurst demonstrates in "Sentence Combining: Maintaining Realistic Expectations," (*CCC*, 34 [February 1983], 62–72), has strictly limited values, and as Michael Holzman suggests in "Scientism and Sentence-Combining" (*CCC*, 34 [February 1983], 73–79), its popularity may be due to a misplaced faith in the measurability of the growth in students' abilities at writing. Studies of relations between discourse, context, and audience, as already noted, have hardly progressed, even though teachers of writing regularly admonish their students to keep in mind the interests, knowledge, and attitudes of readers. (A bibliographic essay on this subject by Lisa Ede, and an exploration of ways of looking at relations of writer and audience written by Ede and by Andrea Lunsford, will appear in *CCC* in 1984.) And error analysis, which seemed so promising a direction when *Errors and Expectations* appeared, has hardly advanced far except in Bartholomae's essay, and has indeed invited some witty counter-arguments, such as Joseph Williams's "The Phenomenology of Error" (*CCC*, 32 [May 1981], 152–68), which demonstrates how much difficulty teachers of writing may find in trying to decide what is an "error." The work in all five of these categories, then, seems to be marking time, and to be at a standstill in some of them.

One reason for the slow progress of this work may be its inability to unite attention to the product of composing, the completed draft or essay, with attention to the activities of the writer that brought the text into being—with, that is, attention to the creative processes that underlie the product we see before us on the page. Those who develop taxonomies of discourse (theories of "modes" or forms) typically start with the finished or nearly finished product; some appear to assume that the writer identifies the structural and stylistic features of various forms, selects a form appropriate to the situation that invites composing, and produces a piece in the appropriate form. The writer, such studies assume, selects and essentially imitates examples from that category. Those who explore the social relationships between writer and reader and the relationships of both to the context in which writing is evoked or proferred have put before students of composition some exhortations and directives, but usually give students little explicit help in carrying out the directives. Those who look at the kinds and sources of error in writers' work, while aware that errors of particular kinds often signal cognitive growth—the growth associated with efforts at mastering new language structures and with willingness to take risks in trying out new ways of using language—nevertheless begin their studies with what writers *have* written, not with what they are writing or plan to write.

The authors in two of my five groups, to be sure, may be in a better position than the authors in the other three groups to combine the study of processes of mind with the study of completed texts. Those who develop heuristic plans make up one such group. They proceed, typically, in one of two ways: some infer from the evidence of effective finished writing the kinds of inquiries that might lead to the production of similarly effective writing; others examine objects or experiences and enumerate the kinds of data an informed observer might gather in compiling a complete record of that object or experience. From these inferences they evolve advice to writers—instructions about mental processes that writers might test out (hence the term "heuristics") in the search for ideas that will assist in solving what the writer has perceived as the problem requiring communication. Inventors of heuristics may be trying to guide the writer's mind without first looking to see whether all minds can benefit from the guidance. But these inventors, at least, are exhibiting (even if they are not yet developing) concerns for directing, strengthening, and making more productive the operations of writers' minds.

Those who advocate sentence combining and other approaches to the "generating" of sentences may come the closest of the five groups of scholars to looking at the minds of writers. But they, too, typically look first at the structure of utterances and the structure of texts to derive rules (more than for heuristics) that they can advise student writers to follow. The central and durable question implied by their work is this: To what extent are the procedures they describe and advocate congruent with how writers' minds actually work in creating language structures? It is a question much like the one we might ask of inventors of heuristics, with the difference that, in psycholinguistics, we may have a discipline that can investigate and answer the question.

Now there are highly reputable scholars and teachers for whom explorations of the workings of writers' minds seem unproductive if not downright futile. Implicit, perhaps, in Peter Elbow's *Writing Without Teachers* (New York: Oxford University Press, 1975), is the conviction that writers would do best when they create strategies, techniques, and social situations that facilitate writing and feedback about one's writing. Elbow describes processes that he follows, and that others might follow, to release natural inventive processes, to keep themselves writing, to find out where their writing is headed, to refine their writing, and to see how their writing is perceived. Examining processes for creating language, for defining problems, for assuring rounded explorations of a subject are less important to Elbow, it would seem, than moving the writing ahead. The same emphases organize and energize Elbow's latest book, *Writing with Power: Techniques for Mastering the Writing Process* (New York: Oxford University Press, 1981). Elbow does not so much disavow studies of the writer's mental processes as ignore them, thus implying that such studies are less helpful to teachers (and to writers) than finding ways to get words on paper, to overcome blocks, to read, critically, one's own writing and then rewrite. Barrett Mandel is much more explicit in discouraging writers from planning extensively in advance of writing—and, perhaps, from encouraging those who study cognitive and linguistic processes from thinking that they have much to tell writers. In two essays, "Losing One's Mind: Learning to Write and Edit" (*CCC*, 29 [December 1978], 363-68) and "The Writer Writing Is Not at Home" (*CCC*, 31 [December 1980], 370-77), Mandel asserts that writers (and, by implication, students of writing) have no way of predicting what will appear on paper before it appears there, even if they think they are planning or "rehearsing" (Donald Murray's term) what they will say. One can profitably edit what one has said after one has said it, Mandel suggests, but editing is different from composing, and composing is, if not unfathomable, at least unpredictable.

But explicit and implicit hesitations about studying the writer's "mind" (perhaps we should refer to the subject as the writer's mental activities) are relatively rare in the scholarly literature of the past decade. Many of our most visible scholars find it productive to contemplate—to observe, to hypothesize about, to gather empirical data about, to develop models of—how writers proceed, in hopes of finding some clues that might help teachers, and students too, understand and practice the processes. In my next pages I discuss only a few of the major contributors to this line of inquiry, which many other people have pursued less extensively and less visibly.

Unquestionably the pioneer scholar to explore by observation, rather than simply by conducting interviews, the processes by which writers compose was Janet Emig, whose study, *The Composing Processes of Twelfth Graders* (Urbana, Ill.: National Council of Teachers of English, 1971), focused on the work of a few students in a Chicago-area high school, and in particular upon the activities of one notably lively and alert young woman. Emig's work introduced teachers to some facts that working writers have probably known also since the first writer wrote anything—that writing is a complex process in which thinking, planning, drafting, rethinking, revising, guessing at the reader's needs, and similar activities go on continuously and concurrently (the jargon term is "recursively") throughout writing, rather than the neatly linear succession of "stages" discussed in many textbooks. Emig overtly focused upon that apex of the famous "communications triangle" occupied by the writer, implying that many elements in the composing process occur irrespective of audience and subject, and also irrespective of other dimensions of what Lloyd Bitzer has termed the "rhetorical situation": the occasion, stimulus, and context within which writing occurs.

Although one can't be exact about the chronology of research on the processes of composing, Emig's monograph seems to have established a new emphasis in scholarship on composition that others willingly continued: an emphasis on addressing the texture of the composing experience, on what practicing writers do when they write, on how (insofar as one can get at the subject) their minds work. The researcher who has attempted what are easily the most comprehensive studies of the composing experience is Linda Flower, who with her colleague John Hayes has published several papers based upon their analyses of "protocols," transcripts of writers' thoughts during the act of composing, as verbalized aloud in response to the researchers' instructions and recorded on tape. Two of Flower and Hayes's most influential studies have appeared in *College Composition and Communication:* "The Cognition of Discovery: Defining a

Rhetorical Problem" (*CCC*, 31 [February 1980], 21-32) and "A Cognitive Process Theory of Writing" (*CCC*, 32 [December 1981], 365-87). In the first essay, Flower and Hayes examine the consequences of their finding that the more successful writers are those who define for themselves—a conscious or perhaps unconscious cognitive act—more successfully and in more detail the rhetorical "problem" they are trying to solve. In the second essay, Flower and Hayes lay out what aspires to be no less than a complete account of what they now know about how composing occurs, from start to finish. The authors present, in continuous prose and in a schematic diagram, a description of composing activities that includes the definition of rhetorical problems, the establishment of goals for writing, the definition of subgoals, the planning of content and strategy, the drafting of text, the revising of text, and the looping recurrence of each of these activities as the writers, and each of their activities, are informed and stimulated by the activities they have just carried on.

One can, of course—and subsequent commentators have leaped at the chance to do so—raise questions about the reliability of Flower and Hayes's research procedures. One can suggest that the artificiality of a setting in which writers are given a prompt and asked to verbalize their thoughts while responding to it calls into question the applicability of the authors' findings to what happens when writers compose for real audiences. And one can assert that what writers utter aloud as they write affords at best a dimly incomplete account of what is passing through their minds. One can even argue that, regardless of the dependability of a protocol, it affords us little insight into the processes by which writers get at their content and at their organizational plans and at the language in which they will compose what they "think." Protocols, one can argue, allow at best highly imperfect descriptions of the texture of composing. Still, Flower and Hayes's work represents the first visible and influential attempt to develop a model of how composing works, a model that may make possible analysis of where, in some writers, the process of composing does not work.

In the last few years, several other scholars have investigated perceptively, but selectively, various elements in the texture of composing that Flower and Hayes studied comprehensively. Among the most luminous of those scholars are Sondra Perl and Nancy Sommers, both of whom have looked extensively at the way writers revise. Perl's major work to date has been a study of composing processes of underprepared writers in college—a study that led her to conclude that inexperienced writers often worry excessively over making small changes in the details of what they are writing, thereby losing momentum and losing also a sense of the whole on which they are working ("The Composing Processes of Unskilled College Writers," *Research in the Teaching of English,* 13 [December 1979], 317-36). Reflecting further on the results of her work with young students and with teachers in workshops of the New York City Writing Project and other groups, Perl elaborates in "Understanding Composing" (*CCC,* 31 [December 1980], 363-69; reprinted as chapter 5, above) her exploration of the "recursiveness" of composing, and adds two important concepts to our understanding of how writers plan their work. Writers often engage, says Perl, in "retrospective structuring," looking back over what they have done to see where they began and how they have progressed, and in "projective structuring," considering how to move forward in such a way as to meet the needs of their subjects and their readers. But Perl recognizes that writers' decisions are not always open to discrete analysis and are often intuitive, not cerebral; writers reach, Perl suggests, what can only be called a "felt sense" of their readiness to put ideas down on a page in words, or of the rightness (or inadequacy) of what they have written. At these points, the writer's mind, Perl hints, may indeed not be open for inspection, though Perl has herself elicited protocols similar to those evoked by Flower and Hayes and has extensively analyzed the contours of composing as revealed by those protocols.

Nancy Sommers' work has also focused extensively on revision, but her principal techniques for inquiry have included interviews with experienced and inexperienced writers and invitations to these writers to describe in writing how they see themselves revising. In "Revision Strategies of Student Writers and Experienced Adult Writers," (*CCC,* 31 [December 1980], 378-88), Sommers tends to oversimplify somewhat her important distinctions, that inexperienced writers (students) often focus in their revisions on replacing words and accomplishing small reconstructions of individual sentences or short passages, while more experienced writers attend to the overall plan and development of what they have written and to the overall appropriateness of what they have done for its intended readers. Sommers is here discussing, as did Perl and Flower, differences in writers' attention to planning—to judging the substance and design of the whole writing in its context as an act of communication—and is thus asserting implicitly, I think, that successful writers undertake deliberate analytical, ratiocinative activities through the recursive processes of composing. If these scholars are correct, it may follow that students and teachers of writing can look with profit for ways of describing, explaining, and teaching others to carry on these deliberate activities.

Research on composing processes has been highlighted most recently by the work of these three scholars, Flower, Perl, and Sommers. But others, somewhat less visible to date, have conducted their own inquiries and have contributed to our understanding of those processes. In "Understanding a Writer's Awareness of Audience" (*CCC*, 32 [December 1981], 388–99), Carol Berkenkotter reports an experiment in the analysis of protocols given by an experienced academic professional writer responding to a prompt developed specifically by Berkenkotter. Berkenkotter found that the experienced writer devoted considerable time to assessing the needs and interests of her audience (a group of teen-agers), to the possible orientation of that audience toward her subject (what her academic field involves), and to the ways in which she might most effectively try to present her subject to that audience. In "Analyzing Revision" (*CCC*, 32 [December 1981], 400–407), Stephen Witte and Lester Faigley differentiate between revisions that affect the "macrostructure" (overall design and meaning) of a text and those that affect the microstructure (local details in particular passages), and note that experienced or older writers *tend* to focus their revisions on the macrostructure of a text, less experienced and/or younger writers on the microstructure. The work of Faigley and Witte tends to confirm, through empirical observation of writers at work, the conclusions reached by Nancy Sommers. Certainly Witte's and Faigley's work suggests that successful revision is a part of the total process of planning and "re-seeing" a work—not, perhaps, a surprising discovery, but one that reinforces the importance of attending carefully, when discussing how writers work, to the cognitive processes of planning. In an essay to be published in *CCC* in October 1983, Witte discusses the signals writers appear to look for in deciding whether and how to revise. Drawing upon recent work in linguistic theory to describe the "topical structure" of a text (the ways in which a text, by the structure of individual sentences, reveals and develops its focal "topics"), Witte examines how students, in an experiment in which they tried to revise a passage of academic prose, achieved more effective or less effective revisions depending on whether they accurately grasped the topical structure of the passage. Not only does Witte's experiment highlight revisers' (possibly unconscious) searches for the cognitive ("topical") structure of what they will revise, it underlines the important connections between writers as writers and writers as readers of draft texts. The mind, Witte demonstrates, has to *interpret* the text on the page in order to be able to improve it.

The last scholar I will discuss in this brief survey of important research on writers' cognitive processes, Mike Rose, has studied some of the causes of interference—blockages in the processes of composing:

those forces that prevent the writer from getting words onto paper. Recognizing that writers can encounter blocks as a result of psychological forces only now being investigated, Rose suggests that blockage may also result from writers' convictions that they must compose a certain kind of writing, and follow particular plans, even though these procedures do not work in the situation in which or on the subject about which they are writing. Drawing upon observations of student writers at work as well as on interviews with these writers, Rose concludes that misguided cognitive strategies ("algorithms" that demand exact reiteration of the same procedure time after time) are at the root of many writers' troubles with writing ("Rigid Rules, Inflexible Plans, and the Stifling of Language: A Cognitivist Analysis of Writer's Block," *CCC*, 31 [December 1980], 389-99).

The work of these scholars, as I have suggested, examines the total structure, what I have called the "texture," of the processes of composing, from the cognitive perspective of how "planning" proceeds. In one way or another, each of these researchers is looking at acts of deliberate analysis and acts of cognition—acts by which the writers determine what they are to accomplish, by what path they reach that accomplishment, how they test and try to improve their efforts, what stands between them and successful achievement. Others have written about composing and revising, but less directly with attention to processes of analysis and planning, processes of deliberate, controlled, cognitive effort. One thinks of Donald Murray looking at the processes of rehearsing and internal revision of language, in such work as "Write Before Writing," (*CCC*, 29 [December 1978], 375-81), and "Internal Revision: A Process of Discovery" in *Research on Composing: Points of Departure* (Urbana, Ill.: National Council of Teachers of English, 1978), 85-103. Murray's work, more informally, through the reflections of a practicing writer rather than through the systematic studies of an academic researcher, has tended to focus on how writers select language and local syntactic structures—a cognitive process of a more focused sort than those studied by Flower, Perl, and Sommers.

But the studies I have attempted to summarize, albeit in the barest of brevity, are not the only inquiries, now going on or recently completed, into the workings of writers' minds, and I cite some of these other strands of inquiry in order not only to recognize them but also to suggest that, at a future date, they may lead to important discoveries. First, *studies in cognitive style*. Scholars at Educational Testing Service and elsewhere, and Lynn Troyka, have been investigating the learning patterns of varied students in order to determine whether they can classify, or at least arrange along some sort of scale, the psychological features and forces that affect how students learn, and thus perhaps how they learn to write. No substantial report of the findings of these inquiries has yet appeared in journals easily accessible to teachers of writing, but readers might be on the watch for such reports. Second, *studies in linguistic and cognitive development.* A good deal of scholarship on writing focuses on continuities and disconti- nuities between speaking and writing, and although we do not yet have important information on how these connections might best be studied or on what activities of mind these connections might reveal, we are often reminded of the need to think about the matter. The work of Lev Vygotsky is frequently cited, and recently James Moffett has investigated developmental patterns followed by young people in moving from speaking to writing ("Writing, Inner Speech, and Meditation," *College English*, 44 [March 1982], 231–46). The National Council of Teachers of English has issued a wide-ranging anthology of essays on the subject: *Exploring Speaking-Writing Relationships: Connections and Contrasts* (Urbana, Ill.: National Council of Teachers of English, 1981). Similarly several scholarly articles about writing draw on the development in humans' ability to organize, classify, and generalize about data and experience, as explored in the works of Jean Piaget (see, for example, Piaget and Barbel Inhelder, *The Early Growth of Logic in the Child* [New York: Norton, 1969] and *The Growth of Logical Thinking from Childhood to Adolescence* [New York: Basic Books, 1958], and Jean Piaget, *The Language and Thought of the Child* [Cleveland: World Publishing Co., 1955], *The Origins of Intelligence in Children* [New York: Norton, 1963], and *The Psychology of Intelligence* [Totowa, N.J.: Littlefield, Adams, 1960]). Piaget's theories have been applied to writing by, among others, Lee Odell in "Piaget, Problem-Solving, and Freshman Com- position" (*CCC*, 24 [February 1973], 36–42), where he offers sugges- tions about how those who are convinced by Piaget's work might develop curricula and assignments based upon it.

Third, *studies in the development of young people's way of seeing the world and of their moral consciousness.* Though it has not yet been subjected to extended research related to the development of writing abilities, the work of William Perry (*Forms of Intellectual and Ethical Development in the College Years* [New York: Holt, Rinehart and Winston, 1970]) on the growth of young people's ways of interpreting their world has been described by some scholars as a suggestive way of looking at cognitive growth. Lawrence Kohlberg's description (*The Philosophy of Moral Development: Essays in Moral Development* [New York: Harper & Row, 1981]) of the moral devel- opment of young people has also been cited as an important description of human growth that is applicable to the development of abilities at writing. Susan Miller has suggested a connection between students' growth in the rhetorical effectiveness of the writing and the development of their moral orientation ("Rhetorical Maturity: Definition and Development," in Aviva Freedman and Ian Pringle, ed., *Reinventing the Rhetorical Tradition* [Conway, Ark.: L and S Books, 1980], 119-27). And Marilyn Sternglass has briefly applied Andrew Wilkinson's model of moral development (along with other developmental measures, including some for stylistic development) to the analysis of student writing (*CCC*, 33 [May 1982], 167-75), and has suggested that teachers recognize signs of evolving moral orientation as they write comments on students' work. Implications of these descriptions of adolescents' and adults' development may be discovered through future research; once again, readers should be alert to reports on such studies.

Fourth, *biomedical studies and studies of cognitive disfunction*. In some of her work after *The Composing Processes of Twelfth Graders*, Janet Emig speculated on whether we might learn about the effective functioning of writers' (and possibly others') minds through study of the minds of people experiencing one or another kind of biomedical dislocation. Though she herself has discussed this possibility, in "The Biology of Writing: Another View of the Process" in *The Writing Processes of Students*, ed. W. T. Petty and P. J. Finn (Buffalo: State University of New York, 1975), the significance of this line of inquiry has yet to be established. The same, I think, is true of research on the function of the various parts of the brain, as exemplified in W. Ross Winterowd, "Brain, Rhetoric, and Style" in *Linguistics, Stylistics, and the Teaching of Composition*, ed. Donald McQuade (Akron, Ohio: U. of Akron, L and S Books, 1979), 151-81. Once heralded as an important path for exploration of how writers work and why they differ in styles of writing, the topic of "hemisphericity" has not been much pursued in recent scholarship. Whether it will be more productive in the future than it has been to date remains to be seen.

Our field has, then, witnessed in the past decade some intensive observational and experimental studies of composing processes and has brought forward some tentative suggestions about possible additional approaches to the writer's mind. But it is essential that we remind ourselves that we still face, and possibly face all the more because of the research reviewed here, extensive and fundamental questions about how writers work. To conclude this review, I identify some of these unanswered questions.

1. How does the impulse to write arise? What leads (besides a professional obligation or deadline) a human being to say to him-

self or herself, consciously or unconsciously, "I want to write about this subject" or "I want to say this to these people"?

2. How does a writer arrive at a perspective, an approach to his or her subject? How does the writer select a way of viewing it (e.g., an instructive analogy for it), a way of entering the subject, a way of connecting details about the subject, a strategy for putting certain details in the foreground, others in the background, in hopes of enlarging a reader's understanding of that subject?

3. Once a writer has, in Linda Flower's terms, defined a "rhetorical problem," how does he or she go about solving it? How does the writer identify the elements needed for a solution, retrieve from memory or find in some other source(s) the items needed in the solution, and then test the trial solution to see whether it answers the problem?

4. How does the writer, having invented concepts and perceptions, defined a problem, and formulated a plan, find language in which to embody these decisions? Or perhaps one should rephrase: how does the writer, having tentatively formulated in language the materials of a piece of writing, select the preferred language that is to go onto the blank page? Sondra Perl's "felt sense" is still of unknown origin. Her discussion leaves much unanswered about how the "sense" arises and how it affects a writer's language.

5. What is the role of feelings, intuitions, cognitively indescribable impulses and acts, in the arrangement of language? In what ways does language arise to respond to and express feeling? How do we explore the workings of the nonrational, nonanalytic side of a writer's art?

Our deliberate, careful studies of composing, of human development, of styles for learning—studies that mostly use, in Janet Emig's term, a "positivistic" inquiry paradigm (see, "Inquiry Paradigms and Writing," *CCC*, 33 [February 1982], 64-75)—don't reach anywhere near adequately, if they reach at all, these questions. And we are left wondering, as we study the writer's mind, are they questions we can ever answer?

Even so, studies of the writer's mind recently have led us to much new information, to substantial new insights into how writers work, and to the threshold of what may in future years be discoveries that will not only enlarge knowledge but enrich and invigorate our teaching. Through these studies we are moving, I think, toward much better knowledge of human beings as thinkers and as writers than we enjoyed before they emerged. Through these studies, indeed, we have enlarged our knowledge of ourselves.

Contributors

Ann E. Berthoff is professor of English at the University of Massachusetts at Boston. She has served on the NCTE Commission on Composition and the executive committee of the MLA Division on the Teaching of Writing and as a consultant at the Bread Loaf School of English. Her textbooks include *Forming/Thinking/Writing: The Composing Imagination* and *The Making of Meaning: Metaphors, Models, and Maxims for Writing Teachers*. A third volume, *Reclaiming the Imagination: Philosophy and the Composing Process*, is forthcoming.

Annette N. Bradford is completing her Ph.D. in Rhetoric and Communication with an emphasis on discourse theory at Rensselaer Polytechnic Institute. She has published on a variety of subjects including rhetoric, technical writing pedagogy, photo-illustration, writing research, and self-regulating speech.

Kenneth A. Bruffee is professor of English at Brooklyn College, CUNY. He has chaired the MLA Teaching of Writing Division, edited *WPA: Writing Program Administration,* and directed a FIPSE-funded national institute in training peer tutors. His book, *Elegiac Romance,* is on modern fiction.

Hugh Burns is associate professor of English at the United States Air Force Academy in Colorado. His investigations in composition theory and computer-assisted instruction continue with publications in *Educational Technology,* CONDUIT's *Pipeline,* and *The Journal of Computers in Mathematics and Science Teaching.* Descriptions of his research have appeared in *The Computing Teacher* and *Education Week.*

William V. Costanzo is associate professor of English at Westchester Community College in New York. A member of the NCTE Commission on Media and the recipient of a recent NEH grant to study classroom applications of filmmaking to the teaching of writing, he writes regularly on literary topics, composition, and film. His book on film and composition is forthcoming.

Robert D. Foulke, professor of English at Skidmore College, was chair of the department for ten years and is now director of the NEH project in writing across the curriculum. He has published a number of articles on critical theory, the curriculum in English, and Joseph Conrad, and is coauthor of *An Anatomy of Literature.* He is a director of the College English Association and has recently been a visiting scholar in literature for the Sea Education Association in Woods Hole and the Williams Program in American Maritime Studies at Mystic Seaport.

Marilyn Goldberg has a Ph.D. in English Education from Indiana University of Pennsylvania and teaches at The Pennsylvania State University, University Park Campus. She has published articles in *Teaching English in the Two-Year College* and *The CEA Critic*.

Janice N. Hays is director of Composition and an assistant professor of English at the University of Colorado, Colorado Springs. Prior to that, she was director of Writing at Skidmore College. She has published several articles on the theory and teaching of writing and is presently conducting a large-scale study on the development of analytic writing abilities.

Karen M. Hjelmervik is completing a Ph.D. dissertation in English, which focuses on the trends in papers written by freshmen in three levels of composition classes at the University of Pittsburgh. Her special interests are teaching reading and writing, and teaching writing with word processing technology. She is currently a writer with the Westinghouse Electric Corporation at their headquarters in Pittsburgh.

Richard A. Katula is associate professor in the department of Speech Communication at the University of Rhode Island. He is education editor of *Communication Quarterly*, has published numerous articles in the area of rhetoric, and is coauthor of a text, *Communication: Writing and Speaking*.

Richard L. Larson, formerly dean of the Division of Professional Studies at Herbert H. Lehman College, CUNY, is now director of Lehman College's Institute for the Study of Literacy. He is editor of *College Composition and Communication* and has published *The Evaluation of Teaching: College English, Children and Writing in the Elementary School: Selected Readings*, and numerous articles. Currently, he is concerned with problems of testing writing ability, of evaluating writing instruction, and of writing in disciplines outside English.

Elaine O. Lees is assistant professor of English at the University of Pittsburgh, where she teaches courses in writing and in the teaching of Basic Writing. She has published articles on composition and pedagogy in *College Composition and Communication* and *The English Journal*, and has coordinated the university's evening-division program in composition since 1977.

Donald McQuade is professor of English at Queens College, CUNY, where he has served as associate chair, director of the American Studies Program, and director of the Writing Program. He has published several books on composition, including *Popular Writing in America; Linguistics, Stylistics, and the Teaching of Composition;* and *Thinking in Writing*. His essays on composition, advertising, and the American culture have appeared in numerous journals. He is also the general editor of the Modern Library college edition series as well as the two volume *Harper American Literature*.

Celest A. Martin is assistant professor of English at the University of Rhode Island and is currently a coordinator of the College Communication Skills Course. She has coauthored a text, *Communication: Writing and Speaking*.

Susan B. Merriman is in the preliminary stage of her dissertation in Language Communications at the University of Pittsburgh. Her major area of interest is the analysis of errors committed in written compositions by college freshmen. She is currently teaching part-time for the English department at the University of Pittsburgh and for the English as a Second Language Program at Point Park College.

Lee Odell is a professor in the department of Language, Literature and Communication at Rensselaer Polytechnic Institute. He is coeditor of *Evaluating Writing* and *Research on Composing*. He is a trustee of the NCTE Research Foundation and a member of the Editorial Board of *College Composition and Communication* and the Publications Committee of *Studies in Rhetoric and Writing*.

Sondra Perl received the 1979 National Council of Teachers of English Promising Researcher Award for her work on the composing process. A faculty member at Herbert H. Lehman College, CUNY, she has served on the Modern Language Association's Commission on the Future of the Profession. Currently she is the principal investigator of an ethnographic research project (funded by the National Institute of Education) documenting teaching the writing process.

Jon R. Ramsey is the associate dean of Student Affairs and an associate professor of English at Skidmore College. He has published a number of articles on Wordsworth and is coediting a volume for MLA on teaching Wordsworth's poetry. His areas of research interest include the Romantic poets, the *fin de siècle*, and depictions of childhood in literature.

Phyllis A. Roth, associate professor of English, is a member of the Writing Committee and co-coordinator of Writing Across the Curriculum Workshops at Skidmore College funded by an NEH Pilot Grant. Author of *Bram Stoker*, she has published articles on Vladimir Nabokov and is currently editing *Critical Essays on Vladimir Nabokov*.

Leone Scanlon directs the Writing Center at Clark University in Worcester, Massachusetts, and assists in a cross-disciplinary writing program. She has presented papers at CCCC and NEMLA and recently attended the Institute on Writing at the University of Iowa.

John C. Schafer is assistant professor and director of Composition at Humboldt State University in Arcata, California. He is the author of "The Linguistic Analysis of Spoken and Written Texts," in *Exploring Speaking and Writing Relationships: Connections and Contrasts* and a coauthor of *Strategies for Academic Writing*.

256

Sandra Schor, a former director of Composition at Queens College, CUNY, has recently been named a "Master Teacher" in the CUNY Faculty Development Program. She publishes stories and poems as well as essays on the teaching of composition. Her textbook (with Judith Fishman), *The Random House Guide to Writing,* is in its second edition.

Marie Secor is assistant professor of English at The Pennsylvania State University, where she teaches upper and lower level composition, editing, humanities, and nineteenth and twentieth century literature courses. Coauthor of *A Rhetoric of Argument,* she also has published articles on composition, history of rhetoric, and literature.

James F. Slevin is associate professor of English at Georgetown University, where he directs the Freshman English Program, the Writing Center, and an NEH-funded project between Georgetown and the D.C. Schools. He has lectured and published on literature and literary theory, on the teaching of writing, and on the goals of collaborative programs between colleges and schools.

Marilyn S. Sternglass is associate professor of English and coordinator of the Basic Skills Writing Program at Indiana University. She has published papers on composition theory and practice and is the author of *Reading, Writing, and Reasoning.*

Robert Viscusi has written on literary and psychoanalytic theory, late nineteenth- and early twentieth-century British literature, Italian-American literature, and American-Italian literary relations. He has recently completed a book on the works of Max Beerbohm. He is assistant professor of English and director of the Humanities Institute at Brooklyn College.

Monica R. Weis SSJ teaches English and Rhetoric at Nazareth College, Rochester, N.Y. has conducted numerous workshops in New York State on teaching writing, presented papers at NCTE, NYCEA, and has published in *The CEA Critic.* She is currently completing a dissertation, "Insight into Composition: A Neurological, Cognitive, and Heuristic View," in Language, Literature and Pedagogy at the University of Virginia.